More Praise for *The Power to Transform*

"A lucid, beautifully drawn map to schools of the future by an exceptional educator who has made the journey. Every teacher should read this book and do it, every administer should read this book and enable it, every parent should read this book and demand it, because every learner aches to experience it."

> —Dee W. Hock, founder and CEO Emeritus, VISA;
> and author, *One from Many*

"Education is in crisis, and therefore our children are adrift and ungrounded, trained to memorize knowledge but unable to cope in a turbulent world. Stephanie Pace Marshall offers a provocative vision of how education can be reinfused with wonder, enrichment, and transformation. She challenges all of us to understand that it is our capacity to learn that characterizes our most essential humanity."

> —James Garrison, president, Wisdom University

"Stephanie Pace Marshall gives us a transformational school model that inspires our children to 'invent their own minds, reconnect to life, and wisely engage in cocreating a sustainable future.' As a financier and social investor, I believe that her 'whole child' model is crucial for species survival. Every human can understand her riveting recommendations and enjoy her delicious story!"

> —Susan Davis, president, Capital Missions Company

"For years Stephanie Pace Marshall has been one of the clearest and most insightful voices on school reform. Her book, *The Power to Transform: Leadership that Brings Learning and Schooling to Life* solidifies this reputation. In this highly readable book, the reader will be provoked into a deeper understanding of what schooling is and, more importantly, what it can become. It is as elegant as it is deep. Simply a must-read for school leaders."

> —Paul Houston, executive director, American Association
> of School Administrators

"This book explores education from a perspective rare in the field: that we become the stories we tell about ourselves and that to create systemic change in education, educational leaders need to craft new stories. The deep insights on learning and children shared by Stephanie Pace Marshall are mirrored in the success of the amazing school she leads. As an antidote to the purely 'data-driven' testing mentality that robs students of joy and the chance for real learning, the ideas in this book help any educational leader facilitate the creation of the kind of environment all students need to properly prepare them for life as they strive to achieve long-term mastery of the challenging subjects they study. This view into the thinking of a renowned education leader should make her ideas a steady topic of conversation among educators for years to come."

— David Thornburg, director, Global Operations, Thornburg Center

"Stephanie Pace Marshall draws from systems and complexity theory, cognitive science, and more in introducing us to the rich body of knowledge waiting to guide us through the sweeping changes we must make in educating the young. It is not easy to restrain one's anger on realizing the degree to which this knowledge and its implications have been so shamefully ignored in school reform."

— John I. Goodlad, president, Institute for Educational Inquiry

"Stephanie Pace Marshall offers a powerful and unique framework for scholars, policymakers, school reformers, and practitioners who have the capacity to shape our children's future. This book aims directly at the heart of our most fundamental educational goal—to nurture the power and creativity of the human spirit. For any leader working to build a new covenant with our children, this book is a must-read."

— Gene R. Carter, executive director and CEO, Association for Supervision and Curriculum Development

The Power to Transform

LEADERSHIP THAT BRINGS
LEARNING AND SCHOOLING
TO LIFE

Stephanie Pace Marshall

JOSSEY-BASS
A Wiley Imprint
www.josseybass.com

Published by Jossey-Bass
A Wiley Imprint
989 Market Street, San Francisco, CA 94103-1741   www.josseybass.com

Jossey-Bass books and products are available through most bookstores. To contact Jossey-Bass directly call our Customer Care Department within the U.S. at 800-956-7739, outside the U.S. at 317-572-3986, or fax 317-572-4002.

Jossey-Bass also publishes its books in a variety of electronic formats. Some content that appears in print may not be available in electronic books.

Credits are on page 244.

Library of Congress Cataloging-in-Publication Data

Marshall, Stephanie Pace, date.
The power to transform: leadership that brings learning and schooling to life / Stephanie Pace Marshall.
p. cm.
Includes bibliographical references and index.
ISBN-13: 978-0-7879-7501-2 (cloth)
ISBN-10: 0-7879-7501-X (cloth)
1. School improvement programs. 2. Learning. 3. Education. I. Title.
LB2822.8.M38 2006
371.2—dc22
2005033965

Printed in the United States of America
FIRST EDITION
HB Printing   10 9 8 7 6 5 4 3 2 1

The Jossey Bass Education Series

Contents

Part Two: Designing the New Learning Landscape   77

Part Three: A Call for Leaders   183

For Robert, the love of my life

And in grateful and loving memory of my mind makers and soul guides:

My mother, Anne Price Pace
My father, Dominick Martin Pace
My brother, Charles John Pace

Preface:
The Call for a Radical New Story
of Learning and Schooling

*Stories become "testaments," old or new, that choreograph
the life of the community.*

—Stephen Larsen, in Phil Cousineau, *Once and Future Myths* (2001)

Eighteen years into my career as an educator, I was invited to create an innovative statewide public residential institution called the Illinois Mathematics and Science Academy (IMSA). Now internationally recognized, this pioneering institution was established to offer a uniquely challenging program for Illinois students (grades 10 through 12) talented in mathematics and science and to serve as a catalyst for the stimulation of excellence in mathematics and science throughout Illinois.[1]

Although neither a mathematician nor a scientist, I felt confident to lead in creating this unique institution: my preparation in mathematics and science was comprehensive; I had almost two decades of successful educational leadership and advanced degrees in learning and organizational development. What more would I need? Within a year, I humbly had my answer. My education and experience taught me to navigate the landscape of traditional schooling, but they were clearly inadequate for creating a generative new landscape for deep and integral learning. I would need to think profoundly differently about learning and schooling.

A New Context *for* Learning

Intuitively, I understood that the dynamics, creative processes, and organizing properties of living systems must guide the design of this generative learning landscape—life must be my mentor. So I asked some members of our science team to teach me about living systems. This simple inquiry changed my mind and my life.

It soon became abundantly clear that life is about learning and that cognition or knowing is the essential process of life.[2] I was fascinated by the deep patterns of wholeness, order, interdependence, and creativity in the natural world. Needing to probe deeper, I sought out pioneering thinkers in a variety of fields and disciplines, especially Margaret Wheatley, Myron Kellner-Rogers, Fritjof Capra, Sally Goerner, Dee Hock, Parker Palmer, and Howard Gardner.[3] Their revolutionary and trailblazing work provided a foundational and illuminating context for my inquiry. From these explorations I gained a deeper understanding of how complex living systems—including our mind-brain—organize, grow, and learn. I sensed that this synthesis—this story—would be the roots of a radical new story of learning and schooling.

Our guiding metaphor of the universe, living systems, and the mind-brain was that of a deterministic, mechanistic, and predictable machine. But science had changed its mind about how the world works: the natural world is now understood as an interdependent, relational, and living web of connections—inherently whole, abundant, creative, and self-organizing. I believed our children's learning would thrive if they could learn as life does, by being immersed in environments that are natural living habitats—"learning arboretums," as one of my students called them, for nurturing integral and wise minds.

This understanding of the dynamic relationships, sustaining organization, and boundless creativity of the natural world as context for learning and schooling is fundamental. Because we unconsciously institutionalize our scientific worldview in our beliefs, assumptions, thinking, and behavior, we shape the structures and processes of our institutions, including our schools, according to the science of our times.

Yet despite new discoveries, rigid conceptions of world-as-a-machine have calcified into unquestioned models of thinking and design principles that continue to shape our language, stories, policies, and institutions. This worldview and its illusions of predictability, precise measurability, and external controllability continue to influence almost every dimension of our culture. But nowhere is the imprint more debilitating than in the processes and structures of schooling, in what and how we ask our children to learn and in how we were taught to lead them.

Watering *the* Roots

Learning is the most natural and creative of all human endeavors. When we jump back from a hot stove for the first time, marvel at ants living intricate lives just beneath the topsoil, stand in awe at the magic and mystery of a rainbow, or simply wonder at the vastness of the universe, we are learning. Yet despite the inherent spontaneity and naturalness of learning, the nature and quality of our minds are powerfully shaped by the nature and quality of the learning environments in which they are immersed, activated, and nurtured. *How* we are asked to learn matters profoundly. Mind shaping is world shaping.

In the absence of a holistic context of purpose, meaning, and connection, our current processes and structures of schooling have restrained our children's access to all of who they are by creating false proxies for deep learning. Finishing a course and a textbook has come to mean achievement. Listening to a lecture has come to mean understanding. Getting a high score on a standardized test has come to mean proficiency. Credentialing has come to mean competence.

During the most formative time of human development, childhood through adolescence, our children are immersed in learning environments and schooling systems disconnected from their deepest learning needs. These environments stifle natural learning and great thinking; they diminish curiosity and constrain our children's natural capacities to explore, create, imagine, and make genuine contributions to their communities and their world while they are young. The nature of schooling as we know it has become the unquestioned answer to educating our children. *It is not.* Knowing what we now know, we can no longer do what we now do. It is time to reconnect our children to their abundant learning potentials and reengage them in the joy of learning.

I know many remarkable educators and schools that swim courageously against this powerful tide and many students who emerge from schooling still eager to learn. Yet despite their efforts and excellence, the current story and system of schooling too often results in tentative and risk-averse learners, ill equipped to creatively reframe and resolve the deeply complex and interdependent problems of our time. As a result, many children feel disconnected from themselves, each other, and the natural world, uncertain of where and how they belong. Over time, this lived story creates a system of schooling that masks or erodes the unknowable potentials our children can so naturally bring to learning.

We know something is wrong, so we try to fix the schools and the children—altering the schedule, increasing standards and course loads, and adding remedial classes. But re-forming or restructuring schools has not transformed our *system* of learning and schooling or the nature and quality of the minds it invites and educates into existence. In the wise words of the Vietnamese Buddhist monk Thich Nhat Hanh, "If you want the tree to grow, it won't help to water the leaves. You have to water the roots."[4] It is such a simple idea. Yet when it comes to deeply educating the minds of our children, we are watering the leaves of schooling and not the roots of learning.

Schools are powerful places for shaping minds. They provide the cultural practice field for how we learn to know about and meaningfully engage in shaping our world. From age three to eighteen, children are in schools that profoundly shape and reinforce their worldview; their orientation to self, others, and nature; and their identity as learners. And although they graduate from its walls, they do not leave the habits of mind created by its boundaries. We cannot underestimate the tenacious hold our current story of learning and schooling has over the growing minds of our children—the leaders and cartographers of our future.

We can no longer "water the leaves" of schooling, continuing our singular focus on reforming its contents. It is time to water the roots of learning—radically transforming its contexts and conditions. This is a paradigm shift. Our current context and conditions of schooling are completely at odds with the creative principles of life and learning and who we naturally are as learners. It is time to author a new story of deep and mindful learning and schooling and to design learning systems and environments that embody the natural creativity and joy of life itself. It is into this unexplored new terrain that we will venture together.

THINKING DIFFERENTLY

As leaders, many of us were trained to manage and measure our system's success through rigid and externally imposed processes and structures that left little room for variance and professional judgment. As a result, we focused on "predictive" cause-and-effect models of learning and change. We separated knowledge into discrete and unconnected "subjects." We reengineered teaching and learning relationships based on efficiency and productivity. We fragmented our selves, our organizations, our learning, and our world. We separated our rich exterior and interior lives and forced unbridled individualism, acquisition, and competition to compete with collaboration, innovation, and exploration.

Our system's roots are not being nurtured. Preparing our children for wise world shaping requires a generative learning system that (1) recognizes the processes and structures of learning as nested and interdependent and (2) understands learning as a continuous natural process of constructing meaning through creative inquiry, sustained engagement, and imaginative exploration and discovery. A generative learning system invites learning that increases our capacity for continuous self-creation and nurtures the development of minds capable of integral and wise world shaping. The properties of life and the principles of learning are the deep roots for creating generative and life-affirming systems of learning and schooling. It is through this natural story of abundance, wholeness, creativity, and interdependence that our children can reclaim their own wholeness, meaning, creativity, and sense of belonging.

As leaders, it is our responsibility to create learning conditions that immerse and engage our children in the creative story of life so that they can walk connected paths and author whole and connected lives. Using life's own design principles, we can reweave our children's frayed and severed connections to the web of life and to one another. We can create natural and generative learning systems by reconnecting our children's schooling and learning to the dynamic and creative story of life itself. Deeper roots will enable us to reach higher ground.

The CALL

My explorations have led me to understand that engaging all our ways of knowing is what makes us fully human and that we can no longer separate our interior (more experiential and intuitive) mind from our exterior (more observational and objective) mind. This call for a radical new story of learning and schooling is a call to reconnect learning to life. It is a call to heal the intellectual, emotional, and spiritual fragmentation caused by denying the legitimacy of all we are in learning. Life is about freedom, interdependence, creativity, novelty, relationships, exploration, and discovery—and so is learning. I believe it is the power of this generative new story of leadership and learning that will transform our system of schooling and enable the creation of integral and wise minds that can reimagine humanity's collective future. It is this new global consciousness that will lead to the emergence of a just, compassionate, and sustainable world.

This book is that call. Rather than offer best practices or prescriptive "solutions," it creates a context for a new story by inviting you to think differently about learning and schooling. It illuminates the why and what of educational transformation and explores its deepest roots. It opens a new conversation about the generative nature of living and learning systems. And it offers new language, new questions, new design principles, and a new map for creating learning landscapes that integrate the dynamic properties of living systems with the generative principles of learning. It is from this natural integration that the new paradigm of learning and schooling unfolds.

I invite you to engage in this fundamental question: What would it take to create a generative and life-affirming system of learning and schooling that liberates the goodness and genius of all children and invites and nurtures the power and creativity of the human spirit for the world? When our children are invited to joyfully engage in and meaningfully experience their learning and their world as a living network of relationships to which they belong and for which they have responsibility, the quality and wisdom of their minds will astonish us and the creative power of their dreams will shape the world.

Mind shaping is world shaping. Our habits of mind and patterns of thinking are shaped and developed through experience and practice.

When our children engage in powerful questions, they learn to explore and inquire; when they engage in discovering connections, they learn to seek and discern relationships; when they engage in solving significant ethical problems, they learn to creatively resolve complex interdependencies. How we engage the minds of our children in learning profoundly shapes the patterns of their thinking and their thinking shapes the world.

There is a new world struggling to be born. This transformation will not initially emerge through the reinvention of social structures and institutions, although that will occur. Nor will it emerge through the reformation of governing policies and priorities, although they too will change. Rather, it will come from an altering of mind—the transformation of human consciousness and the emergence of integral and wise global minds that will creatively live into a new worldview of an interconnected living planet and a sustainable and interdependent human family. It is my belief that the fullness of our humanity and the sustainability of our planet rest with the transformation of human consciousness and the nurturing of decidedly different minds.

I hope there will be passages in this book that deeply resonate with what you have already come to know. If so, they are calling to your imagination. They are inviting you to claim your voice and lead in the creation of a new landscape of learning and schooling that reconnects our children's learning to life and creates learning systems that liberate their goodness and genius for the world.

Now is not the time for a new learning theory. Now is the time for a new learning story. Individually and together, we can become new storytellers and bring the new story to life.

Wheaton, Illinois   Stephanie Pace Marshall
November 2005

Gratitudes

In 1987, Carl Sagan, who later called the Illinois Mathematics and Science Academy a "Gift from the people of Illinois to the human future," wrote, "Our children long for realistic maps of a future they (and we) can be proud of. Where are the cartographers of human purpose?"[1]

I am blessed that I have had remarkable cartographers along the way whose early charts and formative maps gave context and shape to my own emerging understandings of transformational leadership, transformational learning environments, and the inherent connections between life and learning. These pioneers provoked my thinking and captivated my imagination. Their initial charts provided the outline to deeply explore the contours and terrain of my own landscape—that of learning and schooling. I am profoundly grateful to these writers, many of whose works are listed in the Notes, and to their uncommon scholarship, curiosity, courage, and commitment to give voice to another way of being in the world.

In particular, I profoundly thank six colleagues and friends who are indeed pioneering "cartographers of human purpose." They were the mentors for my integration of the principles of life and learning into a radical new story of learning and schooling. They are Margaret J. Wheatley, Myron Kellner-Rogers, Fritjof Capra, Howard Gardner, Parker J. Palmer, and Dee Hock. Without their radical thinking about living systems and human organizations, leadership, intelligences, and learning, this book might not have been written.

Throughout this book I have referenced my own institution, the Illinois Mathematics and Science Academy (IMSA), which is striving to create a radical new landscape and terrain for our children and for other children and teachers in Illinois and beyond. I am indebted to our founders, Nobel laureate Leon Lederman and Governor James Thompson, and to the members of the academy's board of trustees and foundation board who have selflessly and wisely served over the years. Most important, I am profoundly grateful to our amazing alumni, students, faculty, staff, and parents for continuing this transformational work to liberate the goodness and genius of our children and to invite and nurture the power and creativity of their spirits for the world. Their stories, sprinkled throughout this book, helped to illuminate IMSA's work in the world.

In particular, I thank IMSA trustees and IMSA Fund board members Jim Pearson, Jack McEachern, Sheila Griffin, Manny Sosa, Luis Nuñez, Michael Birck, Bob Malott, Susan Snell Barnes, Bill White, Greg Jones, Tom Castino, and Sandra Goeken Miles. And I extend my gratitude to these special friends and colleagues whose unwavering support and wisdom anchored my journey: Michael and Mary Kay Pauritsch, Harold Bush, Cile Chavez, Mary Jarvis, Valerie Popeck, Merre Lynn Hare, Michael Palmisano, Connie Hatcher, Cathy Veal, Eric McLaren, Carol Corley, Linda Schielke, Lu Ann Smith, Jim Gerry, David Barr, Gregg Sinner, Dick Hanke, Marti Guarin, Bill Fritz, Patrick Furlong, Kristin Ciesemier, Gordon Cawelti, Bob Galvin, Jan and Al Conradt, and Sarah Sullivan.

Deep appreciation is extended to my "elder colleagues" whose reading of the manuscript provided essential insights and clarification: Cile Chavez, Michael Palmisano, Sally Goerner, Dianne Musial, Gregg Sinner, Yusra Visser, Jim Garrison, Margot Foster, Dee Dickinson, and Manish Jain.

I am indebted to my remarkable executive assistant, Susan Burke, who literally typed, retyped, formatted, and reformatted every word, every image, and every table in this book and whose generosity of spirit, dedication, professionalism, and magnanimity continue to astonish and humble me. Without Susan, I would not have been able to write this book.

I extend profound gratitude to everyone at Jossey-Bass, but especially education editor Lesley Iura and senior assistant editor Kate Gagnon. Their talent, guidance, and challenge truly shaped the story of this book. I am also deeply grateful to Naomi Lucks for her insightful questions, unwavering commitment to illuminate the ideas in this book, and superb editorial work. Naomi was a true partner on this journey.

I thank my family for the blessings of their love and support: Stacy, Willis, Austin, and Ryan Kern; Scott, Risa, Lani, Jake, and Sarah Marshall; Ted Kinnari; Margaret Ann Flannery; Mustapha Konteh; Ruth Metzger; and Jane Schenck.

And with all the love I hold in my heart, I thank my husband, Robert: my soul mate, soul guide, and life companion throughout this journey.

About the Author

Stephanie Pace Marshall is the founding president of the Illinois Mathematics and Science Academy (IMSA), an internationally recognized public educational institution created by the Illinois General Assembly in 1985 to develop and nurture talent and leadership in mathematics and science. Marshall is internationally recognized as a pioneer and innovative leader, teacher, speaker, and writer on leadership, learning, and schooling, and the design of generative and life-affirming learning organizations. She has published over thirty articles in professional journals and was an author for the Drucker Foundation's series Organization of the Future. She served as an editor and chapter author of *Scientific Literacy for the Twenty-First Century* (2002) and was a contributing adviser to *Learning and Understanding: Improving Advanced Study of Mathematics and Science in U.S. High Schools* (2002).

Marshall was the founding president of the National Consortium for Specialized Secondary Schools of Mathematics, Science and Technology and the president of the Association for Supervision and Curriculum Development (ASCD), one of the world's largest international education associations. She was elected a fellow in the Royal Society for the Encouragement of Arts, Manufacturers, and Commerce in London, England, and serves on the board of the Queen Noor Foundation in Amman, Jordan.

Marshall has been recognized by the RJR Nabisco Corporation as one of the nation's most innovative educational leaders and by the National Association of School Boards as one of North America's 100 Best Educators. She has received numerous awards and recognitions for her leadership, including the Distinguished Service Award from the U.S. Marine Corp, the Woman Extraordinaire Award by the International Women's Association, and the Distinguished Citizen of the Year Award from the Boy Scouts of America. She earned her Ph.D. from Loyola University of Chicago and has received two honorary doctorates in science and in arts and letters.

Marshall has worked at every level of education: superintendent of schools, a district curriculum administrator, a graduate school faculty member, and an elementary and middle school teacher. Along with her formal leadership positions, she consults with national and international policy leaders and practitioners and is a dynamic speaker. As a result of her achievements, she was inducted into the Lincoln Academy of Illinois and was designated a Laureate of the Academy, the state's highest award for achievement.

She lives in Wheaton, Illinois, with her husband, Robert, and, as often as they can, in their home, Kaleidoscope Mountain, in Breckenridge, Colorado.

Prologue:
Songlines

Everythin' we ever knew about the movement of the sea was preserved
in the verses of a song. For thousands of years we went where we
wanted and came home safe, because of the song. On clear nights we
had the stars to guide us, and in the fog we had the streams and creeks
of the sea, the streams and creeks that flow into and become Klin Otto.
There was a song for goin' to China and a song for goin' to Japan, a
song for the big island and a song for the smaller one. All she had to
know was the song and she knew where she was. To get back, she
just sang the song in reverse.

—Bruce Chatwin, *The Songlines* (1987)

In April 1997, immersed in my work at IMSA and deeply engaged in conversations about creating generative and life-affirming learning conditions for our children, I received a remarkable invitation that felt like a knock on the door of my soul: "Come and spend a week with a group of Ngankari, the Medicine men and women 'spirit doctors,' healers, and elder leaders of the Pitjantjatjara Aboriginal Tribe; explore the non-linearity and transparency of ancient ways of knowing, and co-create a new more sustainable human story for the new millennium."

My entire life had focused on developing my mind, not my body, so I knew I would be completely ill prepared for camping, extensive walking and climbing, pit toilets, scarce water, poisonous snakes, scorpions, wolf spiders, and daily clouds of flies. Despite these rather formidable challenges, the mystery and possibility of cocreating a new, more sustainable human story was magnetic. I said yes and several months later arrived in the Red Center of Australia's outback. For two weeks, together with our five Ngankari hosts and their children, eleven other invited leaders and I were immersed in the living world of the Aborigine, welcomed into a vast and intricate web of living relationships that sustained an astonishing sense of living connection to ancestors, family, community, nature, and landscape. This was a world unlike any I had ever known.

SHAPING *the* LANDSCAPE

Aborigine culture has its origin in Dreamtime, or world making. In this time before the world awakened, Aborigines believe their ancestors emerged from sleep beneath the earth and began to meander and sing their way across the continent looking for companionship, food, or shelter. Because the earth was still forming, their wandering and "singing the names of things and places into the land" actually shaped the landscape, creating mountains, watering holes, caves, and plants and animals. Eventually each ancestor reentered the earth, transforming into a part of its topography forever.[1]

As they wandered and sung the land into existence, each ancestor left *songlines,* a "meandering trail of geographic sites" that crossed the vast country and was the result of specific episodes and encounters captured as story. Songlines are not simple trails; they are living stories. Each is a geographical and auditory narrative, "a sort of musical score that winds across the continent, the score of a vast, epic song whose verses tell of the Ancestor's many adventures, of how the various sites along her path came into being."[2]

Songlines are also powerful shapers of culture. They are the roots of Aboriginal identity, relationships, and kinship structures: musical narrative maps of connection, belonging, and sustainability.

At birth, all Aboriginal children inherit a particular stretch of a songline. They know it as their conception site and the place on earth where they feel they most belong. The song's verses are their birthright, and it is their responsibility to nurture both the site and the entire song cycle by continually singing it. It is this continuity of song that keeps the land alive. Because songlines live in the land and its people, "lost" is not a concept in Aborigine culture. By singing and traveling songlines in the appropriate rhythm, Aborigines can find shelter and safety (caves, watering holes) across vast expanses of land. Walking and singing these song-stories tells them where they are. Singing them in reverse tells them how to go home. This profound continuity recreates and revitalizes the landscape, the song, and the story. Sometimes those who share particular stretches of a songline—the owners or "shareholders"—gather to sing the entire song cycle in its precise sequence and cadence, sustaining the vitality of the land and their connection to it and one another.

Changing *the* Story

On very rare occasions, an elder can change the songline's story. When this happens, it changes everything, for we become the stories we tell.

Our group witnessed this profound creation and offering of a new story the night before we left the Red Center. We were gathered around the campfire as the elder, Ilyatari, spoke and danced stories from the Dreamtime. One story was that of the Rainbow Serpents.

The story is about four serpents, two males and two females. The males were very jealous of the females. So when the females decided to venture off to the lake by themselves, the males became angry and sought revenge. They followed the females to the lake and watched them enter the water; then they too entered the lake, swam to the bottom, and emerged to attack and kill the females.

The story of the Rainbow Serpents was a story of lust, envy, mistrust, conquest, revenge, and death. But unbeknown to our guide, an anthropologist who had lived with the Pitjantjatjara for over twenty years, Ilyatari had decided to tell a new story by altering the relationship of the four serpents. This time, when the females decided to go to the lake by themselves, the males became sad rather than seeking revenge. They followed the females to the lake, quietly entered the water, and then emerged to surprise and embrace them.

The new story of the Rainbow Serpents was a story of wholeness, trust, generosity, harmony, relationships, and love. This was indeed the new, more sustainable human story for our future.

Our guide told us that what we had witnessed was extraordinary. In a circle with Western leaders, the elder had transformed an unsustainable story born of his culture into a sustainable and transcendent story for humanity. This was an act of love filled with hope and a deep belief in our collective yearning and commitment to bring forth the emergent new world struggling to be born. The elder had changed the songline's story and had named and offered a new and wise story for humanity.

In the sacredness of the Red Center, a new awareness unfolded: *When we change the songline's story, we change the map. When we change the map, we change the landscape.* We now have the opportunity to change the story and map of schooling and create a new generative landscape of learning for our children.

Sitting around the campfire and sharing its fire and light with the elders, I realized that it is the wisdom leaders—the "elders" of a culture, whether young or old—who name and give witness to possibility. Through wise questioning and deep listening, elders create new contexts and conditions for the emergence of deeper, more collective intelligence, imagination, and wisdom. I had come halfway around the earth to rediscover that the sustaining songline for our future and for a new story of learning and schooling is already embedded in our creative cosmos, in life and in learning.

We can indeed dream and sing a new learning landscape into being. We can immerse our children in the deeper song of life in learning. Our dreams can indeed become our maps.[3]

The Journey
Toward Wholeness

Firestorm or Gift?

The Power of Story

*The stories people tell have a way of taking care of them. If stories come
to you, care for them. And learn to give them away where they are
needed. Sometimes a person needs a story more than food to stay alive.
That is why we put these stories in each other's memory. This is how
people care for themselves. One day you will be good storytellers.
Never forget these obligations.*

—Barry Lopez, *Crow and Weasel* (1990)

'D LIKE TO TELL YOU A STORY.
Several years ago, one week before our residential academy was to
open again for the year, I was told we had erroneously sent letters of
invitation to thirty-two students on the wait list. The staff was dis-
traught. To correct this error, they recommended a plan: call each family, fully accept responsibility, apologize profusely, and not admit the
students.

It was clear the staff had agonized over this decision and wanted
to make it right, but I said no to their recommendation. "Our invitation is our word," I said. "Our name and integrity are at stake. We
must admit these students and welcome them as our own."

The news of my decision spread like wildfire. We needed everything: additional rooms, beds, mattresses, computers, and materials. The buzz, both positive and negative, drowned out any other conversation. We had one week to make it all happen.

My leadership team and I needed to know what the community was saying so we could respond quickly and honestly. I asked several staff to write down every comment they heard and send them to me anonymously. When I studied the comments, I was astounded at the emerging clarity of two dominant patterns. Unbeknown to me and the community, and even to those who made the comments, two "stories of the thirty-two" were taking shape. One I called The Firestorm (a story of impending division and fragmentation); the other I called The Gift (a story of emerging community and possibility).

This experience was an epiphany for me as a leader. Despite my awareness of the power of story to influence behavior, I had never experienced the story as it was unfolding. I had never been able to name its patterns as they were taking shape. I had never been able to create conditions that would enable the community to access its emergent stories and intervene in their manifestation by consciously choosing the story they wished to evoke and live into.

I decided at that moment to use my opening-of-the-year remarks to reveal the patterns of the two emerging stories and present them as two possibilities for the future that were now taking shape unconsciously and invisibly. I prepared two visuals: the first was entitled The Firestorm and had a drawing of a blazing fire in its center. The second was entitled The Gift and had a drawing of a gift box with an enormous bow tied on top. Surrounding each image were the numerous individual comments that told each story.

I presented these patterns to the whole community as two emerging yet to be manifested narratives over which we had complete control: *we could choose which story we wanted to live into.* We could choose The Firestorm story, and likely ensure we had a dismal year, or we could choose The Gift story, and celebrate our new students' gifts to us and ours to them. As the year unfolded and the students thrived, it became clear that the story we had chosen was The Gift.

I later learned from many who wanted to live into The Gift story, but felt they lacked the courage to stand up to The Firestorm supporters, that the public naming of the stories as options had given them not only a place to stand but an authentic voice in cocreating our future. In response to negative comments, they could now say, "You're living into The Firestorm story, and that is not what I have chosen"—and know that the other understood. It became clear that when we change our stories, we change our minds.

I also learned that belonging to a community is not a private matter. We are all connected. Within a community there is no such thing as a random comment; every comment is part of an unfolding pattern or story, and the story matters. We become the story we tell ourselves about ourselves. Context is everything. Our stories become our maps.

The Emerging New Paradigm

For as long as we have gathered around the fire, we have told stories. Stories shape our consciousness and behavior, offering images, symbols, and choices for what we affirm or shun, embrace or fear, and love or hate.

Even in our data-driven culture, the power of story to crystallize an idea, mobilize behavior, and create momentum for often massive social change is disproportionate to the actual information it provides. Rather, the power of story lives beneath its language. It comes from the meaning and wisdom it conveys, the spirit it evokes, the possibilities it inspires, the hope it stirs, and the faith in new images of the future it unfolds. Timeless stories connect us to our roots, enable us to see with new eyes, and serve as a narrative bridge and invitation to explore and try out who we might become. Much of who we are comes from the narratives we live and the stories we have chosen to bring coherence to our world. We are natural storytellers.

Although we are likely unaware of it, the most powerful story we tell is our culture's root narrative, our prevailing paradigm. We often speak of paradigms as constellations of beliefs, assumptions, ideas, and values that shape perception. But a paradigm is also that dominant and potent story that most embodies our worldview and captures our identity, purpose, and sense of belonging. This story shapes our understanding of the past, our perceptions of the present, and our vision for the future. A paradigm shift is actually a shift in a culture's story, and it becomes visible when we become the stories we tell.

Storytellers wield enormous power and responsibility, especially during times of uncertainty when we seek some ground on which to stand. As storytellers, we can weave deceptive tales that diminish our collective wisdom, or we can tell stories that embody our deepest truth and awaken our deepest possibilities. Ben Okri captures this power profoundly: "Beware of the stories you read or tell; subtly, at night, beneath the waters of consciousness, they are altering your world."[1]

Our cultural ground is shifting, and our current paradigm is quietly being challenged. Tiny fault lines are appearing in what were once unquestioned policies, institutions, and lifestyles. Green buildings, alternative energy sources, integral medicine, organic farming, wetland preservation, hybrid cars, small schools, and seeking to simplify our lives are visible indications that the accelerating trajectory of acquisition and competition may no longer be all there is. It is clear that "beneath the waters of consciousness," a deeper, more transcendent, hopeful, and empowering story of life and learning is emerging. Authoring this radical new story—and actually becoming it—can transform our cultural narrative. Grounding a new story of learning and schooling in this holistic new narrative will enable our children to reclaim their deepest selves, embrace their natural learning potentials, and reweave their connection to one another, the human family, our planet, and the web of life. The need has never been greater.

The Current Context of Learning and Schooling

There is no more important work than the education of our children. Yet within the current conditions of schooling, and despite the efforts of the best of our teachers, our children often feel inadequate as learners and isolated and estranged from learning. Far too many emerge intellectually, emotionally, and spiritually disconnected from the natural world, their communities, and their own abundant potentials. They have little sense of meaning, wholeness, connectedness, and belonging. They are ill prepared to deeply understand and creatively resolve complex problems that cross and blur disciplinary boundaries and defy dualistic categorization. In such an imbalanced learning environment, the need for a deeper context of schooling is imperative. Learning and schooling must reconnect our children to their natural learning identity and their place in the web of life. Devoid of a sustaining human context, education cannot advance the human condition.

"What would you like to talk about?" I asked a brilliant, well-known scientist about her presentation to our students. I expected her to say that she wanted to explain her latest experiment. Instead, she replied, "I want to talk about the beauty of the cosmos, the joy and mystery of exploration, and the reason science is so cool."

To scientists deeply engaged in understanding the awesome wonders of the universe and the beauty and harmony of the natural world, mysterious connections abound; but in "school science" there is little room for wonder, awe, or mystery. The same is true for school math, school English, school history, and other school subjects. This reductive story is grounded in a detached way of knowing that exclusively honors the objective, the analytical, and the experimentally verifiable. It views empirical observation as the most important skill and believes that "serious" study and acquiring factual knowledge require learners to disengage from their emotions in pursuit of rigorous scholarship. It holds to the premises that subjectivity endangers the pursuit of objective truth and that there is no relationship between the knower and the known. It fails to recognize that learning occurs when meaning is constructed and that meaning is constructed when emotions are engaged and conceptual relationships and patterns are discerned and connected.

Constructing meaning by developing deep conceptual understanding is the commitment of all teachers. Yet often this understanding eludes our students. Nowhere is this more prevalent than in science. Misconceptions acquired at very early ages remain entrenched and impervious to change and make further scientific understanding almost impossible.

Because of the importance of scientific understanding to our children's future, the presence of deep scientific misconceptions has been documented by the Annenberg/CPB project as part of a video series designed to illustrate the current state of science understanding in our country.[2] Entitled *A Private Universe: Misconceptions That Block Learning,* the video documents the unconscious prevalence of scientific misconceptions of even the most basic scientific concepts held by some of our nation's most highly educated people. It illustrates how these misconceptions distort the learner's ability to construct accurate conceptions of scientific concepts without intentionally designed instructional interventions.

The video begins with all the flurry, excitement, and festivities of commencement day at one of our nation's most prestigious Ivy League universities. Graduates' names are read from the dais, and beaming students receive their diplomas. Then the video's commentator interrupts the celebration "to test how a lifetime of education affects our understanding of science," asking new graduates, alumni, and faculty to explain a basic scientific notion: the causes of the seasons. We watch several of these high achievers stumble confidently but erroneously through an explanation of the seasons and the phases of the moon. One young man, who had given a particularly articulate—yet incorrect—explanation of the seasons, was asked about his college studies in science. He replied that he had studied "physics, planetary motion, relativity, electrical magnetism, and waves."

Following this painful demonstration of "confident error"—the students did not know what they did not know—the commentator concluded: "Regardless of their science education, 21 out of 23 randomly selected students, alumni, and faculty revealed misconceptions when asked to explain either the seasons or the phases of the moon."

What went wrong? How could students considered our best and brightest have excelled at schooling but not at understanding?

The purpose and patterns of our current story of learning and schooling are rooted in scarcity and deficiency—"fixing" and remediating the learner's limitations. This tenacious mind-set leads to prescriptive and uniform processes and structures of schooling and a learning identity of passive acquisition and pragmatic compliance. The antiseptic rationality of our current story diminishes and often destroys the essence of who we are as boundlessly creative, insatiably curious, meaning-seeking, and collaborative learners. It tells us that learning is only about what we can see, count, memorize, and objectively measure; what we can create, invent, imagine, or dream is not important in learning. This narrow view of learning shuts us down and cuts us off. It silences our heart and spirit, marginalizes emotion, and invites only part of who we are into learning. The sad and sobering paradox of our current story of schooling is that to protect themselves from the embarrassment and failure of giving the "wrong" answer or asking the "wrong" question, our children retreat and hide their deepest self.

"Why should I raise my hand?" a student once asked me after I asked why he didn't participate in class. "I'll probably get the wrong answer, and everyone will laugh and think I'm stupid!" Then he got very quiet and looked at me warily. "Do *you* think I'm stupid?" he asked.

Conceived and framed within a context of scarcity, deficiency, and fragmentation, our current patterns, processes, and structures of schooling are not designed to ignite our children's joy, intellectual energy, and imagination. They are not dynamic or integrative enough to enable our children to analyze and solve complex, messy problems and to engage with passion in exploring their real questions about life. And they are not experiential enough to encourage our children to access and experience the mystery and enchantment of their rich interior lives, understand how they belong to the world and one another, and embrace and celebrate their remarkable capacity to sense an emergent future and evoke its creation. They are quite simply irreconcilable with the principles of life and learning. As a result, many of our children have become schooling disabled in a learning-abundant universe.

Our schools must be transformed. Adding wings to caterpillars does not create butterflies; it creates awkward and dysfunctional caterpillars. Butterflies emerge through transformation. So it is with our system of schooling, and so it is with our schools. It is my belief that there is no place in the future for a school in the traditional sense of the word.

Why Can't Johnny *and* Susie Read, Write, Count—*and* Think?

The attributes of our current story of schooling reflect our societal ambitions and predispositions. This "success" has been at an enormous human cost: reductive thinking that perpetuates an orthodoxy of excessive fragmentation, acquisition, consumption, unhealthy competition, speed, and winning—and then wonders why contentment and a sense of meaning and purpose remain so elusive.

Within this context, it is tragically predictable that the criticism of public education rests almost exclusively on inadequate achievement on standardized tests in the basics of literacy and numeracy. "Why can't Johnny and Susie read, write, and count?" is the mantra of school reform. To be sure, these prerequisite skills are essential for all future learning—and they are not enough. Where are the voices that fear as much for the deeper basics—the basics of the human mind, heart, and spirit? Why aren't we at least equally troubled by why Johnny and Susie can't think, can't slow down, can't reflect, can't sit still, can't imagine, can't create, and can't play? Why aren't we deeply saddened that they can't dance, or paint, or draw, or make up a story? Why aren't we worried that they can't cope with frustration and conflict? That it is so easy for them to be bored, cynical, and distrusting of adults and that it is so difficult for them to express deep love, trust, and compassion? Why are our hearts not heavy because their spirits cannot breathe, because they have not experienced the wonder and awe of the natural world, and because they do not know how and why they belong in the world?

Just as we must teach children to read, write, speak, and compute well, we must also create learning conditions that enable them to think—to discern the intricate complexities within and between problems, collaborate in conflict resolution, conceive new ideas and solutions, and become stewards of life.

Obsessed *with* Singular *and* Simplistic Measurement

Albert Einstein wisely said, "Not everything that counts can be counted, and not everything that can be counted counts." Despite his prescient warning, it should not surprise us that we are placing disproportionate value on that which can be easily and quickly observed, quantified, counted, and used. Students pinning their college and career hopes on impressive transcripts with staggering numbers of activities, high grade-point averages, and near-perfect SAT scores are often challenged to recall what they actually learned during their twelve years of schooling. Teachers, feeling compelled to teach to the test, soon lose their passion and enthusiasm for their discipline and for teaching.

This narrowing context and perspective has been relentless, and its vortex of acquisition and competition is inescapable and disabling. The dominant construct in our current social contract is instrumentalism— that which is practical and immediately useful. Consequently, less well-developed and perhaps less immediately "useful" ideas almost inevitably yield to the dominant view. Despite their transformative potential, these new ideas often appear insignificant or naive or are readily dismissed as irrational.

But praising and rewarding instrumentalism at the expense of sustainability, and the illusion of learning at the expense of deep understanding, has created a crisis of mind and meaning. If we did nothing else to endanger our children and their future, this would be enough. Our vast repository of measurement tools has led to an obsession with quantification. The tools have not only defined and determined the task, they have shaped the minds that must now learn how to successfully use them. Our tools for achievement have constrained our opportunities for learning. The authentic reality and value of deep learning has become hijacked by the perceived virtual reality and value of high-stakes test scores. A false proxy has become more real than genuine learning. Just as a corporation's stock price is not an indication of its value, quality, long-term growth potential, or sustainability, the same is true with our children's high-stakes test scores. Of course, we must continuously assess our students' learning, but we can no longer be deceived by singular and simplistic measures. Measuring achievement is not the same as assessing deep learning.

The transformative process of creating a radical new story of learning and schooling must be rooted in our deepest learning priorities.

What We *and* Our Children Have Lost

The profound systemic problems that now cast a malignant shadow over our global community, our own society, and the growing minds of our children will not be resolved until we reconnect to the roots of what it means to be fully human and to what we and our children seem to have lost:

- A sense of personal identity, meaning and purpose.

- A passion for learning.

- A sense of wholeness, connectedness, and relatedness to the natural world and to one another. A deep awareness that we are part of something bigger, more mysterious, wondrous, and more transcendent than ourselves.

- An understanding that we must bring all the ways we uniquely come to know into learning—the analytical *and* the intuitive, the objective *and* the experiential, the scientific *and* the aesthetic, the linear *and* the spiritual.

- The compassionate use of knowledge and a global concern for human and community prosperity and moral action in the world.

- A commitment to ecological sustainability and the embrace of nature as a sacred and healing dimension of our lives.

- The capacity for silence and solitude.

- The intimate connection and collaboration of youth and elders around shared purpose.

- The confidence to challenge current reality and create new possibilities.

Perhaps most distressing of all, we seem to have lost the joy of deeply and imaginatively exploring what we love.

Teachers too are feeling loss. Many who enter the profession eager to teach are leaving prematurely, unable to serve a system they perceive as not serving children. This should not surprise us. Teachers are losing heart. The more we require their adherence to teaching scripts and prescribed "teacher-proof" curricula largely designed for high-stakes test performance, the more we thwart their intuition, imagination, and professional commitment to respond creatively to our children's learning needs. Formulaic instruction, time-consuming test preparation, and a rigid focus on one-size-fits-all processes, strategies, and structures are eroding our teachers' passion for teaching.

I can, with you, name countless great teachers and schools that have defied the system so they could develop our children's deep learning and understanding. But without the continuous support of a generative educational system, their efforts are idiosyncratic, often subject to marginalization, and likely unsustainable. They will undoubtedly nurture scores of individual learners, but they will not transform the minds of a generation. We have taken the self, the heart, and the life out of teaching and teachers. It is now our work to create a way home and back to life.

Our children are also losing heart. Regrettably, they view schooling as synonymous with learning, so they do not believe that learning is natural or relevant. Sadly, they appear indifferent, tentative, and almost uncomfortable when asked to engage in *real* learning. I have seen advanced learners put down their pencils and refuse to tackle a math problem they had never seen before or formally been taught because they feared failure and working together was not considered an option. Many of our children have skillfully excelled at schooling—learning what and how much to do to "get an A"—but deep learning is often an alien and fearful endeavor. What's worse, they believe learning is supposed to be this way because we have told them that competing for and getting top grades will prepare them for the arduous demands of the "real world." They have no way of knowing that they have unintentionally been shortchanged.

Mentally, emotionally, and spiritually out of breath, many children are hyperventilating from frenzied trivial pursuit and excessive activity. They do not know how to reflect in silence, although they crave it. They do not engage or see value in serious inquiry and problem solving, although they seek deeper understanding. They see little connection between themselves, the natural world, and the larger human story, although they yearn for meaning and purpose. They are detached from adults and community, although they seek greater connections and yearn to belong. They live for the moment and do not consider the long-term consequences of their behavior because their sense of connection to what has gone before and what will follow is tentative. They do not believe they have the capacity to evoke the future because reality is perceived to be fixed and everything is a short-term event. Nothing seems connected. Patterns are unclear; only things and events matter. Most children, especially high school students, know they are stressed, but they do not know where or how to begin the conversation that can change things.

Many educators, policymakers, and parents also know that at the deepest, most fundamental human level, the cultural narrative and patterns of thinking and behaving reflected in our current system of schooling are not healthy and cannot nurture minds able to create a meaning-filled and sustainable future. But they too are losing heart. They do not know where or how to begin the conversation to transform it.

The price we pay for these sustained losses is far too high. In denying our need to understand and connect to the unifying and coherent songline of life in learning, we sever the deep roots of belonging that connect us to one another, to all of life, and to our own abundant potentials and transformative capacities. We must now confront and resolve the incongruity between what we deeply know, how we live, and how we educate the minds, hearts, and spirit of our children.

As one of the most stable of all social institutions, schools mirror and reinforce our culture's dominant economic and achievement narratives. But they can no longer be reflectors and transmitters of this increasingly impoverished story. The global consequences of impoverished mind making are staggering. Schools must now embody a radical new story of learning embedded in the mystery and creativity of life itself. Together we can create a generative new learning landscape—a new curriculum for life that immerses our children in essential questions and ideas and enables them to more naturally learn their way into creating a sustainable and just future for all.

The New Story Is Radical *and* Generative

To be radical means to go to the core—to the deepest and most sustaining part of life, to the source of our vitality and generativity. Our new story of learning and schooling is radical because it reconnects us to life, meaning, wholeness, and the deepest roots of what it means to be fully human: creative integration of all of our ways of knowing in learning.

It is this creative integration of potentials that makes our new story generative. Generativity is an intentional and creative process of becoming. It enables the endless emergence of wholeness, connections, and novelty. It is the continuous creation and unfolding of life. Parker Palmer, an internationally recognized writer, speaker, and educational activist, describes generativity as "creativity in the service of the young."[3] Implicit in this wise description is the deep connective thread of nurturing, teaching, and mentoring our children.

Our new story of learning and schooling provides a dynamic map for the intentional design of generative learning communities radically different from our current system. Generative learning communities are life and soul affirming. They nourish and sustain the conditions necessary for life and deep learning to thrive. They create space and time for the passion, wonder, and boundless creativity of our children's intellect, imagination, and inventive genius to flourish. They offer safe and playful practice fields for our children to explore their potentials for bringing forth new worlds and reconnecting to what they have lost.

It is my belief that the fundamental purpose of schooling is to liberate the goodness and genius of children by giving them all the tools they need to become fearless and self-directed learners, to learn how to continuously learn and to reengage and reconnect their thinking in holistic, systemic, and wise ways. When we ignite and nurture the unknowable potentials of each learner, we give them the roots they need for complex disciplinary, interdisciplinary, and transdisciplinary understanding; for knowledge generation; for critical and creative thinking; and for ethical action in the world. It is through immersion in multiple ways of knowing, doing, being, and living together that meaning, purpose, connection, and a deep sense of belonging can emerge.[4] This is the context for the growth of integral and wise minds, discussed in more depth in Chapter Three. Schooling is fundamentally a moral enterprise and it must engage and connect the real lives of our children to the real needs of the world.

Generative learning communities know how to continuously learn. They are teeming with the energy and spirit of life. They stimulate exploration, invite newness, deepen our sense of self and other, and expand our boundless capacity for continuous learning. They enable us to connect to one another, and cocreate the future by bringing forth new relationships and new realities that will create more and more possibilities. Generative learning communities:

- Invite, develop, and nurture each child's multiple learning potentials and natural predispositions for continuous learning—for meaning making, integration, exploration, discovery, invention, creation, and wisdom.

- Reconnect our children to the natural world; their communities; the human family; and the unity, wholeness, interdependence, diversity, novelty, and boundless creativity of life.

- Reengage our children's rich interior lives—emotion, intuition, imagination, love, experience, and spirit—in learning.

- Nurture the potential of each child to wisely advance the human condition and cocreate our future by developing their capacity to discern meaning from patterns, think systemically, take the long view, and act with moral purpose.

There has never been a more important time to reperceive and redesign schooling and the context and conditions within which the minds, hearts, and spirits of our children and our future are grown. The human future will be defined by our children's minds and the nature and quality of their presence on the earth. Now is the time to transform the current reductive, prescriptive, and uniform paradigm of schooling. It is the right moment to create a generative, life-affirming, and personalized story of learning and schooling that stimulates the emergence of whole, healthy, vibrant, and wise minds able to more naturally learn their way into creating a sustainable human future. This new story will become our new map.

The Need for New Language

Authoring this new story will require new language. "To be human is to exist in language," world-renowned physicist Fritjof Capra reminds us. "In language we coordinate our behavior, and together in language we bring forth our world."[5]

Language serves as a context, structure, and process for thinking and perceiving. It weaves patterns and enables us to create abstractions and symbolic imagery. It is no coincidence that our cultural landscape is shaped by the thought patterns (memes) inherent in a language permeated by parts and not wholes, and by the domination of things (nouns), not relationships (verbs and processes).

The language that shapes our culture and current system of learning and schooling is rooted in a militaristic, hierarchical, competitive, and command-and-control framework. Sprinkled throughout our organizational conversations, we frequently hear references to stepping up to the plate, making an end run, raising the bar, following the chain of command, making a game plan, and our many, many references to war—war against poverty, against drugs, against terrorism, against illiteracy.

This analytical and competitive language and the mental model it creates enable us to precisely describe, measure, sort, and control the behavior of seemingly independent parts. But it betrays the existence of the wholeness, flowing interdependence, and networked patterns and relationships of life and learning. It is inadequate for reshaping the public conversation needed to create a generative and life-affirming story of learning and schooling and bring it to life.

It should not surprise us that from the imaginative void inherent in our algorithmic language emerge impoverished stories that cannot liberate our innate sense of wonder, awe, mystery, and surprise. We must pay careful attention to the discourse now emerging in our schools and to the limitations created by using militaristic and market-driven concepts, language and metrics, to define and assess human potential and learning. The pervasiveness of our current commercial, competitive, and quantitative discourse creates mental models that diminish the vibrancy and dynamism of the human mind, heart, and spirit in learning.

When our language is prescriptive, our schools cannot be generative. When our language is controlling, our schools cannot be creative. When our language is derived only from the objectively and experimentally verifiable, our schools cannot honor the wisdom and passion that come from the inner life of children and their intuitive and subjective experience.

Because our worldview is constrained or freed by the limitations or possibilities inherent in language, we need a profoundly different language to create a radical new story of learning and schooling. It will come from the language of nature, and its vitality and creative energy will reignite our imagination.

Only a living language can create living patterns, and only living patterns can create living environments. We have clearly excelled in the language of reductive schooling. It is now time to become fluent in the language of generative learning. By paying attention to the patterns of the natural world, we can move from a reductionist language to a holistic language, from machine-based images to ecology-based images, and from rigid structures to mutable learning environments. Because the limitations of our current language restrict the kind of world we are able to imagine and shape, it is imperative that we learn the language of life and learning and use it to design educational land-scapes that are vibrant and alive. A school cannot come alive and can-not become a sustainable learning community without a living language that enables the design of processes and structures that em-body the generative patterns of life in learning.

This living language is a language of creation, wonder, and enchantment—of mystery and meaning. It is a language of wholeness and unity. Nature's lexicon, as we will see in the next chapter, is a lan-guage of integration, connections, reciprocity, and interdependence. Life explores, imagines, adapts, and improvises; its language speaks of networks, patterns, inherent (not imposed) order, and discovery. It is a language of freedom, vitality, diversity, unpredictability, novelty, and creativity. It is a language of wholes, not parts; of relationships, not things; of meaning, not mandates; of disturbances, not directives; and of abundance, not scarcity. The language of life is a language that en-gages the spirit.

The creation of generative learning communities and the emer-gence of integral and wise minds are inextricably connected to the lan-guage, underlying patterns, and design principles of life and learning. It is this frontier that we now explore.

What Living Systems Teach Us

When we try to pick out anything by itself, we find that it is bound fast by a thousand invisible cords that cannot be broken to everything else in the universe.

—John Muir, 1869

I N THEIR BEAUTIFULLY WRITTEN AND PHOTO- graphed book, *The Sacred Balance,* David Suzuki and Amanda McConnell tell the story of the web of life that unites all living things. The authors identify the seven elements needed by humanity for sustainability: earth, air, fire, water, biodiversity, love, and spirituality. "The exquisite balance of these elements," they write, "creates and maintains the web of life on Earth. We too are part of that web; like all living things, we *are* the sacred elements. We are made from and sustained by earth and air, fire and water. We are part of the totality of biological diversity that maintains the planet's life support systems. We are held together by love. And we express and celebrate our understanding of our place on Earth through the mysteries of the spirit."[1]

As a scientist colleague recently told me, "We are all connected to the universe and are made of stardust." It is this story of unbroken wholeness and interdependence that reconnects us to the songline of life in learning and enables us to create our map of generative learning and schooling.

Understanding how living systems simply and often elegantly organize for sustainability is essential to designing generative learning communities. By placing the reconceptualization and redesign of schooling in the context of life's fundamental organizing principles, we can create vibrant and dynamic learning networks and learning communities that embody the diversity, innovation, interdependence, and creativity of life.

CONNECTING LIVING SYSTEMS *and* LEARNING SYSTEMS

You may believe that connecting learning with life and natural living systems with human systems is a misinformed stretch, or you may find it comfortably metaphorical. But if you are willing to push further, I invite you to play with this possibility: that schools and school systems are indeed living systems and that by applying our knowledge of natural living system organization to the redesign of learning and schooling, we can illuminate and challenge current thinking and practice and offer insights and radical new pathways for educational transformation. This transformation can alter the landscape of schooling by creating learning communities that are bio-resonant—dynamic and creative partners with life.

As we play with applying nature's "principles of organization"[2] to learning and schooling, we must let go of any illusion of "getting it right." This is new territory, and we cannot simply transfer concepts from natural living systems like meadows to human systems like schools. Clearly, a meadow is not a school. Still, it is important that we go through this portal, exploring what we know and connecting what we can, opening up new questions, new possibilities, and deeper insights—always being mindful that they will change as we learn more and engage more freely and creatively with life. It is, after all, what we naturally do best: inquire and creatively explore our way into new discoveries and new learning.

LIVING SYSTEMS ARE COMPLEX, INTERDEPENDENT, *and* NETWORKED

We have always lived in an interconnected, interdependent, and networked world. But until the twentieth century, our scientific worldview was grounded in determinism, linear relationships, and the predominance of independent parts. Remarkable advances in computer modeling enabled contemporary science to usher in a new worldview anchored in fundamentally different concepts: concepts of webs, networks, interdependence, complexity, and infinite potentials.

These discoveries challenged our deterministic worldview, offered us a new way of seeing and being in the world, and changed everything—in particular, our understanding of the interdependence of complex systems, especially living systems, and the dynamic relationships between parts and wholes. We now see that living systems can only be understood within the context of the whole. Parts have no intrinsic meaning outside of the system's diverse, interactive, and reciprocal relationships. This systemic perspective enables us not only to see the interdependence of natural phenomena, but also to see ourselves, our societies, and our institutions as intricately connected to one another and to this living and dynamic web. We are woven into the tapestry of life, "bound fast by a thousand invisible chords," and what we do and don't do affects the sacred balance of the whole. In the natural world of which we are a part, everything we see—and everything we can't see—is interconnected.

OUR MIND/BRAIN/BODY SYSTEM

Sometimes we forget that one of the most remarkable living systems is our own mind/brain/body system. Advances in technology have enabled us to not only observe the patterns and structures of our brains, but the very process of learning as it occurs. We now understand that the brain is not a blank slate or an immutably hard-wired computer. It is a magnificent, pattern-seeking, complex living system whose structures are not fixed.

Continuously evolving in complexity, this dynamic, self-adjusting plastic living network can not only atrophy with disuse, but can also change, "grow" (build extensive and more intricate neuronal connections), and actually reshape itself in response to challenging, stimulating, and sensory-enriched environments. Because thoughts have a powerful role in mind and brain shaping, learning actually changes the physical structure of our brains.[3] Neuroscientists have found that nerve cells that fire together wire together. This amazing capacity of the human brain to transform itself is not limited by time: it is present throughout our lives as long as we continue to actively learn. Fortunately for us, we can indeed teach old dogs new tricks—and nature tells us we must. Continuous learning—growth—is essential for sustainability.

LEARNING *and* INTELLIGENCES

New knowledge has also changed our understanding of learning and intelligence, and this has enormous implications for learning and schooling. We now recognize that human intelligence is not a single fixed measure of immutable inherited capacity but is composed of dynamic multiple potentials that must be intentionally ignited and activated.

Cognition is not a fragmented, independent, and prescribed process of acquiring bits of information. It is both biological and social—a dynamic and self-organizing process of constructing meaning by matching new learning to existing patterns and creating new patterns of connections. Emotions and feelings are not enemies of reason or deterrents to rational thinking; they are essential to learning. It has become clear that our mind cannot be separated from our body and our emotions; cognition and emotion are inextricably connected. We now understand that learning is not a bounded and linear process of acquiring information, but a holistic and networked process of active engagement and knowledge and meaning construction. Just as the mechanistic model of the universe was being discredited, so was the disembodied model of our mind/brain/body system.[4]

A new story of the natural world has emerged. It is a story of unity, wholeness, reciprocity, interdependence, and cocreation. This songline of life is the deeply resonant story that flows through all living systems, including our own. And it tells us that living systems, whether a single cell, an organism, or a rain forest, are fundamentally dynamic learning systems: open, creative, exploratory, interdependent, resilient, intricately networked, and free.

Within these learning networks, the potential for transformation is innate because they are free to preserve, renew, restructure, and recreate themselves. This capacity for creative and self-directed internal adaptation, called *self-organization* or *emergence,* is a key characteristic of all living systems.[5] Unlike closed mechanical systems that change through external pressure, living systems internally respond to external triggers—disturbances and constraints—in ways that are self-sustaining. External forces do not direct or determine the system's response. The autonomy and dynamic interdependence of living systems ensure they are continuously self-referencing and in a cocreative relationship with their environment.

An Ecosystem Is a Natural Learning Community

Perhaps one of the simplest ways to think about creating sustainable learning communities is to understand the creative dynamics and flexible organization of one of life's natural learning communities—an ecosystem. Ecosystems are complex, infinitely diverse, and generative biological communities of plants, animals, and microorganisms that live in a dynamic relationship with one another and their environment. It is this interactive and cocreative relationship that enables their sustainability.

An ecosystem—a forest, a grassland, a pond, or even our planet Earth—is not a collection of species that exist and function independently. It is an interdependent web, a network of diverse species whose sustainability is intricately and inextricably intertwined—a squirrel's waste becomes a tree's nutrients; a tree's branches become a squirrel's shelter.

Like all other natural living systems, an ecosystem is a dynamic and open energy flow system. It receives energy from the sun and changes it into chemical energy, and it continuously recycles nutrients throughout the system. An ecosystem is a self-generating network; it is this network pattern of organization that enables it to structurally reorganize in ways that enable adaptation to changing conditions.

Understanding the organization and organizing principles of ecosystems as communities of diverse, interdependent, and mutually beneficial relationships guides our design of sustainable learning communities.

THE PRINCIPLES *of* NATURAL LIVING SYSTEMS

As self-generating networks, living systems have no independent parts or properties, only infinite variety and diversity within an interdependent whole. Nonetheless, it is important to identify six fundamental properties (three domains of organizing and three phenomena of organization) that comprise their pattern of organization and their organizing dynamics (see Figure 2.1). These properties will ground our design of generative systems of learning and schooling that are co-creative partners with life.

DOMAINS *and* ORGANIZING DYNAMICS *of* NATURAL LIVING SYSTEMS

First, we'll explore the three organizing domains (functions and dynamics) of natural living systems.

Boundary: Autonomous and self-referencing

Living systems exist and creatively organize within a boundary or self. Although this boundary is semipermeable and ensures the system is open to the continuous flow of matter and energy from the environment, the boundary itself is structurally closed. A cell wall is a good example. It is this boundary that establishes the system's identity, distinguishes it from and connects it to its environment, and determines what enters and leaves the system. It also serves as the referent for self-organization: the internally directed process that determines structural change. The autonomy of a living system ensures that it is self-referencing and self-sustaining.

Energy and matter: Energy-seeking, open, and structurally responsive to environmental disturbances

Energy is the currency of all living systems. Hence, living systems are fundamentally dynamic energy flow systems, and they continuously recycle matter. This cyclical flow energizes the system and sustains it. If we want to understand how living systems work, we must

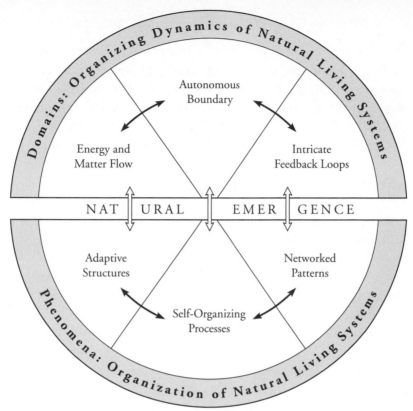

Figure 2.1. Domains and Phenomena of Natural Living Systems.
Note: Natural living systems are energy flow systems and are in a state of
continuous dynamic balance. The curved arrows indicate the cyclical flows of
energy and matter throughout the system's intricate networks and feedback
loops. The vertical arrows indicate the system's dynamic and interdependent
relationships, fluid interaction between all its properties, and capacity for
spontaneous adaptation and self-organization (emergence).

follow the energy. In living systems, energy and matter are the fuel and
source of sustainability.

When an environmental disturbance enters the system and cannot be integrated or absorbed into its existing structures, the system
enters the point of instability from which new structures can emerge.
This happens, for example, when toxins enter a system and can block
or damage the cell's capacity to function. The cell that has the genetic
capacity to adapt can survive.

Feedback loops: Interdependent, intricately connected,
and systems and relationship seeking

Nonlinear relationships are a fundamental property of living systems; these intricate, dense, and closed feedback loops enable nutrients to continuously flow throughout the system, such as an enzyme system in cells.

Life naturally seeks relationships and systems. It seeks mutually beneficial connections with other life in order to create new systems of increasing complexity (networks within networks) that support even greater diversity and novelty. The generative capacity of a living system depends on the flexibility, diversity, and density of its networks of interdependent relationships. These webs of connections keep the system connected to itself and enable it to create more complex systems.

We can see a fascinating example of mutual benefit and interdependence in the relationship between the length of the tube of a *Heliconia* flower on the tropical island of Saint Lucia and the length of the beak of the *Hermit* hummingbird. As the flower tube grew and changed shape, so did the beak of the hummingbird. This cocreative and mutually adaptive process provided "system" guarantees: the hummingbird was guaranteed food because only its beak was long enough to extract food from the flower, and the flower was guaranteed a pollinator!

There is great paradox surrounding the autonomy of life, its freedom to create itself, and its need for relationships to create more life. Although boundaries define the system's identity, the system must exist in an interactive and cocreative relationship with the environment or it will die.

So despite the allure of the concept of independence, it has no relevance or meaning to living systems. *Life is naturally interdependent.* There is simply no such thing as an independent living entity. Without the cooperation, partnership, and reciprocity of the other, the self will simply not survive. The cocreative process of life cannot support isolation. The self-regulatory capacity and sustainability of a living system is inextricably connected to the density, diversity, and intricacy of its interlinked and interactive networks and feedback loops. Self-regulation requires that the system has continuous access to itself. In a living system, relationships are everything.

Organizational Phenomena
of Natural Living Systems

We turn now to the three phenomena of natural living system organization.

Processes: Creative, exploratory, and self-organizing

Within all living systems, self-organization is the fundamental process of transformation and continuous self-creation. This autonomous, exploratory, and novelty-generating process of "self-making," called autopoesis, is the defining property of life.[6] Because life is free to create itself, it cannot be externally controlled; it can only be disturbed, and its structural response to provocation is always self-referential. The system itself directs its response to environmental disturbance. Creativity, invention, and the constant exploration and generation of newness are deeply embedded in life's processes. It is the processes of living systems, not their structures, that give them coherence.

Within an ecosystem, individual species adapt to changing environmental conditions. For example, if a forest falls "behind" in its rainfall, the decrease in water puts many trees under stress. In the short term, trees whose characteristics enable them to be more fit in the drier environment are more likely to survive. But long-term sustainability may require an altered response, such as growing deeper roots.

When environmental disturbances enter the system, expand, become amplified, and can no longer be absorbed and integrated into the system's current structures, the system enters a state of instability from which new structures of greater complexity can emerge. Living systems creatively respond to environmental disturbances through self-initiated structural changes in the pattern of their network and not through a linear cause-and-effect process.[7] Processes are the link between the system's patterns and its structures. It is because of mutual adaptation between the system and the environment that we can say that life and its environment coevolve.[8] This remarkable capacity for cocreation enables the emergence of new systems of greater complexity and diversity.

The complex ecosystem that can emerge in sand dunes is a good example. The community starts off as sand. Eventually a plant species such as grass arrives, grows, and over time stabilizes the sand. When it dies, it begins to provide nutrients to the soil. As the soil increases in nutrients, bushes can grow. The cycle continues, and eventually pine trees and oak trees can survive. The system has become more diverse, more complex, and more stable.

Patterns: Densely networked and attracted to wholeness and order

Living systems are attracted to wholeness and order, and their pattern of organization is a self-generating network. Patterns represent the organized and coherent connections between the elements of the system. These repeated constellations and configurations of relationships give the system its shape and form—its pattern.[9]

We used to describe the interdependent feeding relationships of biological systems as food chains. Now we recognize that they are far more complicated, and we refer to them as *food webs* or *networks*—the pattern of life. This dense and intricate network pattern gives rise to the system's uniqueness, fundamental properties, and process structures. It is the inherent attraction of the pattern that keeps a living system within its boundaries. Living systems can and do change their structures, but their fundamental network pattern does not change. If it does, the system's properties are destroyed, and it is no longer sustainable. For example, humans and chimpanzees have the same cell types, but clearly, we don't look alike. What distinguishes us at the cellular level is the unique configuration of our identical cell types. The differences lie in the pattern of our cell types.

Patterns can be mapped, and the influence of their qualitative effects on and within the system can be discerned over time. It is because the pattern of living systems is a self-generating network that environmental disturbances can travel so quickly through its networks and feedback loops and then return to its origin. The cyclical flow enables the system to be self-regulating and self-organizing. The recognizability, resiliency, and sustainability of a living system are inextricably connected to the intricacy of its pattern of networks. The more complex and intricate its pattern, the more diverse, creative, and resilient the system will be.

Structures: Flexible and spontaneously adaptive

Structures are the visible and physical manifestations of the system's processes and pattern of relationships. They emerge, adapt, and change in self-directed response to environmental disturbances. This capacity for the emergence of new forms of order keeps the system dynamic and able to continuously recreate itself.

In a living system, structures provide both system flexibility and stability. They are the tangible and often temporary forms created to ensure the flow of vital energy and matter into the system. Structural changes represent changes in the system's networks (patterns); they are triggered, not caused, by disturbances from the environment. For this reason, we say that living systems are self-directed and self-organizing. It is the system itself, and not the environmental disturbance, that directs whether and how it will change. Structural changes emerge when energy can no longer be absorbed by the current structures. For example, toxins from a rattlesnake bite can trigger the breakup of our cells' protein structures, resulting in the cell walls' dissolving.

GENERATIVE HUMAN SYSTEMS

I invite you now into relatively uncharted territory: the application of the principles of organization of natural living systems to the transformation of our system of learning and schooling. Until we enable our schools and our school systems to function as the autonomous, creative, interdependent, and self-generating learning systems they are, we will not be able to transform learning and schooling. We may continue to mandate and direct reform initiatives, but we will not alter the system's identity and its fundamental patterns of organization and learning and teaching relationships. This means not only thinking outside the box, but transforming the box into a dynamic learning network.

As we apply—*not* transfer—the organizing principles of natural living systems to the redesign of systems of learning and schooling, we must be mindful of several critical distinctions between natural living systems and generative social systems.

In generative social systems:

1. System identity (what we called *boundary* in natural systems) encompasses the system's shared meaning, beliefs, and purpose. It is the self around which the system intentionally organizes and serves as the frame of reference for system change.

2. System information (what we called *energy* and *matter* in natural systems) is the primary source of system energy and vitality. The continuous flow of meaningful information into and throughout the system is essential for sustainability.

3. System relationships (what we called *intricate feedback loops* in natural systems) represent the system's "neural network"— the fluid, formal, and informal communication pathways that ensure the continuous flow of meaningful information throughout the system. In generative systems, relationships are grounded in trust and collaboration and ensure the system's interdependence.

4. System processes are the ordered, creative, and self-organizing ways the work of the system gets done. To ensure system integrity, processes must be coherent and congruent with the system's identity. How the system works must be congruent with who it is and what it does.

5. System patterns represent its repeated constellations of diverse and intricate relationships or networks that create and define the system's uniqueness—its culture and characteristics. Patterns are both self-generating networks and functional hierarchies. Functional hierarchies are often important for system security and coherence. Self-generating networks are essential to advance, support, and sustain the system's fundamental identity, resiliency, and purpose.

6. System structures are the visible and often temporary forms the system creates to do its work and ensure its desired patterns are embedded. Structures can be both intentionally designed and emergent. Formal structures (departments, divisions, functional teams) provide system stability. Informal emergent structures ensure the system's continuous creativity, adaptation, and change.

In order to extend the dynamics and organization of natural living systems into human systems and to integrate them into the design of generative systems of learning and schooling, I've adapted and applied a conceptual framework first seen in the pioneering work of Margaret Wheatley. The insights of Myron Kellner-Rogers and Fritjof Capra deepened this conceptual map.[10] This new map guides the design of a generative and more natural "ecosystem" of learning and schooling— a "learning arboretum" of which a student of mine once spoke. It is this generative learning system that will embody the wholeness, freedom, creativity, interdependence, and vibrancy of life and invite the abundance and diversity of our children's unique talents and potentials to thrive. Together, the organizing dynamics and organization of living systems create a new map for redesigning learning and schooling.

The Twelve Attributes *of* Generative Human Systems

When we apply the properties of living systems to human systems, specifically our schools, we add another ring to our map (see Figure 2.2)—the twelve attributes of generative human systems: purpose, meaning, trust, collaboration, intricacy, diversity, creativity, order, adaptability, resilience, energy, and vitality. Together these create the context and conditions of authentic learning communities that are bioresonant: in harmony with the songline of life in learning.

Like natural living systems, generative human systems are also in a state of continuous dynamic balance. But the presence of human intention—purpose and meaning—adds conscious choice to the system's dynamics, influencing the nature and flow of its information, the diversity and transparency of its relationships, and the complexity of its processes, patterns, and structures.

Let's look at how these attributes are integrated within the system's organizing domains and phenomena to map our new learning and schooling landscape.

At the heart of every human community—be it a tribe, a community, a school—there is a self: a unique collectively created and shared **identity** or purpose. Over time, the community—the system— becomes organized and creates its work and place of belonging in the world. Deeply shared collective values, *purpose,* and *meaning* develop.

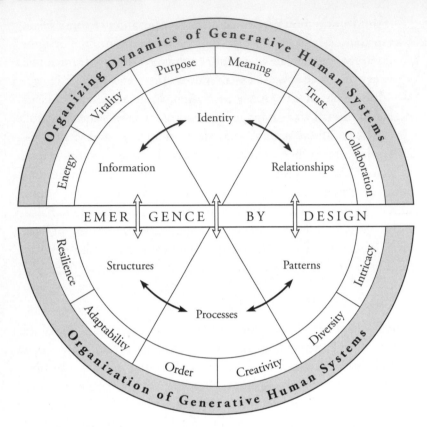

Figure 2.2. Generative Human Systems.
Note: The curved arrows indicate the confluence between the system's dynamics (identity, information, relationships) and organization (processes, patterns, structures). The vertical arrows indicate the fluid interaction and interdependence within and between these properties.

Because the system is open to its environment, continually flowing information (new knowledge, research findings) enters the system; but only **information** meaningful to deepening and advancing its identity is noticed, responded to, and transmitted. Dense and intricate webs of *trusting* and *collaborative* **relationships** and multiple communication feedback loops enable this new and potentially disruptive information to acquire more meaning, become amplified, and be absorbed into the system. There it quickly penetrates and expands, increasing the system's *energy* and *vitality*.

If this information cannot be integrated into the system's structures or these structures become destabilized because they cannot accommodate the new interpretations or perceptions itself provoked by the new information, the system moves into uncertainty and instability. Its current identity has been challenged. It becomes unsure of self. As a result, it can no longer use its history, previous strategies, processes, and relationships to understand, predict, or create its future.

Now the system is at a turning point, or bifurcation point—a fork in the road.[11] Although to system members it feels like the ground is shifting, this point of greatest instability also holds the greatest potential for transformation. Now even the smallest disturbances can disproportionately influence the dynamics and direction of the system. It is at this point that the system can embrace a new self or identity and is then truly able to creatively reorganize itself into new forms.

This is why critical connections, not critical mass, are the essential conditions for change in a living system. The force of the disturbance can be disproportionate to the magnitude of the change.

When this change occurs, *creative* and *coherent* new **processes** and *intricate* and *diverse* new **patterns** of relationships can emerge spontaneously or by design. New networks are formed that give rise to novel, *adaptive,* and *resilient* **structures.** The system changes shape—it has learned—and is now able to integrate this new information into a deeper and expanded sense of self.

Paradoxically, the system has changed and recreated itself in order to preserve its deepest self. To transform learning and schooling, we must bring them to life.

OUR SCHOOLS ARE DYNAMIC LIVING *and* LEARNING SYSTEMS

What could our children accomplish if we stopped trying to externally mandate and structurally direct their learning into existence? Who might they become if we worked with their natural desire to learn—to inquire, create, seek novelty, explore uncertainty, and seek patterns of connection and meaning? What might we create if we use the principles of life and learning to design "naturally right"[12] environments and communities that truly liberated their goodness and genius and provided time and space for them to learn who they were and what it means to be fully human?

Our answers to these questions are embodied in the fundamental unity of life in learning—and it is this integration that grounds the design of a generative and more natural system of learning and schooling. It is this system that embodies the wholeness, freedom, creativity, interdependence, and vibrancy of life and invites the abundance and diversity of our children's unique talents and learning potentials to thrive. When schools and communities are rooted in the deep and resonant songline of life, they are free to engage its creative fire. Because such learning communities embody the properties of living systems, they are naturally autonomous, open, creative, self-organizing, connected, and adaptive. We do not need to fix, remediate, or control them. We simply need to "water their roots" by ensuring that their innate capacities for collective meaning making, exploration, self-creation, and learning are nourished and sustained.

To remain alive and to continue to learn, our schools and schooling systems must be in harmony with life.

Although we are using the principles of living systems as the design principles for creating our new story, living systems in fact do not have design principles. They have natural laws. As designers, we are taking these natural laws—the properties of living systems—and using them as design principles for the new story and system of generative learning. When we create schooling systems in harmony with life, they engage all of who we are, individually and collectively. To create shared learning identity and shared learning purpose, we must engage the whole system. When we enter into the relational dynamics of our schools and schooling systems, we must experience—mentally, physically, emotionally, and spiritually—the dynamic confluence of life and learning in creative motion.

For our schools to act as life does is actually the most natural and ordinary thing in the world. Why would we be excluded from the exuberance of life? We are naturally lured by challenge and the mystery of exploration. We are captivated by the wonder and awe of discovery, and we long for partners and for wholeness, meaning, and connections. We don't have to work at making it so. It is simply who we are.

We Can Transform Our Systems

We cannot underestimate our individual and collective power to consciously provoke our system's transformation in the direction we desire. Shared intention and collective purpose drive system innovation and transformation. This process of self-organization (emergence) is externally provoked but internally determined.

Contrary to our current management view, real change in living systems, including our schools, occurs from the inside out. We and our systems change because we continuously learn. There is a conscious shift in our awareness, perception, and meaning about who we are. Although we try, transformation cannot be externally mandated or directed. It can only be provoked. Change in internal meaning, not change by external mandate, is the source and catalyst for living system transformation.

We know this to be true, yet we continue to direct behavior—trying harder, exhorting more, moving faster, and speaking louder. We know that ultimately it is the community that decides what is meaningful. It is the community that decides what to notice and be disturbed by. It is the community that learns its way into new patterns of relationships. And it is the community that self-regulates (or fails to) and self-organizes into novel, flexible, and adaptive structures that are not only congruent with its new identity, but also deepen its possibilities to continually expand itself.

From the dynamic and continuous integration of system identity (purpose), information (energy flow), and relationships (intricate and nonlinear feedback loops), novel and creative processes (behaviors and ways of working), patterns (self-generating networks), and structures (physical forms) can emerge spontaneously and by design. It is our system's creative capacity to continuously generate diverse new connections and intricate networks and alter its structures that deepens its identity and capacity to achieve its learning purpose.

The drive to continuously learn, adapt, and create keeps our natural world evolving. Recently a science colleague related a remarkable story that underscored this for me. There are essentially two kinds of oak trees, he said: those whose acorns germinate in the fall, and those whose acorns germinate in the spring. A squirrel that buries a fall-germinating acorn in anticipation of spring food will be sorely disappointed. When she goes to find it, it won't be there because over the winter, it sprouted roots and has become an oak sapling. So to survive, squirrels have learned and adapted: before they bury the fall-germinating acorn, they bite the embryo out so it can no longer germinate.

Like all other complex living systems, our schools and school systems must be able to learn, organize, and change through the creative and generative principles of life. They must deepen their learning purpose and alter their learning pattern. They must become self-generating learning networks "bound fast by a thousand invisible chords that cannot be broken to everything else in the universe."

We now turn to the principles of learning and their inseparable connection to life.

3

Nurturing Integral
Habits of Mind

*"The best thing for being sad," replied Merlyn, beginning to puff and
blow, "is to learn something. That is the only thing that never fails.
You may grow old and trembling in your anatomies, you may lie
awake at night listening to the disorder of your veins, you may miss
your only love, you may see the world about you devastated by evil
lunatics, or know your honour trampled in the sewers of baser minds.
There is only one thing for it then—to learn. Learn why the world
wags and what wags it. That is the only thing which the mind can
never exhaust, never alienate, never be tortured by, never fear or
distrust, and never dream of regretting. Learning is the thing for you."*

—T. H. White, *The Once and Future King* (1938)

SEVERAL YEARS AGO AN IMSA GRADUATE STOPPED
by to tell me about her experience as a first-year physics student
in a prestigious university's honors program. The professor was a
young, well-known, and highly accomplished Ph.D. who believed that
intimidation and humility were necessary conditions for gaining the
attention and respect of very talented and, in his view, potentially
cocky first-year honors students. He began class by asking if anyone

remembered a very esoteric formula. As my graduate described, no one did. Worse, the class almost froze—apparently exactly the effect the professor was trying to evoke. Then in the deafening silence, my graduate raised her hand and gave the formula. The professor was shocked. "How did you remember it?" he gasped. "I didn't," she explained. "In my school, we learned how to derive it." When we engage students in deep, meaningful learning, the formulas may fade, but their understanding endures.

Learning is the fundamental process of life and the deepest source of creatively engaging the human mind and spirit. It is a natural and multidimensional process of constructing knowledge and meaning, and its exploratory and improvisational nature invite novelty and discovery. Learning is a continual process of mind making that changes us forever.

We are born learning beings. We naturally imagine, wonder, invent, and explore our way into unknown territories and perplexing and paradoxical questions. Our curiosity and insatiable drive to know and figure things out is innate. Even if we wanted to, we could not stop learning and trying to make sense of our world and our place in it. We could not stop trying to understand who we are, why we are here, and how we belong. From the moment of our first breath, we have learned. We have observed and smelled and tasted and touched and laughed and cried. We have walked and talked and taken things apart and put them together. We have wondered about the blueness of the sky, the vastness of the universe, the depths of the ocean, the awesome complexity of our minds, the intricacy of our bodies, the mystery of our spirits, and the transcendence of our souls. And in our irrepressible quest to know, experience, explore, discover, and play, we create our world.

Although learning is the creative process of life, our current learning story conceives it as a mechanistic, prescribed, and easily measured commodity that can be incrementally and uniformly delivered to our children. This narrative could not be more wrong. Learning emerges from discovery, not directives; reflection, not rules; possibilities, not prescriptions; diversity, not dogma; creativity and curiosity, not conformity and certainty; and meaning, not mandates. Our beliefs and assumptions about learning and about how children learn are the most powerful "rules" in schools—and they are largely invisible. This chapter makes them visible. We turn to two stories of learning and schooling, our current story and the emerging new story, and look more closely at the learning rules that ground them.

Two Stories *of* Learning *and* Schooling

The American Psychological Association (APA) offers a definition of learning in which the generative new story of learning and schooling is rooted: "Learning is a *natural process* of pursuing personally mean-ingful goals, and it is active, volitional, and internally-mediated; it is a process of discovering and constructing meaning from information and experience, filtered through the learner's unique perceptions, thoughts and feelings."[1] (The APA's Principles for Learner-Centered Education are found at the end of the book.)

Amid a world entrenched in misconceptions about learning, this definition offers new understandings and changes the rules. Most Western cultures—and many modern non-Western cultures view *learning* as synonymous with *schooling,* and the result of formal instruction. Learning/schooling is seen as a predominantly externally directed and prescribed process of acquiring and using information.

Although this perspective is contrary to what we know about learning for understanding, its simple logic creates a tenacious hold on how we design schooling. If we view learning as an externally driven and reductive process of incrementally acquiring more and more information, then *input* (delivered information) equals *output* (what is acquired and learned). It follows that the more information children are formally given, the more they will achieve, the better they will test, and the more successful they will become. This perspective is deeply ingrained, and its erroneous beliefs and assumptions about learning serve as de facto design principles for our current story and system of schooling—a story antithetical to deep learning and com-plex understanding.

Reconnecting learning and schooling to life and to the way we naturally learn provides new understandings and new design princi-ples that can ignite our children's goodness and genius and awaken them to a world of creative possibility. There is an enormous discon-nect between the reductive story of schooling grounded in deficiency, prescription, uniformity, and acquisition and the integral story of learning grounded in abundance, meaning, holism, and engagement.

When we compare the "rules"—the learning beliefs and assumptions—that ground the current and the new stories of learning and schooling, their profound differences emerge. And each set of rules creates a learning landscape that invites the emergence of profoundly different minds and ways of thinking. Table 3.1 shows this clearly. (The two stories of learning and schooling are contrasted in greater detail at the end of the book.)

SHALLOW LEARNING *or* DEEP LEARNING?

We only need to compare the body language and emotional expression of children actively engaged in solving problems with those passively sitting in a classroom to understand that the exploratory and inquiry-based ways we naturally learn and construct meaning are completely at odds with the silent, detached, and unnatural ways we are currently taught and asked to learn in most schools. Our children's response to this unnatural design of schooling is often shallow learning, not the deep learning so essential for complex thinking and creative knowledge generation and use.

Shallow learning

Shallow learning estranges the learner from her deepest self. It separates her from the experiences, stories, and questions that foster meaning and connections and from a sense of deep relationship and belonging to others and to something much bigger than herself. It asserts the preeminence of rapid coverage and acquisition over engagement and more deeply constructed understanding. In so doing, it distorts the learner's knowledge of herself as learner, prevents her from accessing her abundant potentials, and disconnects her from the depth of her own creativity and imagination.

The sobering reality is that shallow learning most often results in risk-averse, uncurious, and emotionally disengaged learners who believe either that they are inadequate or that they understand far more than they really do. In either case, they emerge ill equipped to respond to the intricate, ethically complex, and very messy problems we face that defy simplistic categorization, linear analysis, and rapid resolution.

TABLE 3.1. *The Two Stories of Learning and Schooling*

	Reductive Learning and Schooling	*Integral Learning and Schooling*
Identity	1. The context and mental model of learning is scarcity and deficiency—diagnosing, remediating, and "fixing" the learner's clearly identified and often tenacious limitations. The focus of learning is memory—passively acquiring information and accepting external authority for learning.	1. The context and mental model of learning is abundance—activating, developing, and connecting the learner's multiple and indeterminate potentials. The focus of learning is meaning—developing understanding and internal authority for learning.
	2. Competition, threats, sanctions, and fear are the most powerful external motivations to learning. Learning is shaped and driven by external mandates and sanctions.	2. Autonomy, meaning, creativity, exploration, and the quest for novelty are powerful and sustainable intrinsic motivations for learning. Learning is shaped and driven by personal purpose.
	3. Intelligence is a singularly defined, immutable, stable, and heredity-determined capacity distributed along a normal bell-shaped curve. Potential is finite and can be precisely determined. Every learner possesses a single general intelligence quotient (IQ) that remains relatively fixed throughout life.	3. Intelligences are dynamic, multidimensional potentials for information processing, product creation, and problem resolution, not fixed immutable capacities. They are shaped through the dynamic interplay between heredity and environment and can be intentionally activated. Every learner possesses a unique and vibrant constellation of unknowable potentials.
	4. The holistic engagement of the learner's mind, body, emotions, and spirit in learning detracts from rigorous inquiry. Passion, wonder, awe, joy, and the emotional and spiritual dimensions of who we are generally interfere with, detract from, or significantly derail rigorous inquiry, scholarship, and integrative work. Learning is understood as pragmatic compliance.	4. The holistic engagement of the learner's mind, body, emotions, and spirit is essential for rigorous inquiry and integrated work. Inviting passion, wonder, joy, and the emotional and spiritual dimensions of who we are into learning enables meaning and creativity. Learning is understood as transformative engagement.

TABLE 3.1. *The Two Stories of Learning and Schooling, Cont'd.*

	Reductive Learning and Schooling	Integral Learning and Schooling
Information	5. Prior knowledge and experience are not relevant to future learning and are often encumbrances and detractors.	5. Prior knowledge and experience are essential foundations for linking and integrating future learning.
	6. Data, information, and knowledge are the same. A student who has acquired data and information is presumed to have gained knowledge and understanding. Knowledge is not viewed as cocreated meaning. It is detached from the learner.	6. Data, information, and knowledge are profoundly different. A student who has acquired data and information is not presumed to have developed knowledge and understanding. Knowledge is relational, embedded in context, and continuously constructed by the learner in community.
	7. The more information acquired, the better. Rapidly acquired information is more important than slowly constructed knowledge and understanding. The capacity for complex and systemic problem solving rests solely with increased information.	7. Depth and complexity of understanding are more important than the quantity of information acquired. Understanding creates meaning, wholeness, and integration. Complex and systemic problem resolution emerges from integral minds—from the capacity to understand the dynamic relationships within systems and to discern and connect patterns.
Relationships	8. Learning is grounded in a detached epistemology (ways of knowing). This epistemology honors only one way of knowing: the objectively verifiable, the analytical, and the experimental. It views empirical observation as the most important skill, believes knowledge acquisition requires the disengagement of the learners' emotions and that subjectivity and individually constructed meaning endanger the pursuit of objective truth. It asserts that learning is a totally rational process, that there is no relationship between the knower and the known, and that connection to self is not essential to learning.	8. Learning is grounded in a relational epistemology (ways of knowing). This epistemology affirms integral ways of knowing, believes meaning and connections are constructed by the learner, and believes that the learner's passion and love are essential for deep learning. It asserts that relatedness and engagement are at the heart of learning, that there is a profound connection between the knower and the known, and that connection to one's self and a coherent sense of self are essential to learning.

TABLE 3.1. *The Two Stories of Learning and Schooling, Cont'd.*

	Reductive Learning and Schooling	*Integral Learning and Schooling*
	9. Learning is a detached and inert process. Learners of the same age are far more alike than they are different and have similar learning needs. Effective and efficient instruction requires whole groups of chronological age peers to learn and advance together in a prescribed sequence.	9. Learning is inherently relational. Relationships and interdependence enable us to meaningfully connect and belong in community. Deep learning is more likely when a multiaged and multigenerational community is purposefully learning, exploring, and cocreating together.
Processes	10. Learning is primarily a passive, individual, and incremental process of acquiring preselected, externally controlled, and often mandated information devoid of personal or social context, relationships, experience, or environmental influences. It is the quantitatively measurable result of a stimulus-response process.	10. Learning is a purposeful, exploratory, and creative process of discovery. It is a natural goal-directed process of constructing meaning through pattern formulation and active engagement in complex issues and problems.
	11. Individual and collaborative inquiry and the creative exploration of messy, ill-structured, and interconnected questions and problems relevant and meaningful to the learner are interferences to prescribed time allocation and established standards and curriculum and will not prepare students for success on high stakes tests or work.	11. Individual and collaborative inquiry and the creative exploration of messy, ill-structured, and interconnected questions and problems relevant and meaningful to the learner are the processes through which children acquire the knowledge and repertoire of strategies and skills needed for developing deep understanding and expertise.
	12. Schooling is fundamentally a utilitarian enterprise. The purpose of schooling is to rapidly acquire information, cover content, memorize and reproduce facts, and decrease variance between students on standardized achievement tests. Developing "practical" wisdom is too illusive and value-laden to be a function of public schooling.	12. Schooling is fundamentally a moral enterprise. The purpose of education is to transform minds—to acquire and construct knowledge, develop deep understanding and wisdom and demonstrate learning through discovery, reflection, and the exploration and resolution of essential questions that advance the human condition.

TABLE 3.1. *The Two Stories of Learning and Schooling, Cont'd.*

	Reductive Learning and Schooling	Integral Learning and Schooling
Patterns	13. Broad curriculum coverage, content segmentation, and incrementalism are the most efficient and effective ways to learn a discipline. Disciplinary information can best be acquired if we teach a large number of discrete topics independently. Interdisciplinary and transdisciplinary learning are "soft," largely superficial, and distort the rigor of disciplinary boundaries. Discerning and integrating disciplinary knowledge and inquiry patterns are not essential for acquiring information.	13. Deep understanding gained through pattern recognition and concept integration promotes wholeness and the flow of knowledge within and between domains. Disciplinary knowledge and understanding can best be encouraged if we teach disciplinary, interdisciplinary, and transdisciplinary organizing principles, patterns, and concepts in a coherent and integrative context.
Structures	14. Learning is credentialed by the calendar and by the predetermined amount of time spent (and assumed to be sufficient) acquiring pre-selected information. Learning time is a fixed commodity and credentialing occurs when the scheduled learning time is finished. Learners are not capable of participating in the assessment of their own learning or that of their peers.	14. Learning is demonstrated, assessed, and credentialed by multiple forms of evidence and by exhibitions and performances of deep understanding, anytime and anywhere. Learning time is variable. Learning is assessed whenever the learner is ready and is credentialed when learning is demonstrated. Learners actively participate in the assessment of their own and their peers' learning.
	15. Rigorous, meaningful, reliable, and legitimate measurement and evaluation of learning can only be objective and external. Only that which can be quantitatively and objectively measured demonstrates genuine learning. Frequent high-stakes testing is the most effective means to determine student achievement.	15. Rigorous, meaningful, reliable, and legitimate assessment of deep learning is dynamic, flexible, and systemic. It includes both quantitative and qualitative evidence of understanding. It is self-correcting and is demonstrated in authentic contexts and settings that enable complex responses.
	16. It is unnecessary for the curriculum to be connected to the learner's experience, the community's needs, or the world's problems. Most important learning happens in classrooms. Life is not the school's curriculum.	16. Meaningful curriculum must be connected to the learner's lived experience, the community's needs, and the world's problems. Life must be the school's curriculum.

Deep learning

Deep learning is radically different from shallow learning. While shallow learning validates only one way of knowing, deep learning is holistic and inclusive: it recognizes that we are living in a both-and universe, not an either-or one. It understands that it is often through the integration of polarities and seemingly disparate ways of knowing that genuine understanding and wisdom can be created.

Deep learning is both active and reflective. By immersing the learner in the interdependence and wholeness of the world and meaningfully engaging her in the big ideas, questions, paradoxes, and ambiguities of the human experience, deep learning transforms her. It reignites her passion and insatiable curiosity and weaves a tapestry of connection and a timeless web of belonging that grounds her learning in the roots of personal meaning and purpose. Deep learning provides a context of connections and wholeness that reconnects children to all the ways they come to know and reestablishes their physical, cognitive, and spiritual intimacy and resonance with the natural world and one another.

Deep learning is our radical connection to all of life, and it invites and ignites all the ways we come to know:

- The power of the intellect *and* the power of the imagination
- The power of information *and* the power of relationships
- The power of externally validated, analytical, and experimental ways of knowing *and* the power of internally validated, personal, and communal ways of knowing
- The power of rationality and objective truth *and* the power of subjectivity and experiential truth
- The power of the algorithmic *and* the power of the aesthetic
- The power of observation *and* the power of intuition
- The power of reason *and* the power of passion
- The power of skepticism *and* the power of wonder
- The power of expertise *and* the power of wisdom

Deep learning creates self-directed, reflective, inquiring, and fearless learners. As one of my students so beautifully wrote, "I have learned the importance of taking risks everyday; it is the only way to keep growing. I discovered that failure is not always a bad thing. In fact, it can be a positive experience, depending on how the situation is handled. But I think the biggest challenge for me has been that I have learned to be reflective—I have learned the importance of thinking about my thinking, a concept that used to be foreign to me."[2]

Nurturing Integral Habits *of* Mind

The nature and quality of our children's minds will shape who they become, and who they become will shape our world. There is a world now being mapped into the minds of our children; it is one of scarcity, fragmentation, competition, and winning. To many, this world feels like a firestorm. But as mapmakers and architects of our future, our children must experience the world as a gift, engaging joyfully in its cocreation and experiencing its abundance, wholeness, connections, and interdependence. To meaningfully engage requires integral[3] and wise minds able to bring a holistic, connected, and imaginative context to experience and to how we ethically act within and make sense of our world. The most significant work of our time will be integrative. The learned dispositions and habits of mind of integral ways of knowing create a new cognitive map for identifying, understanding, and ethically resolving the complex problems we now face. As future cartographers, our children must see the world as an integral whole.

A child immersed in integral thinking seeks wholeness and integration and perceives and understands parts only in relationship to the whole. She discerns patterns, looking for symmetry in the presence of perceived randomness and asymmetry in the presence of perceived order. She embraces knowing and doubting as partners.

Rather than overrely on any one form of knowing, children immersed in integral thinking develop both-and minds, fluidly navigating within and between analysis *and* synthesis, objective *and* subject knowing, and scientific *and* aesthetic insight. They integrate their minds, bodies, emotions, and creative spirits, reconnecting to the fullness of their learning potentials and how they can uniquely contribute to sustaining the web of life.

The significance of educating for integral thinking is the power of an altered worldview. When we perceive and experience wholeness, we are transformed. We no longer see nature, people, events, problems, or ourselves as separate and unconnected. Wholeness enables us to hear the generative songline of life in learning.

Integral minds seamlessly weave together four contexts of knowing:

1. The multiple ways we come to know, perceive, and belong to our world and one another: the objective, analytical, and experimental *and* the personal, communal, experiential, and transcendent. Integral minds connect our exterior *and* interior ways of knowing and our scientific *and* indigenous ways of knowing.

2. Our unique combinations of multiple intelligences: linguistic, logical-mathematical, spatial, bodily-kinesthetic, musical, interpersonal, intrapersonal, and naturalistic.

3. The languages of disciplinary domains: their organizing concepts, symbol systems, and modes of inquiry.

4. The multiple dimensions of learning: learning to know, learning to do, learning to be, and learning to live together.[4]

Let's explore each of these contexts.

Multiple ways of knowing and belonging to our world

A fourth-grade teacher recently wrote to me about her experiences with problem-based learning (PBL), an instructional strategy that immerses students in messy, ill-structured problems for which they must create a resolution that is defensible to external experts. Students frame the problem, identify its components and interdependencies, assume a stakeholder role, and form teams to research and investigate its multiple components—scientific, legal, ethical, political, and so on.

"I am loving the whole PBL experience," she wrote. "The problem that I am running right now is a blast! The kids have gone far deeper than I ever thought possible for nine year olds. This week we have an animal behaviorist coming to talk about synthetic chemicals and the impact on the environment. One of my students discovered that male polar bears with high levels of synthetic toxins in their systems begin acting like female polar bears and they won't mate. This is playing havoc on the bear population! I have so much exciting stuff to share with you."

After this unit was over, she said, the students planned and held a fundraiser for polar bears. This unit was one of a series of animal studies in which students engaged in problem-based learning to improve their reading scores as measured by district tests at several points during the year. She found impressive growth in reading skills as well as significant gains in their motivation and interest in reading. When we create conditions that invite children to have a genuine stake in a problem that matters and deeply engage in exploration and discovery, their achievement and insights can astound us.

The questions that hold the greatest challenge for mind making are not, "*What* did you learn in school today?" but rather, "*How* did you learn in school today, and *who* are you now?" Not *what* did we teach, but *how* did we teach, and *who* have you become as a result? "Every way of knowing becomes a way of living," Parker Palmer said. "Every epistemology becomes an ethic. . . . Every mode of education, no matter what its name, is a way of soul-making."[5] How we teach and how we ask our children to know will become how they live.

The predominantly depersonalized, and reductive ways we currently ask our children to know in school have indeed become a "way of living," an "ethic," and a "way of soul making," and the results are painfully predictable: too many children who are technically competent and efficient but woefully ill prepared to meaningfully and creatively explore and navigate the messy and unpredictable terrain of life. Far more damaging is that the disproportionate time and value placed on objectivity, speed, high-stakes, and short-term measurement and taking things apart has often silenced or siloed our children's creative spirits and made them feel insecure or even fearful when invited to explore their more sensory, intuitive, and imaginative ways of knowing.

Within the current context and conditions of schooling, we are asking our children to know, think, perceive, and become empirically— to rely on objective observation, reductive analysis, and quantifiably verifiable measurement as the most worthy means to define and defend absolute truth. We have almost become blind to wholeness, connections, relationships, and the vibrant and healing energy of our senses and creative imagination. We cannot wholly know or belong to the world until we integrate all of our learning capacities. Table 3.2 illustrates the contrasts between reductive and integral ways of knowing.

TABLE 3.2. *Reductive and Integral Ways of Knowing Contrasted*

Knowledge Skill	Reductive Thinking	Integral Thinking
Defining and discerning truth	Truth is immutable, and it can be discovered if we disengage from what we are seeking to know. Emotional connections and intuitive insights are impediments to seeking and finding objective truth and to rigorous scholarship and complex thinking. Empirical observation is the most important skill for objective knowing.	"Truth" is neither absolute (immutable) nor relative (individual and idiosyncratic). It is not a fixed state to be achieved or acquired. Rather, it is a communal, continuous, and dynamic process of disciplined and engaged inquiry. The search for truth evokes deeper and deeper questions, not final answers.
Acquiring and generating knowledge	Knowledge is the sum of numerous propositions—bits of factual information that must be dispassionately acquired piece by piece. Subjectivity and individually constructed meaning distort and endanger the pursuit of a discipline's objective truth.	Knowledge is complex and integrative understanding, and its generation and construction require the total engagement of the learner's mind, body, emotions, and spirit. Relatedness, connection, and meaning are at the heart of learning and knowledge acquisition and creation.
Engaging in learning	There is no connection or relationship between the learner and what he or she is learning. Meaning and connection to the self are not essential to learning and are actually detractors and contaminators.	There is a profound connection and relationship between the learner and that which is to be learned. When knowledge is viewed as a subject and not as an object, and when learning is viewed as an engagement and not a transaction, it invites a relationship.
Constructing meaning	Knowledge and truth reside within disciplinary experts and require their explanation for understanding. Students are not yet ready to access or personally engage with the subject itself. This engagement requires an expert interpreter to ascribe meaning. The learner's own construction of meaning is naive and often irrelevant. Objective truth can be accessed only through a hierarchical structure grounded in relationships of power and control.	The "expert" and the "novice" sit together and cocreate meaning by exploring the mysteries and patterns of the subject. The discovery of truths comes through reciprocal engagement. Meaning and understanding are constructed by learners in a community as they mutually seek to understand and cocreate their world.

The integral mind invites and naturally integrates both of these ways of knowing—the more objective and empirical, the more personal and relational—and moves wisely within and between them. These unique and essential ways of knowing are a part of an integral way of living, an integral ethic, and an integral process of soul making.

The integral mind invites the depth and insight possible when scientific dispositions and ways of knowing (those associated with logic, analysis, observation, and experimentation) and indigenous ways of knowing (those associated with relationships, patterns, community, and personal experience) are deeply connected. The integral mind is neither fearful of uncertainty nor obsessed with certainty. It is rooted in wholeness, buoyed by curiosity, grounded in skepticism, comfortable with ambiguity, and committed to the search for possibilities and the passionate pursuit of deepening truths.

Over time, this passionate pursuit leads every great scientist to establish a deep relationship with the subject he or she is striving to understand—James Watson and his "beautiful molecule,"[6] Barbara McClintock and her love of corn and "feeling for the organism,"[7] and George Washington Carver, who said, "Whatever you love opens its secrets to you."[8] Each eventually understands that great science is not detached or neutral observation. Great science and great learning are about passionate inquiry, rigorous skepticism, wonder, and awe. "It is an art, this history," one of our students said. "Breathtakingly beautiful and filled to the brim with evidence to be discovered by the human mind." Clearly it is discovering and engaging the subject—the great idea—that ultimately holds the mysteries, and these mysteries are revealed when we listen to what they are making available to us. Love's affinity for deep connection, meaning, and wholeness enables the subject to "open its secrets" and emerge whole. The integral mind's intentional engagement in living encounters enables its deep resonance with life.

We must indeed learn to love the subject and hold it at the center of our inquiry. The integral mind deeply engages in objective, analytical, and experimental ways of knowing, *and* it knows that absent personal, relational, and intuitive ways of knowing, the deepest and most transcendent and transformative mysteries of the subject cannot be seen, heard, or understood.

Unique combinations of multiple intelligences

We know that each child is a unique learner, but we are often not aware of the depth, complexity, and variability of this uniqueness. Noted cognitive psychologist Howard Gardner illuminates this kaleidoscopic view of learning with his theory of multiple intelligences. He currently identifies eight, possibly nine, multiple intelligences, rather than a single general ability (often called "G"). (The complete list of Gardner's multiple intelligences can be found at the back of the book.)

Gardner defines an *intelligence* as "a biopsychological potential to process information that can be activated in a cultural setting to solve problems or create products that are of value in a culture."[9] His powerful assertion is that *every* learner possesses all forms of these intelligences, but in unique combinations. Our intelligences are not "things that can be seen or counted," he says, but "potentials . . . that will or will not be activated, depending upon the values of a particular culture, the opportunities available in that culture, and the personal decisions made by individuals and/or their families, school teachers, and others."[10]

It should not surprise us that the current conditions of schooling ensure that, as Gardner says, the "values and opportunities available in our culture" and the "personal decisions made by individuals and/or their families, school teachers or others" are primarily directed toward the development of linguistic and logical-mathematical intelligences. Intentionally activating these intelligences is of course fundamental to all learning. But our almost exclusive focus on verbal, written, and numerical ways of knowing and processing information creates an invisible yet palpable field of irrelevance around all the other potentials our children have for constructing meaning. It ignores the value and worth of these potentials in finding and solving problems, figuring things out, exploring new worlds, and creating new knowledge. Equally damaging, it actually prevents our children from accessing and connecting their multiple potentials in learning, such as using music or drawing to learn reading or math. In school, being smart currently means being smart linguistically and logically-mathematically. Being smart in any other way is simply not considered smart. As Gardner once remarked, "It is not how *smart* we are, but *how* we are smart" that really matters.

When we create conditions that invite our children to develop, deepen, access, and freely explore all the ways they can know and represent the world, we set them free to invent their own minds.

The languages of disciplinary domains

Each time I interview a prospective faculty member for a position, I ask two questions: "How does the 'language' you speak, the concepts and organizing principles of your discipline, inform and enhance the 'languages' of mathematics and science? How do the 'languages' of mathematics and science inform and enhance the 'language' you speak"? For some, the idea of a discipline serving as a language is foreign. Even those with advanced degrees and extensive experience struggle with this question.

Yet integral understanding, or the ability to "think with knowledge according to the standards of good practice within a specific domain," requires that we help students make these connections.[11] Deep understanding comes from engaging with knowledge and constructing personal meaning around it. It is developed in three primary contexts: disciplinary, interdisciplinary, and transdisciplinary learning.

DISCIPLINARY UNDERSTANDING.   This refers to understanding a specific discipline's knowledge structures, relationships, and ways of thinking and brings a systemic and multidimensional context to "thinking with knowledge" and solving problems. Each discipline's unique modes of inquiry (designing and conducting experiments, deriving formulas, or researching primary source materials), enduring questions, conceptual organizers (concepts and principles), symbol systems (numbers and musical notes), and strategies for knowing and making sense of the world influence the nature and quality of minds our children invent.

The tools and strategies for developing disciplinary understanding vary within each discipline. For example, children who are fluent in mathematical thinking seem to understand physical phenomena best when they create an algorithm or a computer model. Symbolic representation helps them to visualize physical relationships and discern patterns. By contrast, historical thinking is rooted in understanding the context and conditions of social phenomena by analyzing the relationships and patterns found in human artifacts such as maps, diaries, and treaties.

Just as world languages acclimate and connect us to the culture of a country, disciplinary languages acclimate and connect us to the culture of a discipline. They not only enable us to communicate within an established community of practice, but they frame and shape how we think about, navigate within, and interpret the world.

Deep disciplinary knowledge and ways of knowing are essential for interdisciplinary and transdisciplinary knowing. We cannot connect what we do not know. Yet it is important to be aware of the difference between teaching for disciplinary understanding and teaching for content accumulation and memorization. Absent deep disciplinary understanding, the fundamental organizing principles and concepts of a discipline can easily be lost, and a shallow and naive mind results. Deep disciplinary understanding enables the power of the discipline's great ideas to truly illuminate our children's understanding of the world.

Borrowing from an essay by the poet Rilke, Parker Palmer uses the phrase "grace of great things" and defines the "great things" our children should be engaged with:

> I mean the subjects around which the circle of seekers has always
> gathered—not the disciplines that study these subjects, not the texts
> that talk about them, not the theories that explain them, but the
> things themselves. I mean the genes and ecosystems of biology, the
> symbols and referents of philosophy and theology; the archetypes of
> betrayal and forgiveness and loving and loss that are the stuff of litera-
> ture. I mean the artifacts and lineages of anthropology, the materials
> of engineering with their limits and potentials, the logic of systems
> in management, the shapes and colors of music and art, the novelties
> and patterns of history, the elusive idea of justice under law.[12]

INTERDISCIPLINARY UNDERSTANDING. Interdisciplinary understanding is the ability to think deeply in two or more disciplines. It enables learners to look across, between, and within disciplinary boundaries and "soften" them so they can fluidly connect their concepts, symbol systems, forms of knowledge representation, and modes of inquiry. Interdisciplinary thinking enables children to significantly use and transfer concepts from one discipline to another in order to illuminate and deepen understanding and creatively solve complex problems.

Interdisciplinary learning does not homogenize disciplines so they become fuzzy or indistinct. Rather, extending a specific discipline's

---

Integrating Mathematical Thinking Within Social Science: An Illustration

This illustration demonstrates how essential concepts in two disciplines—mathematics and social science—can be authentically connected and assessed in a way that deepens and extends a student's understanding within both domains. Although the example is primarily one of assessment, it is grounded in integrative and concept-centered curriculum and inquiry-based instruction that enable children to not only demonstrate understanding but also generate new learning.

The following assignment from a former IMSA social studies teacher, Bernard Hollister, was given to high school sophomores talented in mathematics. The assignment was called "The Story of an Equation," and this is what the teacher presented to the class:

In this activity you are asked to develop an equation that mathematically represents the relationship between multiple variables in the emergence of civilization. Historians are in rather general agreement that once humans ceased being hunters and gatherers and became farmers and herders, the first great revolution in *Homo sapiens* lifestyle took place—the emergence of civilization.

As you know, humans seem to have a love-hate relationship with nature. Some scholars have argued that all of historical time has been one of struggle by humans attempting to master nature. There has been heated debate over the nature of the relationships between factors such as technology, population, population growth, urbanization, and change in general and just how they "produced" civilization.

It is your task to develop a working equation for the birth of civilization that will mathematically and historically portray the relationship of these factors in the emergence of civilization. Here are the factors:

C = civilization
T = time
C = change
TC = technology
P = population
A = area
E = energy
Ag = agriculture

The students were given an opportunity to add any other variables they chose. The results of this assignment were fascinating. Some of the variables the students added included:

G = stability and effectiveness of the government
Q = quality of the lives of people
SB = shared beliefs
ES = environmental stress
CM = creative minority
Cu = culture
UM = unwashed masses
R = religion
ME = morals and ethics
E = education
H = health

The equations and their written descriptions were as diverse as the students. What is critical in this example is how an integration of a deep understanding of mathematical relationships with an understanding of the factors critical to the growth of civilization can deepen understanding in both mathematics and history. Using the representational language of mathematics illuminates historical, social, and economic patterns and relationships in unique and powerful ways.

knowledge into the problems of another domain deepens and broadens the learner's capacity for complex problem solving. Here's another example of one student's rudimentary foray into interdisciplinary thinking:

> In school today, in English class, second hour, I thought of something. Socrates and special relativity have a lot in common. For Socrates, different perceptions may produce different truths or realities. In special relativity, the velocity of an object is relative to the observer—it changes.
>
> For Socrates, there is no true reality. In special relativity, there is no real velocity.
>
> For Socrates, God's reality is the only real one, but we can never really know it. In special relativity, the speed of light is the ultimate reality, but we can never really reach it.
>
> For Socrates, each point of view, each reality is valid if it can withstand interrogation. For special relativity, each different velocity is valid if it is congruent with the equation for velocity [the student included the equation in her notebook].
>
> In addition, Socrates says not to give blind respect and judgment to people and things. The unexamined life is not worth living, he said. So, if you don't understand and examine questions, it's pointless.
>
> What good are they if you don't know where they came from, or why they work.
>
> I don't know if the way I worded these comparisons makes a whole lot of sense, but it was perfectly clear to me in English today.

Although several physics faculty gave this first-semester sophomore a passing grade, her comments illustrate the power of consciously seeking unifying patterns, trying to think in more integrative ways, and using the concepts in one discipline to illuminate the concepts in another. Although this student had just begun her interdisciplinary journey, she was gaining comfort in thinking across disciplinary boundaries. Thinking about special relativity in English class is not typical!

If students don't have deep disciplinary understanding, attempts at interdisciplinary teaching may be inconsistent, nondiscriminating, and superficial. Yet we cannot wait for disciplinary mastery before we introduce interdisciplinary work. We must enable our children to become comfortable with interdisciplinary ways of thinking by providing extensive practice for them to connect concepts learned in one discipline to the problems of another.

In practice, interdisciplinary learning actually deepens disciplinary understanding. It challenges students to explore, explain, and use fundamental connections within and among the disciplines and to seek the organizing principles and patterns that make them coherent. It enhances the depth and power of the learner's capacity to understand and resolve intricately connected problems that defy single-discipline solutions.

Creativity typically emerges at the boundaries of a discipline. To intentionally provoke and stimulate the creative synergy that emerges through interdisciplinary connections, children need lots of practice solving problems at the edges. They must be immersed in questions and challenges that cannot be resolved from a single disciplinary perspective.

TRANSDISCIPLINARY UNDERSTANDING.   Transdisciplinary understanding goes even deeper and further by embracing all the ways we come to know: knowing through disciplines, knowing across or between them, and, most important, knowing beyond disciplinary boundaries. The purpose of transdisciplinary learning is to understand the unity of knowledge by identifying principles and patterns that go beyond a single domain and are common to all of them.

Let's consider an example. Suppose we pose this question to students: "How do I come to understand the natural world and my place in it?"[13] Initially they might view this as a science question, or more specifically a biology or ecology question, and confine their responses to the content of these domains. But how might they respond if they were specifically asked to do so through the lenses and languages of multiple disciplines? How might literature inform their response? What about mathematics, history, music, art, poetry, ethics, or psychology? Each domain offers a unique portal into understanding that is distinctive, and when they are integrated, they form a far deeper, more holistic, and wiser story. This is the realm and arena of *beyond*. If we keep asking children to respond to questions such as this through multiple disciplinary and transdisciplinary lenses and help them to seek and discern the wholeness, patterns, connections, insights, and new meanings that unfold over time, we design conditions that invite integral mind making and world shaping. We invite them to invent whole new minds.

The ability to go beyond is essential to integral mind making. Beyond invites our unexplored questions, our search for meaning, and our need to connect and belong to the whole. Beyond honors our creative and imaginative energy and our yearning to deeply engage in the world so we can cocreate a sustainable future. Beyond represents the field in which so many of the world's deeply complex, integrated, and systemic problems reside. Global peace, environmental sustainability, and universal human rights are transdisciplinary challenges whose resolution exists beyond the boundaries of individual disciplines.

Basarab Nicolescu, president of the International Center for Research in Transdisciplinary Studies, writes, "Transdisciplinarity complements disciplinary approaches. . . . It offers us a new vision of nature and reality. Transdisciplinarity does not strive for mastery of several disciplines but aims to open all disciplines to that which they share and to that which lies beyond them."[14] Transdisciplinary knowing emerges from a lasting relationship and apprenticeship to life. It is from this deep and eternal center of dynamic wholeness that the integral mind can best be nurtured.

Multiple dimensions of learning

UNESCO identified and advanced four pillars of learning: learning to know, learning to do, learning to be, and learning to live together. Together they constitute a new integrative framework for a global agenda for holistic education for the twenty-first century.

We are now coming to understand that the resolution of complex, systemic, and globally interdependent problems such as poverty, AIDS, and hunger requires integral minds that have learned to think holistically and wisely. These minds can emerge only when our deepest sense of self is connected to our deepest sense of other—when our personal identity, efficacy, and well-being (learning to be) are seen as inextricably linked to the identity, efficacy, and well-being of others (learning to live together). These four pillars reframe the global educational conversation, redefine and integrate each of these knowledge paths, and assert their equal value and essential importance to creating a sustainable future for all.

Under this new framework, the concept of learning to know is moving away from an exclusive emphasis on passive content acquisition to one of engaged knowing for understanding, discovery, and exploration. Learning to learn and integrating multiple disciplinary ways of knowing and modes of inquiry are now viewed as essential to learning to know. We are moving away from only learning what to know to also learning how to know.

The concept of learning to do is also being deepened. No longer viewed exclusively as developing prerequisite skills (usually physical) for a specific vocation, learning to do now emphasizes the development of a broader range of intellectual competencies that are adaptive and transferable to multiple vocational and avocational endeavors. Creative problem solving, conflict resolution, and interpersonal communication are now viewed as essential to learning to do.

Learning to be and learning to live together are emerging as indispensable knowledge paths for a vibrant and just economy, a healthy planet, and a sustainable world. Learning to be is fundamentally rooted in autonomy and the freedom to be and become one's self (identity). It recognizes the imperative to holistically develop the fullness of our potentials. It affirms the need to invite emotions, imagination, creativity, and spirit into our learning and our work. It recognizes and honors the innate dignity and right of every person to develop all of whom they are.

Learning to live together is fundamentally rooted in respect for cultural differences and diversity, in choosing dialogue and collaboration over competition, in choosing nonviolence and peace over violence and conflict, and in creating shared identity and meaning. Recognizing interdependence and creating collective purpose fosters a new context for respect, empathy, reciprocity, community, and stewardship; enables us to discover and enroll the gifts of others; and permits us to deeply understand the common in the common good.

Table 3.3 illuminates the habits of mind of integral learners in the context of the four pillars of learning: learning to be, learning to know, learning to do, and learning to live together.

TABLE 3.3. *The Habits of Mind of Integral Learners*

Learning to Be: Integrity and Intuition	*Learning to Know: Inquiry and Integration*	*Learning to Do: Imagination and Innovation*	*Learning to Live Together: Inclusion and Interdependence*
Aware of and connected to one's identity and integrity as a self-directed learner.	Learns from diverse experiences.	Inquisitive, persistent, imaginative, inventive, and passionate.	Has shifted perception from self as an independent entity to self as a part of the web of life.
Learning and meaning making are driven by personal purpose and goals.	Continuously seeks new information, generates provocative questions, and is driven by inquiry and hypotheses.	Suspends judgment; takes risks; challenges "facts," authority, and the "logic" of arguments; weighs conflicting "truth claims."	Possesses a sense of joy, awe, wonder, and reverence for the mysteries and sacred nature of life in all its forms.
Understands that there is an integral wholeness to the natural world and an integral wholeness to us.	Is insatiably curious.		
	Possesses deep levels of disciplinary, interdisciplinary, and transdisciplinary understanding.	Pushes boundaries and continuously constructs questions and generates knowledge that deepens understanding.	Seeks connections to the human community.
Knows that our fundamental identity (self) is embedded in the identity of the whole.	Uses the rules of evidence within multiple disciplines yet looks beyond them.	Spontaneously takes ideas and things apart and puts them back together in original ways.	Possesses a sense of oneness—a sense of belonging to the natural world and to others.
Demonstrates "existential intelligence"—a concern for ultimate human issues and questions (Howard Gardner) and a high level of moral conscience.	Constructs meaning and connections by probing one's own knowledge to expose beliefs and assumptions, clarify ideas, and identify and resolve misconceptions.	Seeks novelty and new possibilities.	Self and other are inextricably connected around significant issues, great ideas, and questions of long-term consequence.
		Possesses skills of both analysis and synthesis.	
Is intuitive and introspective.	Critically and creatively integrates, synthesizes, and transfers (extends and applies) knowledge, skills, and modes of inquiry learned in one domain to understand another.	Recognizes the importance of wonder and surprise in learning.	Ethical behavior and the compassionate use of knowledge are embedded in a natural sense of stewardship.
Recognizes that wisdom and discernment come from honoring and inviting all our ways of knowing and being.		Fluidly integrates the seeming polarities within multiple ways of knowing and being.	Concern for human prosperity and moral action in the world.
		Able to hold the tensions inherent in paradox, ambiguity, and uncertainty.	

TABLE 3.3. *The Habits of Mind of Integral Learners, Cont'd.*

Learning to Be: Integrity and Intuition	*Learning to Know: Inquiry and Integration*	*Learning to Do: Imagination and Innovation*	*Learning to Live Together: Inclusion and Interdependence*
Understands that deep learning comes through the construction of meaning, the integration and creation of knowledge, the cultivation of relationships, and the reengagement of intellect with heart and spirit.	Integrates information gained from accessing multiple ways of knowing—the objective and analytical, the subjective and experiential.	Is not bounded by more traditional ways of thinking. Is inventive and improvisational.	Weaves together multiple perspectives and contexts of meaning to create new relationships and new connections.
Reflectively and creatively pursues wholeness and meaning.	Seeks multiple perspectives and diverse and conflicting information about significant issues and problems of fundamental importance to the human community.		Listens deeply. Actively engages with others in inquiry and problem finding, formulation, framing, and resolution.
Continually regulates, assesses, and monitors own learning.	Understands that learning is driven by inquiry and that knowledge generation is dynamic.		Creates diverse networks—real and virtual—to learn with and through others.
Thinks in holistic and systemic ways.	Acquires, generates, and uses conceptual and procedural knowledge from multiple disciplines to solve complex and ill-structured (messy) problems.		Accepts the rights, responsibilities, and shared commitments of belonging to a diverse community.
Acute reader of context.			
Intuitively seeks connections within and among disciplinary domains.			
Seeks new information that deepens its relationship with the subject.	Creates conceptual maps and knowledge frameworks around the organizing principles and knowledge structures of disciplinary domains.		

TABLE 3.3. *The Habits of Mind of Integral Learners, Cont'd.*

Learning to Be: Integrity and Intuition	Learning to Know: Inquiry and Integration	Learning to Do: Imagination and Innovation	Learning to Live Together: Inclusion and Interdependence
	Experiments with multiple forms of knowledge representation: for example, drawing, poetry, literary and scientific writing, and mathematics.		
	Discerns and evaluates the deep patterns inherent in knowledge.		
	Seeks to understand the unity of knowledge—the patterned logic and organizing and unifying principles that give coherence to multiple disciplinary domains.		

Integral habits of mind—learning to know, to do, to be, to live together—form a natural confluence with the integral design principles of living systems. Indeed, the integral mind can be thought of as the mind of life. It is:

- Autonomous, meaning making, and self-referencing. (Identity)
- Information seeking and generating and open and structurally responsive to meaningful environmental disturbances. (Information)
- Interdependent, intricately connected, and system and relationship seeking. (Relationships)
- Boundlessly creative, exploratory, and self-organizing. (Process)

- Pattern seeking, densely networked, and attracted to wholeness and order. (Patterns)
- Structurally flexible and spontaneously adaptive. (Structures)

INTEGRAL MINDS ARE WISE MINDS

I have used the phrase "integral and wise" to describe the nature and quality of thinking essential for a sustainable future. Now we pause to shine a light on wisdom—its unique nature and its life-affirming contributions to understanding integral ways of knowing.

Contrary to popular belief (and perhaps personal experience, if you are living with a teenager!), acting wisely does not exclude the young. Wisdom is not an inaccessible or ordained quality available only to those of uncommon intelligence or knowledge. In fact, wisdom is very different from intelligence. It is a holistic process of reflection and judgment. It is a way of thinking, analyzing, synthesizing, and creatively acting that enables us to understand and respond to the world in interconnected and balanced ways in order to justly and sustainably shape the future. Wisdom takes the long view. It enables us to see beyond events and moments and to bring deep awareness and reflective context to finding, framing, and resolving complex problems and questions. It enables us to hold paradox and ambiguity, discern patterns, seek what is enduring, and purposefully integrate our more objective and subjective ways of knowing. Wise minds know what they don't know. They understand the power and limitations of knowledge. They embrace the tensions and treasures of holistic and systemic thinking. They are context seeking and sense making, and they can more readily find and imaginatively connect the dots into new patterns and new stories. "Wisdom," says Jim Garrison, president of Wisdom University, "is the integration of intelligence and compassion." It is a "natural resource of the spirit" and its "focus is how to live in harmony with nature and all other sentient beings."[15]

We face formidable challenges to nurturing wisdom in our children. Educating for wisdom is radical. It challenges and disrupts our current schooling narrative and dislodges the power of its reductive, competitive, and easily quantifiable metrics for defining and measuring achievement. Schooling is currently about parts and thinking in compartmentalized ways. Wisdom is about the whole and thinking in interconnected ways.

Teaching toward wisdom recognizes learning behaviors that transcend the traditional definitions of success in schools. It is not enough to educate children to think critically and creatively. We must also educate them to act wisely. One way to do this is to provide opportunities for authentic experiences in community service. One of our students who spent several weeks in Mexico as part of a community service project returned profoundly changed. She told me, "I used to think that wealth was all about money, about material things and what we could acquire. Now I understand that wealth is about how much we give; it is about how much and who we love." This is what the wisdom of children looks like. We can hear in her words the echoes of the songline of life in learning and the promise of a more sustainable world.

We Are Embarking *on a* Synthetic Odyssey

Integral minds connect the fullness of our learning potentials. They integrate our multiple capacities for learning to know, do, be, and live together. They seek wholeness, notice patterns of relationships, and possess a connected sense of self and other. They are awake, holistic, full of wonder, and wise, and their vibrancy and wisdom come from their creative engagement with life. Integral minds navigate the landscapes of objective and relational knowing, scientific and indigenous knowing, and empirical and experiential knowing. They synthesize, fluidly weaving webs of connection between seemingly disparate concepts and perspectives.

Nurturing integral ways of knowing, doing, being, and living together is akin to embarking on an odyssey to explore an unknown landscape. It is a reflective, disciplined, and imaginative process of engaged inquiry, exploration, creation, and self-discovery, and new possibilities and deeper and more expansive clarity emerge with each forward motion.

But make no mistake: we will encounter significant challenges and tension in nurturing the growth of integral minds. Dualism, unexamined certitude, and rigid adherence to linear analysis provide great security to many. But so do relativism, subjectivity, imprecision, and endless qualification. Unfortunately, this mode of thinking can also distort serious inquiry, impair rigorous observation, and erode the skepticism and experimentation essential for authentic learning.

Integral thinking does not reject either of these ways of knowing. Rather, the insights of both experience *and* disciplinary knowledge, of intuition *and* rigorous experimentation, and of perception *and* empirical observation are integrated in defining and resolving deeply complex and interconnected issues. The uncommon curiosity, open-mindedness, and evolving wisdom of integral thinking enable us to engage in uncommon inquiry—to take risks, push boundaries, move beyond the status quo, and be comfortable in our knowing and our not knowing. This is clearly not safe territory, but it mimics how life explores and recreates itself.

Ultimately the evolving integral mind develops a relational and connected internal model for learning—seeking to deepen understanding and create new knowledge—by looking for patterns as well as disparities in information. It fluidly reorganizes the terrain of individual disciplines in order to both understand and challenge the distinctive contexts and perspectives each one brings.

To be sure, deep disciplinary thinking also creates knowledge; but the fluent "multilingual" repertoire of integral minds and the holistic context within which they navigate promotes uncommon conceptual and representational connections. Most important, they foster unsettling and irreverent questions that jar conventional wisdom and liberate possibilities for creating new knowledge and new worlds. This capacity to generate questions fundamental to understanding what it means to be fully human will more likely come from children who have moved beyond the boundaries of disciplinary knowing, into the unifying waters of wholeness and connections, and the interdependence of their life with life. The essence of the integral mind is that it sees a fundamentally whole and connected world. It lives a fundamentally whole and connected life. It wisely engages in the fundamentally connected problems of the world to seek sustainable resolutions for the whole.

One of my former students described her education in this way:

I learned how to think, how to reflect and how to learn. I was instilled with a true passion and commitment to be a lifelong learner and developed the skills necessary to be fearless in the face of ambiguity. Although I gained a great deal of knowledge in a variety of academic subjects . . . one of the most important skills I developed was the ability to learn . . . it is not adequate to be an expert in a particular field, one must be truly agile and flexible, continually learning new skills and coping with shifting paradigms. I have been well prepared to be unafraid of the unknown, and to embrace new experiences and possibilities.[16]

The current story has schooled our children away from their wisdom, from accessing their relationship to nature, and from understanding and engaging in the world's deeply systemic and interconnected problems. It is now our responsibility to bring the new story to life and design generative learning landscapes in which integral minds can more likely be nurtured. The maps for this design remain with life and learning. What might this system look like? We now explore its landscape.

A New Learning Landscape

Aspen Grove by Design

> *Struck forte or pianissimo, novelty is the designer's main note. The*
> *most impressive designs are those that seem naturally right,*
> *unimprovable, inevitable.*

—Arthur Lubow, "Inspiration: Where Does It Come From?" (2003)

T HE DESIGN OF OUR CURRENT STORY OF SCHOOL- ing often feels like a management contract with our students. We seem to tell our children that in exchange for following the rules of schooling—coming to class on time, paying attention, completing assignments, and passing tests—they will receive a diploma. The design of the new story feels quite different. It is transformational, not transactional. It is a learning covenant with our children—a promise as well as an agreement.

It is a promise to mentor and help our children develop the fullness of their potentials, invent their own minds, reconnect to life, and wisely engage in cocreating a sustainable future. By intentionally creating this restorative story of learning and schooling and shaping its generative landscape by design, we will invite children to reclaim what they have lost through the old story and learn the deeper basics of integral thinking essential for lifelong learning. There can be no greater purpose of schooling than to awaken children to the wonder of their life and to free their minds and spirits in learning.

Life is a dynamic, perpetually creative learning process. Our children must know that they learn just as life does. When children become authors of their own lives and experience their personal learning narrative unfolding, they rejoin the story of wholeness, creativity, and interdependence woven into the natural world. When they reconnect to this generative songline, they know that they are not alone because they are at home in the world. As Carl Sagan wisely said, "Our children long for realistic maps of a future they (and we) can be proud of. Where are the cartographers of human purpose?"[1] Our learning covenant with our children must be our promise to create generative learning environments that prepare them to wisely assume their role as mapmakers for the future.

Imagine *a* "New School"

What might it feel like to learn in the midst of this generative learning landscape? What might our children experience within vibrant networks of learning designed to embody the dynamics and animating context of life? What kind of learners might our children become if learning was seen as a joyful and mentored odyssey—a "courageous journey that changes everything"?[2] What kind of mind might they invent, and what kind of world might they shape if they see learning as a transformative relationship and a live encounter with great questions and great ideas, and a lifelong process of exploring and discovering the hidden connections between their unfolding story and the unfolding "stories" of the cosmos, the planet, and the human family? Estranged from their story and its deepest roots in the great stories, our children cannot know who they are and how they belong.

The context of story may appear too elusive to ground the redesign of learning and schooling, but its potency must not be underestimated. "The true mentor, the soul guide," Cousineau says, "sends his or her pupil in search of the story that will reach the heart, not an easy thing during the difficult, sometimes gawky adolescent years. Without the story—or the *wrong* story—young people are agonizingly alone. Armed with the story that signals the 'absurd good news,' to borrow from Chesterton, our youth finally know they are not alone."[3]

Until such time as the wholeness, meaning, and connectedness inherent in life and learning become embedded in our psyche, cultural stories, and social discourse, we must imbue our language with new meaning. So when I use the phrase *new learning community* or *new school,* it is to imbue the word *school* with new meaning and new images so we may envision and shape new possibilities.

It is essential to imagine this new school as part of a living and connected whole. It is but one of many small multiage and often multigenerational learning centers embedded in a dynamic learning network—a living system—that connects the communities' "curriculum" and its intellectual and creative resources (personal and institutional) with the learning needs of its children. Such new schools move beyond the rigid boundaries of established places and times and situate learning in diverse locations, institutions, and facilities. They also recast the concept of public education and accountability. Not only does public accountability mean reporting information about student learning to the public, it also means engagement in children's learning *by* the public. Intergenerational learning can revitalize and restore a community.

Welcome *to the* Aspen Grove Center *for* Inquiry *and* Imagination

Let's visit a possible new school: a learning center for primarily ten to sixteen year olds, the Aspen Grove Center for Inquiry and Imagination.[4] I say *possible* because Aspen Grove represents a synthesis of learning conditions that already exist in some of our nation's schools.

An aspen grove is a powerful symbol for the new learning and schooling story. Although an aspen grove looks like a forest of individual trees, it is actually a single organism connected at its roots. Within a grove of aspens, most, if not all, the trees are related. Like an aspen grove, the generative new story of learning and schooling supports a wide variety of unique learning centers, but they remain connected at the roots, part of an intricate learning network and system.

Learning experiences are personalized and intergenerational

As we enter the dynamic and technologically rich learning spaces, engagement, respect, and freedom are palpable. Aspen Grove serves as an incubator for inquiry and imagination. It feels like an experimental laboratory, an interactive hands-on museum, an entrepreneurial think tank, and a reflective retreat center. Aspen Grove invites and exudes life. Its space is open, colorful, and fluid. There are lots of windows for natural light and comfortable furniture that beckons conversation and problem solving. Learning studios and tutorial and production studios have telephones, copiers, fax machines, wireless tablets, digital cameras, and other materials to ensure students can access and create what they need. Plants are everywhere, and students take care of them. There is even a flourishing vegetable garden that the children tend, and once a month they prepare a meal for a community group. A large outdoor labyrinth invites their reflection.

There are no bells to signal the end or beginning of classes. Learning experiences, learning time, and even learning locations are driven by the goals and commitments of the children and the nature and complexity of their work. Clusters of children of different ages, teachers, mentors, and community members, as well as national and international online partners, are working together. Intergenerational learning is pervasive.

Learners are not segregated by traditional age cohorts or grades. Rather, personalized learning plans cocreated with the children and their families drive the design and creation of learning experiences and multiage learning clusters. Because learning is explicitly linked to the community's life, students are engaged in learning year round and not confined to the traditional school day. In fact, Aspen Grove is part of a global learning network where learning happens any time and anywhere.

Curriculum weaves deep understanding

The curriculum is not textbook driven. Textbooks are just one resource. Students have Internet access and can retrieve information and generate knowledge from multiple sources.

Student learning is guided by learning inquiries—significant disciplinary and interdisciplinary questions—contained in curricular frameworks, developed by faculty and staff. The curriculum is integrative, inquiry based, centered on significant questions and complex problems, and grounded in specific learning competencies created by the community.[5]

Students are immersed in disciplinary, interdisciplinary, and transdisciplinary inquiry. They are learning how to learn, engaging in collaborative problem framing and resolution, and creatively using knowledge learned in one discipline to inform the questions raised within others. They are learning about their own abundant and unique potentials, developing their own internal authority for learning, and developing a fluid repertoire of learning strategies essential for deeper and more complex and creative understanding.

The larger community is engaged in learning

Each year, in collaboration with the city council and the elected trustees of the learning board (which replaced the school board), the volunteer leadership of the community learning network (which includes student leaders) chooses the most significant problems facing the community. These problems are integrated into the curriculum and become the work of interdisciplinary and intergenerational problem-based learning teams. Sometimes the teams work at Aspen Grove; sometimes they work at other community sites. What is so powerful about this experience is that children and adults are living and resolving problems together.

On this particular day, we observe as problem-based learning teams (which meet weekly) analyze the results of their research using computer simulation, modeling, and concept mapping and share them in an electronic forum with teams from other new schools.[6] They are also in conversations with national and international practitioners and experts who have been working on the same problem in diverse settings and from different disciplinary perspectives.

The resolution of each team's work will be presented to several community panels: disciplinary experts and industry practitioners, representatives from the learning board and the community's learning network (through the cable network and the Internet), and the city council, whose decision it is to accept, adapt, or reject the team's recommendation. The students' work and the panel's assessments will become part of each student's digital learning portfolio, a dynamic collective record and narrative of his or her personalized learning plan.

Learning is collaborative, creative, and exploratory

As we continue to explore and experience this deeply engaging, reflective, and playful learning environment, we pass a mathematical investigations studio where groups of students are constructing small bridges in response to geometry problem sets designed by a team of math faculty, local engineers, and architects. Prior to construction, prototypes were electronically designed and created using design software. We watch the teacher stop at each table and talk with each child, asking questions, probing for understanding, listening, and providing instruction when necessary. When a new insight or a misconception emerges, the teacher calls the entire group together.

These students do not appear to be afraid to actively engage in mathematics, nor do they appear to be afraid of learning. Though some struggle, the respectful, collaborative, and nurturing atmosphere gives them the confidence they need to be successful over time. They remain challenged, not threatened. They seem to really believe that making mistakes is a valuable and necessary part of learning.

We move into the scientific inquiries studio and once again see teams of students working together, sometimes with and often without their teachers. A team is working on a laboratory experiment in nanotechnology with a research scientist, biotechnologist, and two graduate students from a nearby university; a team is preparing and videographing their presentation for the annual Inquiry and Research Symposium (which is also broadcast on a local cable network); a team is discussing their museum mentorship project; a team is analyzing data electronically sent in real time, from an experiment being conducted a thousand miles away; and a team is working with their teacher and a visiting bioengineer to probe the future implications of living technology. Another student team is exploring the social, ethical, and economic policy implications of their artificial intelligence research with a social science instructor who has joined them. Eventually the social science and science teachers and several invited clergy from many faiths engage the students in integrating the scientific, economic, and ethical concepts they are studying.

We also pass fine and performing arts studios where students are practicing an instrument, singing, painting, sculpting, and working both independently and with practicing artists. Teams of faculty—mentors, older students, elders, and community members—are preparing materials and learning experiences. Older children are tutoring younger children and collaborating with them as junior investigators.

Community-centered learning networks are welcomed

As we conclude our visit, we notice that staff and volunteers from many of the community's learning and health agencies are integrated into the learning life of Aspen Grove. These include prenatal care; reading and computer literacy; medical, dental, psychological, and social work services; family planning and counseling; employment and housing counseling; vocational training; and child care and child development counseling. Community college, university, park district, museum, and business mentors and liaisons are a natural part of this vibrant learning network.

This intergenerational learning center is one of many dynamic hubs in a dense and ever growing learning network. This network is sustained by deeply shared beliefs about children and their learning, a clear learning identity and purpose, continuously generated and widely disseminated information about the children's and the system's learning, intricate learning relationships, fluid learning and communication patterns and networks, collaborative and creative processes that activate and engage learning potentials and promote system innovation, and flexible learning and teaching structures that honor each child's uniqueness and the system's self-organizing capacity.

To be sure, you will recognize some dimension of the Aspen Grove landscape in schools and systems you already know or are a part of. These learning communities are essential contributors to the learning and schooling "future struggling to be born." The storytellers who are already engaged in bringing this landscape to life will help to lead the way.

PRINCIPLES *for the* DESIGN *of* GENERATIVE LEARNING *and* SCHOOLING

Like life, the new story of learning and schooling will creatively unfold in an infinite variety of ways. To be sure, the physical structure of Aspen Grove is uniquely configured. Clearly the vast majority of schools do not have the financial resources to start all over. But the essence of Aspen Grove is neither its architecture nor its innovative space. It is its generative learning context, its identity as an intergenerational learning center of inquiry and imagination, and its vibrant community-centered learning networks. The essence of Aspen Grove is the integrity of its generative design principles, which embody and evoke the wholeness, abundance, interconnectedness, creativity, and diversity of life and learning.

These are the fundamental principles for the design of generative learning landscapes:

- Ensure learning environments are bioresonant and rooted in the principles and properties of life and learning—how living systems organize for sustainability and how the human mind learns.

- Immerse children in meaning, wholeness, connections, and belonging.

- Create time and space for deep and slow learning, problem resolution, and the holistic development of integral ways of knowing, doing, being, and living together.

- Create learning experiences, materials, and pathways that identify and ignite each learner's unique constellation of learning potentials.

- Ensure that the system's information generation, application, and evaluation processes are open, fluid, transparent, connected, and designed to secure, create, and continuously share meaningful knowledge about learning.

- Foster personalization and community engagement. Ensure that learning relationships are inclusive and that the whole system is dynamically connected to and accountable for its shared learning purposes.

- Immerse learners of all ages in creative inquiry, exploration, and discovery. Embed individual and collaborative opportunities for meaning making and invention in the system's learning processes and structures.
- Ensure learning structures are flexible, temporary, and adaptive, and embody the principles and properties of life and learning.
- Understand the profound connection between mind shaping and world shaping. Ensure learning and schooling environments and experiences are designed to engage children in wise and sustainable world shaping.
- Surround the system in meaning, wonder, joy, and love. Liberate human goodness and genius, and ignite and nurture the power and creativity of the human spirit for the world.

These "naturally right" design principles are not static constructs. They are fundamental relationships and patterns that sustain system creativity, vitality, and continuous learning. They enable us to intentionally link learning to life and schooling to living systems. In so doing, we create learning landscapes that reconnect our children to the songline of wholeness, meaning, and connectedness that flows through them and the natural world, and we bring our children and our systems back to life.

Grounded in these generative design principles, the new story links our personal stories to the world's story. It is this deeply embedded and interlocking story that claims our place of belonging in the web of life and reconnects our children to life, one another, and the natural world. The new story of learning and schooling profoundly changes the context of why, what, when, where, how, and with whom we learn.

The radical new design of learning and schooling reconnects us to the roots of our capacities to become fully human by reweaving the severed connections of mind, heart, body, and spirit in learning. It is not a new technique, strategy, or best practice. It is a sustaining context for mind and world shaping. Our children will more naturally and meaningfully learn when they are free to develop and connect all of who they are in learning. Each of our children is a marvel, and they do not know it. The new story invites them to embrace their gifts with joy and without apology.

Earlier I invited you to think differently about the current story of schooling and its influence on mind shaping. I invited you to play with the possibility that schools and the systems within which they are embedded are living systems and that applying our knowledge of life and learning to our understanding of schooling would illuminate current practice and offer new pathways to altering the present landscape and for creating learning environments that are creative partners with life.

Generative systems of learning and schooling learn—grow, adapt, and change—as life does. They are:

- Autonomous, meaning making, and self-referencing. (Identity)
- Information seeking and generating, open, and structurally responsive to meaningful environmental disturbances. (Information)
- Interdependent, intricately connected, and systems and relationship seeking. (Relationships)
- Boundlessly creative, exploratory, and self-organizing. (Processes)
- Pattern seeking, densely networked, and attracted to wholeness and order. (Patterns)
- Structurally flexible and spontaneously adaptive. (Structures)

Integrating the properties of life and the principles of learning creates a powerful map for designing the landscapes and terrains—the contexts and conditions—of generative and life-affirming schooling. The chapters that follow illuminate the landscape of the new system—the confluence of its generative identity, information, and relationships, manifested by design in its generative processes, patterns, and structures. Although we'll explore each property, it is only to shine a light on its distinctive attributes. Two things must be kept in mind: in any complex system, none of these properties is independent, and each property is present at each level of scale: individual, classroom, school, district, and community.

Within living systems, there is only interdependence. There are only dynamic relationships in continuous motion.

Designing the New Learning Landscape

Integrity

Naming and Owning Our
Integral Learning Identity

*System learning identity is purposeful, personalized, and
transformative engagement.*

S EVERAL YEARS AGO, A DEAR FRIEND WHO WAS
the superintendent of a local school district asked me to address
his first staff meeting of the year. There was great excitement in the district because they were opening a new middle school. I talked with the
staff about the conditions they would need to create in order to enlist
the children in deciding how they wanted to live and learn together in
their new space. I shared three "Rules for Belonging Together," which
we had created with our students.[1] The rules were very simple: Take
care of yourself. Take care of each other. Take care of this place.

A few weeks later, I received a note from my friend thanking me
for my comments and telling me what happened as a result. His story
astounded me. He said the middle school staff had resonated deeply
with the three rules and decided to talk with the children about them.
As a result, the whole school community chose to embrace them as

their own rules for belonging together. During a heavy thunderstorm, he said, the fire alarm had sounded and all six hundred students had to go outside in the rain. Upon returning to the building, every child took off his or her shoes so they would not get mud on the new carpeting. They told him they were "taking care of this place."

This strong sense of meaning linked to personal identity did not arise solely from the rules. It arose because the school nurtured each student's authentic connection to the community. In the new story of learning and schooling, personal identity and community identity always work in harmony.

CREATING *and* DEEPENING LEARNING IDENTITY

As human beings, learning is our essential and core competency. It is also our system's core purpose and work. The learner's construction of meaning and understanding through purposeful, personalized, and active engagement is at the heart of deep learning and the system's culture of inquiry and imagination. Generative schooling develops each learner's capacity and confidence as a learner, activates his or her multiple learning potentials, and nurtures the development of holistic, integral, and wise ways of thinking.

Our sense of efficacy, creativity, and tenacity as learners grows from the clarity and depth of our learning identity. Whether we feel competent or inadequate, smart or "dumb," confident or fearful as learners depends on our deeply embedded perceptions of ourselves as learners. For better or for worse, our personal learning story creates a powerful and resilient learning identity, becoming a self-fulfilling prophecy that drives the nature and quality of our present and future learning.

Several years ago, at a conference designed to ignite our multiple learning potentials, I met a woman who told me she couldn't sing. She began the conversation in a lighthearted way but quickly became serious when I asked her how she knew she couldn't sing.

"Because my third-grade teacher told me," she replied immediately.

I was stunned. "But that was fifty years ago! Surely you've sung since then?"

"No," she said. "From that day I stopped singing—even in the shower."

> ## Beliefs That Ground Generative Learning and Schooling Identity
>
> - *The context and mental model of learning is abundance—* activating, developing, and connecting the learner's multiple and indeterminate potentials. The focus of learning is meaning—developing deep understanding and internal authority for learning.
>
> - *Learning is shaped and driven by personal purpose.* Autonomy, meaning, creativity, exploration, and the quest for novelty are powerful and sustainable intrinsic motivations for learning.
>
> - *Intelligences are dynamic multidimensional potentials for learning*—that is, for information processing, product creation, and problem resolution—not fixed, immutable capacities. They are shaped through the dynamic interplay between heredity and environment and can be intentionally activated. Every learner possesses a unique and vibrant constellation of unknowable learning potentials.
>
> - *The holistic engagement of the learner's mind, body, emotions, and spirit is essential for rigorous and imaginative inquiry, ethical and creative problem solving, and integrated work.* Inviting passion, wonder, joy, and the emotional and spiritual dimensions of who we are into learning enables meaning and creativity. Learning is understood as transformative engagement.

If you are and have always been a confident learner, you likely can't imagine this happening to you. But if you are not, this story may resonate all too clearly.

Our learning identity emerges from many factors: heredity, past and current experiences, learning opportunities, curiosity, emotions, motivations, and learned thought patterns and strategies. It is also shaped by the context and conditions of the learning and schooling story and the landscapes in which we are placed to learn. What and, most important, how we learn, shape who we become as learners. And who we become drives whether we can access the will, desire, and commitment to continue to learn deeply—to wonder, explore, question, imagine, invent, and take risks with new and even absurd ideas.

When I asked one of our graduates to describe her IMSA experience from the perspective of her identity as a learner, she wrote this thoughtful response:

> Before coming to IMSA, I had lived in the same small, conservative suburb of Chicago my entire life. I went to school with the same students year after year, and we shared similar beliefs, values and morals. Our community was somewhat intolerant to new ideas or different ways of living. My ideas and all I knew were accepted by my peers, I was comfortable, and I never was asked to think about why I believed something.
>
> When I came to IMSA, suddenly my way of thinking was not shared by all. For the first time, I had to support what I believed—my ideas weren't simply accepted. It was difficult and uncomfortable at first—I never had to think about my thinking. However, I now know my identity will always be changing. As I learn more about the world around me, as I meet different people, and am exposed to different ideas and beliefs, I must continue to grow. Ideas must not be accepted simply because they are popular.[2]

Learning is all about the freedom to construct one's own knowledge and meaning and to continuously recreate one's self. Freedom is the wellspring of deep learning, inviting the mystery and transcendence of the human spirit and awakening us to the possibilities inherent in exploration and discovery. Who we believe we are as a learner creates a context and story that frees or constrains who we believe we can become. A child immersed in a generative learning environment becomes self-directed and actively engaged in generating and pushing the boundaries of his or her own knowledge and understanding. Within this landscape, the locus of control for learning shifts from the teacher to the learner.

Children Need Access *to*
All *of* Their Intelligences

We know that every learner is unique, but we are often unaware of the depth, complexity, and variability of that uniqueness—even, and perhaps especially, our own. Howard Gardner's theory of multiple intelligences reminds us that each of us possesses multiple intelligences (detailed at the end of the book), but in varying degrees and unique combinations. Our multiple intelligences are not countable entities, he contends, but are "potentials . . . that will or will not be activated, depending upon the values of a particular culture, the opportunities available in that culture, and the personal decisions made by individuals and/or their families, schoolteachers, and others."[3] In general, the earlier we activate and develop our potentials (through meaningful experiences, creative inquiry, sustained practice, and continuous feedback), the more likely we can use them to generate new knowledge and deepen understanding.

Currently, our system of schooling is primarily designed to develop two intelligences: linguistic and logical-mathematical. These intelligences ground our ability to think logically, effectively use language, and perceive and use numerical relationships. They are clearly foundational to all learning. However, our one-size-fits-all approach to developing these intelligences creates a field of irrelevance around all our other potentials. This sense of insignificance actually denies or constrains their value and power for learning language and mathematics, solving problems, figuring things out, and creating new knowledge.

Paradoxically, when we do not activate (or, as often happens, dismiss) our children's other learning potentials, we actually diminish their ability to develop their linguistic and logical-mathematical potentials. Creative and innovative problem solving requires us to have access to the breadth of our intelligence repertoire—naturalistic, kinesthetic, musical, and spatial. Why would we ask our children to construct a complex "house" with only two tools in their tool box? Whether by design or default, our exclusive reliance on linguistic and logical-mathematical ways of knowing clearly tells children who possess different combinations of intelligences that their learning potentials are simply less worthy. Being "smart" in school is so narrowly defined that it rejects the very nature and synergistic interdependence of all of our learning potentials.

This is often true of children from first-language cultures other than English whose distinctive and often highly developed ways of knowing may extend into other forms of intelligence, such as naturalistic, kinesthetic, spatial, and musical. As a result of this cultural variability in preferences for how information is first accessed and processed, each learner uniquely constructs his or her own meaning and understands the world through the patterns of connection created by his or her own knowledge, experience, and understanding. Although learning unfolds within common developmental patterns, learners process information and construct meaning differently.

Despite our good intentions and the sincere efforts of committed teachers, the conditions within our current system of schooling often send debilitating and distorted messages to our children about how "smart" they are and how well they can learn. Over time, these messages can shape timid and tentative learning identities that mask and even diminish our children's potentials for further learning.

THE CURRENT STORY DISTORTS INNATE LEARNING IDENTITY

Imagine sitting down with a child whom you love and telling her the following story.

YOU ARE BORN EITHER SMART OR NOT SO SMART. Your intelligence is in your genes. It is fixed at birth, and you can't do much to change it. You can try as hard as you want, but your capacities and potentials are limited. You can't change the quality of your mind very much, but you must work hard anyway.

REALLY SMART PEOPLE ARE GOOD AT ALL SCHOOL SUBJECTS—MATH, SCIENCE, READING, WRITING, ENGLISH, AND HISTORY. They are also good at taking tests and writing papers. You can be talented in art, music, dancing, poetry, or athletics. You can be really "good" at building or inventing things, figuring things out, or taking things apart and putting them back together. But being good at these things doesn't make you smart in school.

EVERYONE SHOULD LEARN AT THE SAME TIME AND IN THE SAME WAY. Mostly this means sitting in a classroom and listening to a teacher. If you learn differently—by drawing, making models, creating music, taking things apart, or physically moving—you are probably not as smart as those who learn the way you are expected to in school. You are different and probably not well suited for education beyond high school.

YOU CAN TELL HOW SMART OR INTELLIGENT YOU ARE BY HOW WELL YOU DO ON TESTS (USUALLY STANDARDIZED AND HIGH STAKES). If you don't do well on tests, you are probably not very smart. If you get A's, you are smart; if you get C's, you are not smart. You do not need to understand how you learn best. You simply need to do what is expected and what everybody else is doing.

SCHOOLING AND LEARNING ARE THE SAME THING. Learning mostly happens in school, and if you are not successful there, you probably won't be very successful in life. The learning you do outside school really doesn't matter very much.

COMPETITION IS ESSENTIAL TO SUCCESS. You must look out for yourself and not spend too much time trying to help others be successful. If you do, they may achieve a higher grade point average (GPA) than you do. The higher your GPA and class rank, the more competitive you are.

LEARNING IS A SOLITARY ACTIVITY. You must learn and study alone. Learning is not a joyful, creative, exploratory, or collaborative process of making sense of things, building something, or solving a problem that you, your peers, and your community really care about. If you are learning with others, especially if they are your friends, you will likely get distracted and learn less. Learning is serious and rigorous work, and if you are really engaged and having fun, you are probably not learning what you should. Solving problems that affect your community and perhaps the world is too complex and hard for you now. You'll be ready to work on them when you are older. Just be patient.

WHAT PROFESSIONALS TELL YOU ABOUT YOUR INTELLIGENCE, LEARNING ABILITY, AND FUTURE IS PROBABLY TRUE. They can tell whether you are smart or not, capable or not, and likely to be successful or not. Only they can really interpret the results of the tests and the tests tell the story of how smart you are and how successful you will be.

YOUR PASSION, EMOTIONS, INTUITION, AND SPIRIT ARE NOT WELCOME OR VERY USEFUL IN SCHOOL. They distract you from the requirements of the curriculum, generally waste time, and get you, the teacher, and the class off track. Besides, none of that stuff is on a test, so it is not very important.

YOUR GOALS AND DREAMS ARE PROBABLY UNREALISTIC, AND YOU WILL LIKELY OUTGROW THEM WHEN YOU GET INTO THE REAL WORLD. The real world isn't about dreams. It's about acquiring things, winning, being successful, making money, and doing better than others. One person can't really make a difference or change the world.

These are harsh lessons, and to some they may seem preposterous. "We don't tell kids this," they protest. But for some children, this is indeed what they hear every day. The learning identity that emerges from our children's subliminal immersion in this story of learning deficiency and fixed and finite potential cannot possibly invite their creative engagement, cannot inspire possibilities, cannot stimulate their development as independent learners, and cannot instill a sense of connection and belonging. It can only constrain and diminish.

As leaders, our role is to awaken and ignite our children's potentially vast learning repertoire. It is to deepen, expand, and diversify our children's learning experiences by meeting them where they are and nurturing each of their intelligences. Diverse and flexible learning opportunities must be created for each of them to emerge confident, connected, and whole.

DEVELOPING INTERNAL AUTHORITY *for* LEARNING

Emotions and motivation are two of the most powerful influences on the nature and quality of our thinking. Motivation is influenced by our emotions and the depth, richness, and complexity of our interior lives. It is also influenced by our beliefs, values, goals, sense of self, and efficacy as a learner. It is emotions that drive attention, and it is attention that drives learning.[4] We must create conditions that authentically invite and motivate our children to learn.

What engenders a strong desire to learn? In general, goal-directed and purposeful challenge, novelty, and surprise stimulate learning. Positive emotions such as wonder, curiosity, and even mild uncertainty and confusion seem to increase motivation, focus attention, and invite deeper and more complex learning. Even some stress, frustration, and anger can direct a learner's attention and challenge greater levels of achievement and performance. However, threatening conditions that yield intense negative emotions like fear, panic, and deep anxiety generally interfere with learning and create a blockage that prevents the learner's natural curiosity and creativity from emerging.[5] For many children, learning in schools is threatening because they feel impotent within its walls. The most powerful motivation for learning is meaning and the belief that you can influence the context, conditions, and outcomes of your own learning and your own life. Neuroscience tells us that we shape our world from the inside out: thinking and learning affect the chemistry and structure of our brain. Hence, we can only see what we believe is true and possible. Believing is seeing, and not the other way around. Our children must believe they are capable and worthy before they can see their remarkable potentials for world shaping.

The concept of locus of control or internal authority for learning is an often overlooked but critical dimension in understanding the power of motivation and emotions. Learners engage when they can be self-directed cocreators in learning; when, what, when, and how they learn is personalized; when learning goals and questions are driven by them; and when they believe they can be successful despite the degree and nature of challenge. Teachers can design engaging experiences, offer insights, illuminate patterns, and weave interdisciplinary connections, but they cannot prescribe or construct the learner's meaning. Learners coconstruct their own meaning within a community. Meaning can be informed, ignited, and deepened, but it cannot be imposed. The depth and complexity of knowledge, understanding, and meaning constructed by the learner are linked to the nature, depth, and complexity of the learning experiences we create and immerse them in by design and the emotions and potentials these experiences are likely to activate. Internal *author*ity for learning means children can *author* their own lives, because they have unencumbered access to what they want and need to know, do and be.

The New Story Honors Each Child's Unique Learning Identity

Let's contrast the messages the current learning and schooling story inadvertently sends to our children, with those intentionally sent by the new story. Now imagine sitting down with a child whom you love and telling her a new story.

Your brain can actually grow when it is challenged. Our brains don't actually get bigger, but our brain's remarkable networks of connections become denser and more intricate because more connections grow as we learn. We can actually increase the number of connections in our brain through learning, even as we get older. The human brain is amazingly flexible and adaptive. We never stop learning, so continue to challenge yourself.

Intelligence is not a single capacity and is not fixed at birth. Just like a diamond, intelligence has many facets, and each of us possesses many different types of intelligence. But they will remain dormant or hidden if we do not actively use them. The nature and quality of our learning experiences are major factors in what and how we learn, and they are created by the decisions of teachers, families, friends, communities, and, most important, you. You are ultimately responsible for your own learning and for shaping your own mind. You must decide what your learning questions and goals are and what you want and need to learn in order to develop your mind well. So do not limit yourself, and do not take the easy way out. Creating your own mind and authoring your own life is the greatest gift you can give yourself and the world, and learning is your pathway to get there.

Schools are currently designed to teach and reward primarily two of your potentials. It is these logical-mathematical and linguistic or language intelligences that have largely defined whether you are smart in school. But each of us has a unique combination of many intelligences, including language and mathematics. So do not wonder *if* you are smart. Instead, find out *how* you are smart.

Learning is a naturally social and collaborative activity. As humans, we naturally seek cooperation, not competition. Despite all the messages to the contrary, independence and competition are cultural choices, not innate biological ones. You will learn more deeply if you learn with others.

UNDERSTANDING CONCEPTS, PURSUING QUESTIONS THAT MATTER TO YOU, AND SOLVING MEANINGFUL PROBLEMS ARE WHAT LEARNING IS ALL ABOUT. Doing well on standardized tests does not define or determine your intelligence; tests are important, but they provide only one piece of information about your achievement in school, not your potential for success and contributions in life. We need you to understand and help us resolve the problems in our community and our world now. You do not need to wait, and we will not ask you to.

YOU ARE A UNIQUE LEARNER. THERE IS NO ONE ELSE IN THE WORLD EXACTLY LIKE YOU. You must learn in your own way and in your own time. Making mistakes, taking risks, exploring, failing, and asking for help are essential to learning. Discover what you love, and pursue it with passion.

WE ARE ALL WORKS IN PROGRESS. Never lose sight of your dreams; they are as possible as anyone else's. Pursue them with knowledge, courage, and determination, and don't be afraid to bring your passion, your heart, and your spirit to learning. Learning, exploring, discovering, and creating are the most joyful things we can do, but they take focus, persistence, and commitment. Never shortchange your life by deciding to stop wondering and learning.

THE EARTH AND ALL OF LIFE, INCLUDING EACH OF US, COMPRISE A DYNAMIC LIVING SYSTEM. We are all connected. If this system were a gigantic machine and we were each a tiny part, we could make no difference: machine parts have no freedom and certainly no "minds" of their own. But this is not the story of life. In a living system, every living being, no matter how small, can significantly affect the direction and behavior of the whole system because we are all connected. This is called the *butterfly effect*—a butterfly in one part of the world can literally move its wings and affect the course of weather in another part of the world. It seems impossible that such a tiny creature can have such a far-reaching effect, but it does because we are literally all connected in the web of life. One tiny movement can make an enormous and unpredictable difference. You too can have a dramatic effect on the world, for good or for ill. Be wise about your choices and the fluttering of your "butterfly" wings. They could change the world.

These are the messages our children must hear so they can begin to believe them. And this is the conversation we can have with them now.

The generative learning identity inherent in these messages is based on learning abundance and a commitment to develop the unknowable potentials of each learner by design. How smart are we really? How smart are our children really? The truth is, we have no idea. But I believe it is safe to say that we and they are far more capable, far more imaginative, far more creative, far more courageous, and much, much smarter than test scores might have us believe. We must ensure that schooling does not define our children's limits, silence their spirit, demean their passions, undermine their dreams, or deny their access to learn whatever they desire. Generative schooling and deep learning must be reconnected before another generation is denied access to knowing who they are and becoming what they dream.

The nature and quality of our minds are inextricably connected to the nature and quality of the learning arboretums in which they are invited to grow. Now let's explore the identity of generative learning system.

Everything Emerges *from* Identity

Identity is the source of system integrity, its context for sustainability, and its animating force for creating a shared and deeply felt sense of connection and belonging. Identity holds our system's collectively created and shared beliefs and intention, shapes our cultural norms and commitments, and provides the frame of reference from which continuous learning emerges. Whether for good or ill, everything emerges from identity.

Our system's identity emerges from its clarity, meaning, and depth of commitment to its learning purpose, beliefs, and values. A clear and compelling learning identity (its purpose) grounds our system's capacity for self-reference and self-organization (an intentionally chosen structural change) because it holds the deep self around which we and our system can continue to organize.

Uncertainty about our system's learning identity (its purpose and fundamental beliefs) leads to a lack of institutional focus and confusion of means. We cannot ignite and direct our collective intelligence toward achieving our goals unless they are clear. If students are not clear about what is expected of them, if teachers are confused by changing priorities, and if administrators are frustrated by lack of autonomy to create conditions essential to student success, the system becomes closed and unstable.

When our system's identity is clear at the roots—when there is only one self to radiate purpose and possibility and when we are free to explore and creatively organize around this learning identity—we invite trust and more expansive and imaginative expressions of the system's purpose to emerge. We feel both secure and free in systems where boundaries are rooted in meaning and where identity is internally created, not externally prescribed and imposed. It is the process of continuous self-creation that gives generative learning systems their spirit, energy, motion, and life. A compelling identity creates a deep sense of meaning, community, and continuous learning. Table 5.1 shows some of the sources of system identity.

The LEARNING IDENTITY *of* *a* NEW SCHOOL SYSTEM

What is the learning identity or self of a new school? What is the identity or purpose of the new learning and schooling system within which it is embedded? Simply, it is to develop integral and whole minds by igniting our children's boundless capacities for self-directed lifelong learning. It is to nurture critical and creative thinkers able to wisely advance the human condition. The identity of generative schooling is to transform minds by activating, engaging, and integrating the fullness of each child's intellectual, emotional, physical, and spiritual potentials.

This life-affirming system identity is grounded in a relational worldview and a context of abundant learning potentials. It is focused on developing meaning and internal learning authority, and it is centered on deep learning and holistic engagement. It provides the sustaining roots of generative schooling. A life-affirming learning identity enables us to say yes to our system's transformative learning purpose in the world. The story that began this chapter is a powerful example

TABLE 5.1. *Seven Sources of System Identity*

History	Our founding and sustaining stories, legends, traditions, and rituals. Our heroes, warriors, villains, healers, and spiritual leaders. Our chronology of achievements and disappointments. Our joys and sorrows. Our expressions and acts of courage, bravery, and cowardice.
Beliefs and values	What we believe about learning and our work and purpose in the world. The learning commitments and values we name and seek to embody in our vision, mission, processes, structures, and relationships. What we accept as fundamental and basic "truths." What we hold as nonnegotiable. Who we believe we are.
Vision	The field of intention created by what we proclaim as our greatest possibility and what we declare as our highest purpose. What holds our hearts and feeds and sustains our souls.
Mission	The unified and shared learning purposes that have called us together. What we articulate as the essence and reason for our creation and existence and what we wish to bring forth in the world.
Goals	Declarations of our learning and teaching intentions. What we hold ourselves accountable to achieve. Our mile markers for realizing our mission.
Shared knowledge	Why and how we collectively gather, create, share, and use knowledge in order to achieve our purpose. What we collectively know and share about our fundamental work and how we uniquely define and position ourselves in the world. Our distinctive competencies and capacities. What we notice and continue to learn about ourselves in order to both preserve and transform ourselves and how we share and expand learning throughout the system.
Principles of belonging	How we define the nature of our relationships and work together; what we espouse and embody as our guiding, fundamental, and sustaining norms, "rules," agreements, and commitments for learning and belonging together as a community.

of what can happen when our personal identity is in harmony with our system's identity.

Generative and life-affirming schooling links the identity of each learner (child and adult) to the identity of the whole system. This synergy of identities creates a confluence of shared meaning that enables the system and each learner to continually create and learn. Our children's resonance with their school's learning purpose comes from its congruence with their own purpose. They can see themselves in the system. It is this clear connection to the whole that invites them to fully engage and feel they belong. There is astonishing power in simple rules of belonging. Shared identity keeps the system true to itself.

One day I was leaving my office when I saw a student intently reading our belief statements posted near the staff entrance. He was fumbling around for something in his backpack but still kept his eyes focused on the belief statements. I asked him what he was looking for. "Paper and pencil," he replied. "These are so good. I want to write them down." I was astounded and couldn't resist a conversation. I knew these beliefs were powerful to me, but why did a teenager actually want to write them down? So I told him our story of how these beliefs were born and how as a community we had created, challenged, and "blessed" every word. I asked him which ones resonated with him the most. He named these two:

- Meaning is constructed, not prescribed.
- The survival of global civilization depends primarily upon the quality of education provided to all people.

"Why do you want to write them down?" I asked.

He replied, "Because I now see what our community really is and what we are trying to be."

We simply must be able to see our selves in the system's learning identity we have created.

Grounding Learning *and* Schooling *in* *an* Identity *of* Learning Abundance

The distinctions between learning and schooling grounded in an identity of learning abundance rather than learning deficiency are profound.

An abundance identity asks what is possible, not what is wrong. It asks how the community might cocreate new learning conditions, not who's to blame. It asks how we might invite and release all the potentials of our children, not how we can fix them. Because the context of our questions creates conditions for the quality of our responses, a deficiency identity cannot lead to generative thinking or action. Whether our system's conception of learning is rooted in a mind-set and model of abundant potentials, invitation, empowerment, and engagement, or deficient capacities, remediation, domination, and transaction makes a profound difference in how we conceive and design learning environments. Unless we profoundly alter our awareness and understanding of our current learning and schooling identities, we will not be able to transform their processes, patterns, and structures.

The Role of Leaders

Understanding the coherence and potency of a generative and life-affirming learning and schooling identity is essential to understanding the real dynamics of school change. Like other living systems, we and our schools change or learn when we choose to—when new information triggers a change in meaning and this challenges how we perceive and define ourselves. We resist externally imposed control, but we seek autonomously created change. Meaning and choice are the catalysts for systemic change. The system, not an external authority, chooses if and how it will respond to environmental disturbances. And if it changes, it does so in a way that deepens the integrity of its self—its identity.

As leaders, we often ignore this understanding of change and continue to direct our systems. We must understand that like life, we and our schools naturally resist any attempt at external control.

Many school leaders are weary of excessive mandates and often feign compliance to preserve their integrity. But deep down, we all long for and seek deeper awareness and bold new insights about our self and our possibilities. We crave greater meaning and purpose. And we look for new and challenging partners to create more learning, more life, more connections, and more complex systems. The generative and life-affirming learning identity of the new story of learning and schooling reaffirms who we are as naturally creative and collaborative learners. It affirms our unique and indeterminate potentials and infuses our schools and our children's learning with vibrancy and fire.

This chapter begins a series of Leadership Inquiries that can be used to engage our communities in new conversations about learning and schooling. It is often through deeper and slower conversations that our shared commitments and highest purposes emerge.

To create generative and life-affirming systems of learning and schooling by design, we must first become what we seek to create. Soulful conversations safely held can invite our deepest self to emerge. It is from this deep center that we can bring the new story to life.

LEADERSHIP INQUIRIES *About* LEARNING *and* SCHOOLING IDENTITY

Creating generative learning and schooling systems means engaging our communities in deeper questions about learning and schooling identity. I offer the following questions to get you started:

• *Who am I as a learner?* What must I learn to live the life that is mine to live, do the work that is mine to do, and advance the purpose of my life and the purpose of my community? What will it take for me to reconnect my full capacities of mind, heart, and spirit to the work of this community? What is my heart asking me to be courageous about? How would I be different if I decided to surprise myself? What is my stake in the community's work now?

• *Who are we as a community of learners? What is our learning vision and purpose?* What called us here, and why have we come together? What are our collective vision, mission, learning purpose, and goal? What gives our system meaning, integrity, and coherence? What is the self we are referencing and wish to organize around? What do we want to create together? What are our deepest beliefs and commitments about our children's learning from which our actions emanate? What do we believe we can create and achieve together that we could not achieve alone?

• *Who are our children as learners? What if there are no limits to their potentials?* When we listen to the voices and yearnings of our children, what do we hear them say about their lives, learning, schooling, community, and future? What is our faith in the capacities of our children? What do we believe about their intelligences and potentials?

What do we believe about teaching and learning and activating and nurturing capacity? How will we ensure our beliefs are manifested in our behavior?

• *Who are we as leaders and learners?* How might we and our children be engaged together in a life of learning that is meaning filled and purposeful? What is our faith in the intelligences and potentials of our community? Who must we become, and what must we do to manifest the new story of learning and schooling in our community? What community capacities and resources need to be reconnected in learning?

• *How can we make schooling worthy of our children's passion, creativity, and imagination?* What is standing in our way? What don't we want to talk about? What do we believe is impossible? How must we change? What grounds our courage and commitment?

• *How shall we name and articulate our real work in the world?* What language, metaphors, and stories best capture our learning identity? What is the most compelling possibility we seek? What principles of belonging might we create to ensure our learning community continues to learn? What do we want to be able to claim about our work and its impact?

Vibrancy

Generating and Using Abundant Learning Information

System learning information is dynamic, abundant, accessible, self-generating, and imbued with meaning.

OR THE FIRST TIME LAST SPRING, OUR INSTI-
tution's entire adult community—all faculty, support staff, and
administration—gathered to learn about the state of our students'
learning. Although instructional teams, counselors, and residential
staff regularly reviewed student learning information, we believed that
all staff needed to understand the data that informed our assessment
of how well our children were learning.

Engaging the whole system in meaningful conversation about
student learning is a challenge, but because our community is so
small—250 staff—we can physically come together. So we are now
experimenting with an annual State of Learning Colloquium—a community convening designed to share student learning information generated over the past year and integrate its results into previous years'
data. For our initial colloquium, a comprehensive data-based learning

report was prepared and distributed to all staff. That day, the research and assessment team focused the conversation on patterns of achievement of current students, as well as longitudinal data on graduates. A student panel provided insights on their learning and the conditions we created that either enhanced or constrained their thinking, creativity, and ethical decision making. Students responded to such questions as: In what ways do you think IMSA has prepared you to conduct inquiry within a given discipline? In what ways do you think IMSA has affected your ethical thinking over three years? In what ways do you think IMSA has engaged you in understanding your own thinking and the ways you evaluate information and draw your own conclusions?

Following the more formal presentations, curricular, instructional, or programmatic interventions that could enhance learning were discussed. In the afternoon, teachers offered workshops on specific curriculum goals and strategies directed toward our Standards of Significant Learning, those habits of mind we were working toward. This was followed by instructional team conversations and work by faculty curriculum assessment leaders. This year we are creating a richer process for more informed and engaged conversation.

We know the structure of our State of Learning Colloquium will change over time. What will not change is our collectively held commitment to generate and share comprehensive and meaningful information about how deeply and well our students are learning. Standardized test data will continue to be part of our evidence base. But the knowledge, skills, and habits of mind we asked our students to address on the panel remain the primary drivers for learning data collection: evidence of engagement in disciplinary and interdisciplinary inquiry, creative and ethical thinking, and thinking about their own thinking. Designing the conditions essential for deep student and system learning requires that staff and students have continuous access to many forms and sources of learning information. For our children to learn well, their learning must activate and engage all their potentials, be linked to their prior knowledge and experience, be embedded in meaningful context, and be driven by their own questions. For our systems to learn well, the same conditions are needed. Generative learning and schooling systems are open and vibrant information systems. They continuously seek, generate, share, and integrate meaningful information about how well they are learning and achieving their learning purpose.

Living systems require a continuous flow of nutrients: energy and matter. Without them, the system is not sustainable. As we've learned, the currency of natural living systems is energy. So to understand the system, we must follow the energy flow. The same is true for us. Human systems also need a continuous flow of nutrients, but the primary source and currency of our energy and vibrancy is meaningful information about our own and our system's learning identity. To understand a learning system, we must follow its flow of learning information. Within the new system of learning and schooling, there are two distinct dimensions of learning information: information for learning (what we ask our children to learn, that is, the curriculum), and information about learning (what the system seeks, generates, and uses to determine how well our children are learning). We'll begin with information for learning—what we ask our children to learn.

Information *for* Learning Is What We Ask Our Children *to* Learn

Although most curricula prescribe the information—knowledge and skills—we want our children to learn, what they actually *do* learn is decided by them. This decision, conscious or not, is based on how motivated they are, how relevant they believe the information is to their experience, and how meaningful it is to their personal goals and purpose. Although information that jars our understanding, challenges our thinking, or creates discomfort and uncertainty may be the catalyst for learning, it is not its source. Only information that truly challenges or illuminates our understanding or interpretation of our learning identity has the greatest potential to provoke meaningful changes in our thinking and behavior. We learn because the information matters. And it matters because it has personal significance to who we are now and who we wish to become. This is true for us as individuals, and it is true for our systems.

When children connect to and authentically integrate new knowledge in ways that alter who they believe they are now, they experience "Aha!" moments. They feel as though they see the world with fresh

> ## Beliefs That Ground Generative Learning and Schooling Information
>
> - *Prior knowledge and experience are essential foundations for linking and integrating future learning.* Without a context of understanding and experience, it is very difficult to integrate new information into a pattern of meaning and connections.
>
> - *Knowledge is relational, embedded in context, and continuously constructed by the learner in community.* Data, information, and knowledge are profoundly different. Acquiring data and information does not presume understanding.
>
> - *Depth and complexity of understanding are more significant than the quantity of information acquired.* Understanding creates meaning, wholeness, and integration. Complex and systemic problem resolution emerges from integral minds—from the capacities to understand the dynamic interrelationships within systems and to discern and connect patterns.

eyes. Their world expands, familiar things take on new meaning, and they see and experience deeper and broader connections between their new self and their new world. This transformative and live encounter feels almost magical. It happens so infrequently, especially in schools, that we are often surprised.

As leaders, we can design learning conditions that invite these magical moments to unfold far more frequently. We can ensure that the information (the knowledge and experiences) we immerse our children in, encourage them to explore, and ask them to construct is meaningful to them. We can ensure that their learning is connected to significant problems, intriguing questions, and paradoxes that challenge their current understandings and invite them into further exploration and discovery.

To do so requires that information for learning is:

- *Real* and *relevant* to whom they are becoming as a learner
- *Rigorous* and *responsive* to the questions they are asking
- *Relational* and connected to the larger human story and their place in its coevolution

Information of "optimal novelty and difficulty" (one of the APA Principles, listed at the end of the book), meaningfully linked to what the learner already knows or has experienced, becomes the context and foundation for an expanding base of knowledge and promotes learning competence and confidence. Absent these intentional linkages that allow children to create patterns and mental maps, new information cannot easily be remembered, understood, or integrated. This confidence or even "fearlessness" with respect to learning information is captured in this student's comments:

> We often were asked questions that motivated us to discover the necessary information for ourselves. We learned various methods and gained many different skills to help us gather accurate information . . . we used traditional sources of information and electronic resources including the Internet and World Wide Web. By senior year we had dealt with many real world issues including validity and relevancy of information, and we understood there was often more than one solution to a problem. We were able to handle almost any situation we were given—from determining what a data set of more than 3000 points told us, to collecting our own data through experimentation . . . my IMSA experience has helped me develop a type of "fearlessness" with information.[1]

Undeniably our students' experience and current knowledge are both the filter for and the base of their future knowledge. For our children to acquire and construct new knowledge, understanding, and meaning, they must have continuous and unencumbered access to learning information that is relevant to their personal learning goals. We will return to this dimension of information for learning in our discussion of curriculum.

INFORMATION *About* LEARNING
IS WHAT *the* SYSTEM SEEKS

A generative learning system continually accesses, creates, and shares information about learning to determine how well it is achieving its fundamental learning purposes. The story that begins this chapter is a good example.

Without the stimulation, flow, and formal sharing of information (that is, evidence) about learning and how well the system is manifesting its beliefs and achieving its learning goals, the collective intelligence and imagination of the system cannot be ignited and mobilized. To engage the creative capacities of our system and each learner, information essential to deepening and sustaining learning must be generated, gathered, shared, and used in decision making. To know if and how well our system is achieving our learning purposes and goals, we must strategically use research and meaningful evidence-based information to assess the congruence between our learning results and our learning intentions. A system that does not generate and circulate meaningful information about its own and its children's learning, or that blocks or distorts the flow of authentic yet potentially disruptive information, becomes closed, loses its resiliency, and can no longer learn. Without valid and reliable evidence, unexamined assumptions and perceptions of success can become rigid convictions that make new learning almost impossible. Ideology can easily trump reality. As leaders, we must ensure that our systems have unencumbered access to accurate and meaningful evidence (information) about the quality of our children's thinking, what they genuinely know and understand, and how they are learning. Although system information is the catalyst for constructing new meaning, only information that brings new knowledge and understanding about our children's and our system's learning has the potential to provoke systemic transformation. Within generative learning systems, information about purpose is amplified and circulated throughout the system; it is not regulated or controlled. When the whole system is able to seek, notice, generate, collect, share, and use information vital to its learning purpose, it continues to learn. By focusing the system on monitoring and assessing the congruence between learning intention and learning achievement, and by continuously generating information about its "learning identity," the intelligence, creativity, imagination, and leadership of the system are engaged, and the system continues to learn.

This is especially critical now with our obsessive reliance on the learning misinformation generated by high-stakes, multiple-choice, norm-referenced standardized tests. Testing is not the culprit; it is the nature, quality, and frequency of testing that is so fundamentally flawed in its ability to authentically portray authentic learning over time. Although most parents, educators, community members, and even students recognize that the learning they really care about and that really matters—deep understanding, critical thinking, ethical problem solving, creative inquiry, and learning how to learn—is not demonstrated on these tests, externally imposed and often punitive mandates require their administration despite their failings.

To be sure, school systems can supplement this testing by creating their own formative and summative learning assessments. These assessments can enable children to demonstrate their understanding by conducting experiments, solving problems, drawing or creating models, writing stories, or designing conceptual maps. But the external pressure to ensure students do well on high-stakes tests, often coupled with punitive consequences if they don't, creates an oppressive atmosphere of teaching to a bad test and relying on a single, narrow, one-shot indicator of student achievement. The fear and embarrassment of falling from grace (and losing federal funding) are not incentives to risk, even if the minds and future of our children are at stake.

This requires designing processes and structures that ensure the system accurately captures, generates, and uses meaningful learning information—evidence that it deeply cares about. It must gather and share evidence on whether and to what degree its learning outcomes are congruent with its beliefs, vision, and mission. It must gather and share evidence on whether and to what degree each of its children is learning deeply, understanding well, and moving toward the development of integral habits of mind.

Within a generative system of schooling, information essential to the system's integrity does not come from isolated data bits or externally imposed mandates for data collection. It comes from specific, self-generated knowledge about the health of the system's learning identity—its purpose. Unless the system and each learner explicitly know whether and how well they are achieving their unique learning purposes, they lose their capacity for continuous and creative learning.

LEADERSHIP INQUIRIES *About* LEARNING *and* SCHOOLING INFORMATION

Creating generative learning and schooling systems means engaging our communities in deeper questions about learning and schooling information. I offer the following questions to get you started:

• *What do we need to know?* What internal and external information (evidence) about learning—our students' learning, our systems' learning, and our own learning—does our purpose call us to notice, seek, generate, share, use, and hold ourselves accountable for in order to deepen our capacity to achieve the learning purpose (identity) we espouse?

What do we believe our children must know (competencies), do (skills), be (habits of mind), and experience (actively engage in) to learn deeply, become authors of their own lives, fluently speak multiple disciplinary languages, and live together well? What learning evidence are we currently collecting, generating, sharing, monitoring, and using? How does it inform our purpose and ensure program quality? Are there gaps between what we want to know and what we currently know about our children's learning? Do our learning intentions match our learning results? What new information must we generate and collect?

• *How shall we ensure that the learning information we value is generated, captured, and shared?* How do we ensure our collective knowledge is made visible so that our entire system has abundant, transparent, and freely flowing access to its own intelligence? How does information about learning move within our system and our community so that it can be used to continuously improve our children's and our system's learning? What information distribution mechanisms are available to us—radio, TV, publications, Web sites, intranet—that would enable us to share learning and information? How are we using them now? How might we use them differently?

• *How can we ensure that provocative and potentially disruptive information essential to our identity is invited into, noticed, and generated by the system?* How do we foster innovation, experimentation, and external connections so that new information is continuously created? What are our rules for discerning, processing, and integrating information? What might we be fearful of learning about ourselves? Are there tools and strategies we need to help us uncover and make sense of vital information that may be hidden? What critical learning achievements and competencies are we failing to notice because we are not assessing them?

CHAPTER 7

Interdependence

Inviting and Sustaining Collaborative Learning Relationships

*System learning relationships are inclusive, collaborative,
interdependent, and trust centered.*

MANY YEARS AGO, AS A NEW SUPERINTENDENT
of schools in a midsized K–12 school district (we had four elementary schools, one middle school, and one high school), I struggled
with how to connect our siloed elementary, middle school, and high
school faculties. Clearly our teachers shared our children over the
years, but rarely did they engage with one another in conversation
about our children's learning over time. As a consequence, teachers felt
disconnected, students experienced abrupt and often confusing transitions from one school to another, and parents were often frustrated
with inconsistent rules and expectations. Less visible, but even more
significant to me, was the recognition that we were not functioning
as a system. We were six independent—not interdependent—schools.
I believed that unless we became an authentic learning system, our
remarkable yet untapped talents would likely not be available to us.

In an effort to try something that would begin to bridge this enormous divide and begin the process of reconnecting our system to its self, I asked the board's blessing for an experiment: we would close half the district for a day in the first semester and have all the high school and middle school teachers spend that day paired with elementary teachers in their classrooms. The second semester we would close the other half of the district and pair the elementary teachers with high school and middle-school teachers in their classrooms for a day. The pairing would be random. Once all teachers knew their learning partner, they had to call that person, explain what they were teaching that day, send materials if necessary, and design opportunities that engaged their colleague in the children's learning. The principals also participated, visiting their colleagues and joining their daily routines.

To say that this was a profound experience for everyone—teachers, students, and principals—is both trite and true. The stories that emerged were powerful. The high school math department chair struggling to tutor a second grader in math told his learning partner that he had never known how hard it was to teach second-grade math; he asked for her help, and later thanked her for what she had taught him about teaching mathematics to seven year olds. The high school English teacher confessed to a sixth-grade teacher that she had always blamed the elementary schools for not teaching writing but now understood this was not the case. She asked how they could work together long before the kids got to high school. The high school football coach asked by third graders to hold their jump rope during recess saw firsthand the energy and enthusiasm children have for play when it is not bounded by competition and winning. And the elementary teacher was dazzled by her middle school science colleague's knowledge and insight in engaging the attention of eighth graders in a science experiment.

Parents were equally enthusiastic, reporting that their elementary children thought it was "so cool" to see high school and middle school teachers in *their* building. They saw them now as helpers, and not so scary. A third-grade teacher told me that she later received a note from her middle school partner, congratulating her and "our" kids on their success in the district's science fair. By intentionally creating conditions that connected teachers around what they cared about the most, the children and their learning, a different district—a generative learning system—began to emerge.

Learning is a naturally relational and social process, and it is significantly influenced by the nature and quality of our learning relationships. Relationships that foster natural learning are cocreative and collaborative, and they enable learners to discover more of who they are. Learning can be seen as a "mentored odyssey" in which teachers and learners construct knowledge and meaning together.[1] To learn deeply, a relationship must be established between the learner and what he or she is seeking to understand. Generative learning systems are continuously learning because their intricate learning relationships, communication pathways, and feedback loops generate trust, encourage risk, and keep the system continuously connected to its learning self.

Beliefs That Ground Generative Learning and Schooling Relationships

- *Learning is grounded in relational ways of knowing.* This relational context affirms integral ways of knowing and believes meaning and connections are constructed by the learner and that the learner's passion and love are essential for deep learning. It asserts that relatedness and engagement are at the heart of learning–that there is a profound connection between the knower and the known and that connection to self and a coherent sense of self are essential to learning.

- *Learning is inherently relational.* Relationships and interdependence enable us to meaningfully connect to and belong in community. Deep learning is more likely when a multigenerational community is purposefully learning, exploring, and cocreating together.

Five Interconnected Learning Contexts

In learning as in the rest of life, relationships are everything. When I use the term *relational learning,* it is to describe five interconnected learning contexts.

• *The relationships between our children's own unfolding stories and the stories of the natural world.* If our children understood that they are an integral part of the web of life and therefore have infinite creative possibilities, might they embrace uncertainty and exploration with greater confidence, knowing that this is what life and they naturally do?

• *The relationships between and within our children's multiple intelligences.* How might a child's ability to hear and compose music inform and enhance his logical and mathematical reasoning? How might a child's ability to visualize and mentally manipulate space increase her geometric problem solving?

• *The relationships our children can have with great questions and great ideas.* How might we ignite our children's desire to creatively engage with great ideas in science, mathematics, music, history, and literature? What might they discover about themselves from studying and getting to know a historical document, map, musical score, or piece of sculpture? What connections might they make between their personal story and the stories that ground a discipline's search for truth? How might our children learn differently if we invited them to love the subject?

• *The relationships between learners of all ages.* How might we create an intergenerational learning community to identify and resolve shared problems?

• *The relationship of each learner to the community's informal learning institutions.* How might we engage our children in the "curriculum" offered within the community's diverse learning networks of museums, libraries, nursing homes, hospitals, and arboretums?

We need to keep these fundamental learning contexts in mind as we design learning environments and experiences for our children. They have much to teach us about authentic engagement. We have already discussed the first three contexts of learning—the relationships between our many ways of knowing. Now let's turn to the last two contexts: the intergenerational and community-based dimensions, which reinforce the social context of learning.

The SOCIAL CONTEXT *of* LEARNING RELATIONSHIPS

Learning is a social and communal process of constructing meaning from information and experience. Although we are often attracted to the concept of independence in learning, the perceived importance of the lone learner is simply a myth. Learning is inherently relational. It is profoundly influenced by social relationships and meaningful connections. It is a dynamic, interactive, and collaborative process of meaning and sense making, and it requires authentic engagement with others.

Creative, adaptive, inquisitive, and resilient learners are not only aware of who they are as learners—the potentials they uniquely bring to learning—but they seek and encourage the potentials of others as well. Self-directed learners eagerly seek learning partners. They know that these expanding learning relationships can illuminate and enrich their understanding and open doors to unexplored and even unknown territory. Without authentic learning partners, our learning self can become deformed. Learning is a cocreative process, and we cannot prosper in isolation. What, where, how, and with whom we learn significantly shape the learner we become.

One of the most significant, far-reaching, and often life-changing and magical learning relationships is the one between a student and teacher. The sheer joy of a truly generative learner-teacher relationship can be transformative. It changes and recreates us. We learn things we never dreamed of. We see possibilities we never imagined. We become bolder, braver, and wiser. When teachers ignite a child's passion for learning, they open a portal to a new sense of self. The comments of one of our young graduates describes this special relationship:

> The faculty . . . didn't teach me in the traditional sense—instead, they helped me to learn. They helped me become a problem-solver and a risk-taker, and allowed me to become responsible for my own learning

and discovery. Before IMSA, most of my classes consisted of a teacher spoon-feeding us information and then requiring us to memorize facts for a meaningless exam. We were on a strict schedule, and had to cover certain topics on certain days. Our learning felt rushed and somewhat choppy. Our instructors worked and learned with us . . . as colleagues in the classroom, they acted as peers rather than authority figures. Some of the bonds I formed with the faculty and staff were as strong as those I formed with students.[2]

One of the paradoxes of learning is that individually constructed meaning is not an exclusively individual phenomenon. Individual meaning is influenced and shaped by social context. It is codiscovered and cocreated. We simply cannot underestimate the extraordinary power of social context in mind shaping. Although schools are but one context for learning, they remain our culture's dominant structure for formal learning. For this reason, the conditions we design to invite and enhance learning have a profound impact on the growing minds of our children and the future they will be able to envision and create.

Currently, most students view school learning as unrelated and irrelevant to their lives. Because we do not ask them to learn within their communities, they learn apart from them. We do not ask them to learn together, create together, explore together, or construct meaning together. We do not ask them to learn with and from younger or older children or adults. We do not connect them to the multiple resources and vital learning curriculum within their communities or life itself. We do not ask them to learn *with* us.

Understanding the relational and social context of learning makes us more mindful of how we must engage our children's natural predispositions for collaborative learning. Student-generated and -led learning networks created to solve real problems in the community or the world generally do not naturally emerge in school. This isolation severs critical connections. Understanding the relational and social context of learning challenges us to design learning environments that ensure students engage with their peers, teachers, parents, and communities around issues of deep and shared significance. Relatedness and engagement are at the heart of learning. We need to be in relationship to one another to fully understand who we are.

Learning Relationships Connect
the System *to* Itself

Relationships represent the dynamic, self-generating learning network of our systems, and they establish its capacity for collaborative inquiry, engagement, innovation, and knowledge generation. Unless we are deeply connected to our system's identity and work, we cannot be drawn into its purpose or even notice or generate information essential to its continuous learning.

Belonging to a learning community is not a private matter. When we choose to join a community, we assume responsibility for its purpose and accept accountability to one another. Despite our current preoccupation with structural reform, it is the system's kaleidoscopic and fluid network of information and communication relationships that enables its collective intelligence, curiosity, and imagination to freely move within it. As social institutions, schools and schooling systems have both formal and informal institutional and operational relationships (roles). However, in generative environments, most learning relationships are not prescribed. Who "bumps into whom" is driven by the information and communication needs of the system's shared purpose and the work that needs to be done to achieve it. It is not predetermined, controlled, or regulated by positional authority. Everyone is encouraged to generate, collect, and share information about learning. It is the interactive, interdependent, and relational capacity of the system—its intricate, diverse, and complex communication networks and feedback loops—that establishes its resiliency and adaptability and increases the system's trust, vibrancy, and creativity. Without purposeful connections and relationships that continuously weave the system together, diversity can create fragmentation. But when the system is intricately connected to its deepest learning purpose, diversity fosters newness, surprise, abundant creativity, and deeper levels of complexity.

Generative learning relationships are essential for system transformation. They promote interdependence and a sense of belonging. They link learners of all ages into networks focused on achieving the system's purpose. It is this interdependence and the density and intricacy of the system's communication loops that enable information vital to the system's purpose to permeate the system rapidly. The system can continuously access itself and learn.

One of the powerful attributes of living learning systems is the dynamic balance between self and other. Simply, the self is best understood, expressed, created, and re-created in relation to others. Although life continually asserts its self, it never stops seeking connections to other life. Generative schooling fosters simple agreements about how we wish to learn and belong together in our work. When everyone is connected to everyone else around learning, the system remains energized and vibrant. We simply must be connected and in partnership with others in order to continue to learn.

LEADERSHIP INQUIRIES *About* LEARNING *and* SCHOOLING RELATIONSHIPS

Creating generative learning and schooling systems means engaging our communities in deeper questions about learning and schooling relationships. I offer the following questions to get you started:

• *How does information critical to our purpose circulate seamlessly and quickly through the entire system so that it can be responded to and so our community and each individual can continue to learn?* How is our whole system available and continuously connected to its self?

• *What are the informal and formal webs and networks of communications and relationships within our system?* How might we increase and deepen our multiple feedback loops and learning networks to ensure that everyone within the system, including the larger community, has transparent and seamless access to essential learning information and our system remains healthy, connected, and continuously learning?

• *What are our agreements for belonging together in the work and for ensuring ownership and accountability for collective purpose?* How does our community invite all of who we are into achieving our purpose? How are relationships around the institution's work invited, nurtured, and sustained? How do we invite the larger community into the work of learning?

• *Who are our natural partners, and with whom do we wish to partner?* How shall we attract the real pathfinders and risk takers who are seeking new ways to collaborate in creating a new generative system of learning and schooling? Who needs to be in this conversation? What relational and communication capacities must we develop to position ourselves as a pioneering partner in the development of the new story and system of learning and schooling?

• *How does our community invite, nurture, and integrate diversity of all kinds into our work?* What does it mean to be a diverse and connected learning community?

• *How have we defined power and leadership?* Are these understandings congruent with our purpose? How is generative leadership nurtured and distributed throughout the system?

• *What do we wish the nature and quality of the learning relationship to be with parents? Between students and students? Teachers and students? Teachers and teachers? Students and the external community?* How are we and our children engaged together in learning? What would an authentic intergenerational learning community look like? Have we created competitive or collaborative learning environments? Is this the relationship we seek? What is possible now? How are we explicitly connecting the work and goals of teachers to one another?

• *How are we explicitly connecting: each person to his or her own purpose, each person to our system's purpose, our system to its self, and our system to the community and the world?* What does it mean to liberate individual and collective goodness and genius for the world?

The Generative Confluence *of* Identity, Information, *and* Relationships

Although each of these three domains—identity, information, and relationships—has its own dynamism and motion, it is their confluence and synergy that create the generative landscape essential for individual and system wholeness, meaning, and connections. It is this landscape that enables generative processes, patterns, and structures to emerge. Without clarity at the core, without unfettered and continuous access to abundant information about its learning purpose, and without multiple learning networks and feedback loops for innovation and communication, our children, our schools, and our schooling systems cannot deeply learn. To learn, we must be free to explore, invent, inquire, risk, seek novelty, and recreate ourselves as we engage more deeply in our environment and with one another.

Despite all we now know about change in living systems, virtually all our efforts at educational and school improvement—reform, restructuring, and reengineering—begin at the wrong place. We begin at the level we think we can fix: the processes and structures of schooling. Somehow we believe that if we restructure or realign the more tangible hard things before we engage the whole system in cocreating the intangible soft things—its beliefs, values, vision, and mission about learning—we will make our schools and children more productive, efficient, and successful.

Life teaches us otherwise. Life teaches us that we must first reconnect ourselves and our systems at the level of meaning. We must first clarify our beliefs, values, purpose, and principles of belonging together in the work. To create a generative and life-affirming system of learning and schooling by design, we must first work deep within the dynamics of our system, at the place where our learning identity is forming. It is from this deep sense of learning identity and purpose that generative processes, patterns, and structures can emerge. A generative system will continuously create what is important, what makes sense, and what works. It will notice and choose what it needs to learn, and it will create conditions to continuously renew and sustain itself.

We now leave the context of our generative landscape of learning and schooling to explore its conditions. The generative identity, information, and relationships of the new story's landscape enable us to shape natural habitats for wholeness, meaning, connections, and belonging. In order to fully activate our children's multiple potentials for learning and nurture the development of integral and wise minds, we must immerse them in dynamic learning environments of personalized and creative engagement, exploration, and connectedness.

Coherence

Stimulating Creative and
Self-Organizing Learning Processes

*System learning processes are creative, inquiry driven,
exploratory, and coherent.*

A FRIEND WHO WAS A TEACHER RECENTLY RE-
counted a magical yet sobering story of her local elementary
school. One afternoon many years ago, while working in her garden,
she heard a joyous commotion. The principal was enthusiastically lead-
ing a joyful band of more than three hundred students as they proudly
marched down the street in their annual book parade celebrating all
the books they had read during the year.

The delight, pride, and sense of genuine accomplishment on the
faces of the children, and the sheer joy on the face of the principal,
were contagious. My friend remembers tears filling her eyes and feeling blessed by the moment. But then she said, "I haven't seen that
parade in years. I wonder what happened?" Any answer, of course, is
pure speculation. But my fear is that the current story of schooling has
eroded our ability to celebrate our children's authentic learning by

117

sending out the message that with all there is to cover and test, there is simply no time for parades.

There is an inherent exuberance and flow to the processes by which living systems continuously recreate and sustain themselves. They are neither linear nor formulaic. Life is simply free to be and become. It is free to explore, seek new relationships and partners, generate novelty and playfully discover, invent, and cocreate new meanings and new possibilities. Because life is free to recreate itself and connect to other life, it resists any external directives, controls, or prohibitions that stifle, thwart, or erode its endlessly creative quest to discover and learn.

Learning is a boundlessly creative, curiosity- and inquiry-driven, and exploratory process of meaning construction and discovery. It is a natural, purposeful, goal-directed, and playful process of acquiring and creating knowledge and constructing meaning within a social context. Generative schooling systems experiment with creative ways of working and organizing. They encourage improvisation and innovation and bring the whole system together to achieve its learning purpose.

LEARNING IS *the* PROCESS *of* LIFE

There is no better mentor for engaged learning than the process of life itself. Cognition is the sustaining process of living systems, and it is marked by autonomous exploration, discovery, and the creation of meaning.

Meaning simply cannot be prescribed for living systems. Noted educational psychologist Mihaly Csikszentmihalyi has called this natural learning experience the "flow" experience. He describes it as "the spontaneous, effortless experience you achieve when you have a close match between a high level of challenge and the skills you need to meet the challenge. . . . You have a goal and you are getting feedback. The experience is almost addictive and very rewarding."[1]

Sadly, it is often difficult to see this inherently messy, improvisational, and exploratory process of meaning making and discovery fostered in the current processes, patterns, and structures of schooling. We witness it every moment as young children learn to explore their

> ## Beliefs That Ground Generative Learning and Schooling Processes
>
> - *Learning is a purposeful, exploratory, and creative process of discovery.* It is a natural, goal-directed, and continuous process of constructing meaning through pattern formulation and active and experimental engagement in complex issues and problems.
>
> - *Deep understanding and expertise develop through immersion in complex questions and messy problems that require continuous practice of critical and creative thinking.* Individual and collaborative inquiry and the creative exploration of ill-structured and interconnected questions and problems relevant to the learner are the processes through which children construct knowledge and meaning and acquire a broad repertoire of learning and thinking strategies and skills.
>
> - *Schooling is a moral enterprise.* The purpose of education is to transform minds—to acquire and construct knowledge, develop deep understanding and wisdom, and experience and demonstrate learning through discovery, reflection, and the exploration and resolution of essential questions that advance the human condition.

world, but it seems to diminish as they become older and more "schooled." Exploration, discovery, and knowledge creation are forced to yield to uniformity and prescribed information acquisition, even though we know that imaginative meanderings and trial-and-error experiments are what children need to do in order to learn. To understand and connect to their world, to build confidence in their emerging learning identity, and to feel safe in paradox and uncertainty, our children must be able to challenge and test boundaries and learn as life does.

Play Is *an* Essential Process *of* Learning

For young children, every moment is an unfolding learning adventure—a test, a trial, an experiment, a question. We must know as we watch them, often in awe of their intelligence, capacities, and wisdom, that we did not teach them to engage in this messy process of learning and meaning making. It is who they—and we—are. It is what we do. We are born meaning-seeking, creative, and continuously learning beings. We are born natural scientists, mathematicians, writers, poets, historians, geographers, musicians, dancers, painters, explorers, and discoverers. We are born attuned to the endless possibilities of bringing forth new worlds in relationship with other explorers.

One of the essential processes of learning is play. Play enables us to spontaneously experience and connect to life, joyfully engage in exploration, and create something brand new, both together and alone. We expect and encourage play in the learning of young children. But as we get older, play is marginalized or removed from formal learning. Learning becomes serious, and there is no longer time for play. Except sometimes. We still play an instrument, we play music, and we play tennis and soccer and basketball. Why can't we "play" mathematics, science, and poetry? What would happen if we did? The insidiously destructive consequences of demeaning and ignoring the power of play in formal learning are staggering.

"I Love This Place!"

When a learning environment invites playful learning, students will find new connections in all sorts of places. Here's an excerpt from an IMSA student's thinking log:

> This is the strangest place I've ever been. It is the only place I know where people can sit around at lunch and argue honestly about the velocity of a falling blob of ketchup. (Yes, that really happened. I was arguing as well, but my point was from how high you dropped the ketchup.) I think that this is the only place where people can sit around and discuss physics and feel NORMAL while doing so.

. . . As soon as sophomores arrive here, [the school] begins to affect them. I know it is affecting me. People I know have observed this changing, and have told me about it.

[Yesterday my friend] was drinking soda from a glass cup, and for some reason all the foam stayed at the top so that while the liquid went down in the glass, the foam remained up so that there were gasses in between.

She shouted, "Hey, look!" We all rushed over and stared at her soda for a few minutes. Then we tried to figure out why it did that. Finally, one of my [friends] grabbed a camera and took a picture of it for our photography class. It was really an interesting occurrence.

I love this place!

Stuart Brown, founder of the Institute for Play, offers a sobering assessment of the absence of play in his essay "Evolution and Play." He writes, "What is shared by mass murderers, felony drunk drivers, starving children, head-banging laboratory animals, some anxious students, most upwardly mobile executives and all reptiles? They don't *play*. What do MacArthur 'genius' grantees, historically renowned creative artists, successful multicareer seniors, and animals of superior intelligence have in common? They are full of play throughout their lives. There is something profound about play."[2] Although this natural and playful learning self is our inheritance, it can be thwarted. And if it is silenced or extinguished, by neglect or design, our deepest self ceases to be. "Play forms the basis for trust," Brown reminds us in the PBS series *The Promise of Play*. "It reduces the social distance between individuals . . . it is the means by which adaptability and flexibility are added to the player's existence . . . play serves as the grounding core of learning."[3] How do we ensure that our children's natural predispositions, unknowable capacities, and insatiable desires for learning deepen and expand as they engage in more formal and complex learning? What can we do to invite meaningful learning—knowledge acquisition, generation, and use? What can we do to ensure that our children remain confident inventors, resilient explorers, and courageous and playful discoverers?

Learning Is *a* Process *of* Live Encounters

I believe we must enable children to experience learning as a live encounter. Together with our children, we must cocreate meaning-filled contexts and compelling questions and problems that actively engage them in owning their own learning, generating knowledge, and constructing meaning using all the ways they must come to know and understand the world and their place in it. This means immersing them in genuine inquiry and real problems so that they can acquire, generate, and use multidisciplinary strategies to develop conceptual knowledge and understanding.

Strategies for learning how to learn, systemic and complex thinking and reasoning, and creative disciplinary and interdisciplinary problem solving are not simplistic procedural rules or tactics to be memorized. They are essential frameworks and tools for more autonomous, creative, and disciplined inquiry, exploration, and discovery. This process of authentic discovery will enable our children to stimulate their appreciation for the importance of ambiguity, imagination, and intuition in problem solving and will fuel their passion for inquiry, exploration, and continuous learning. It will rekindle their sense of wonder, awe, and understanding of the interdependence and mysteries of the natural world, and deepen their understanding of disciplinary, interdisciplinary, and transdisciplinary concepts. It will enable them to become confident learners who know that they have the knowledge, skills, and habits of mind to learn anything at any time in any place.

Learning how to learn

These strategies enable children to acquire the knowledge and skills they need for continuous lifelong learning. They learn to:

- Generate, monitor, and assess their own learning, understanding, and performance goals (metacognition).
- Identify and use their unique potentials for processing information and representing knowledge (for example, using numerical, pictorial, artistic, or musical representations of

knowledge) to increase understanding and to solve complex problems.

Systemic and complex thinking and reasoning

These strategies enable children to find, define, and frame problems to clarify their essential questions and deep systemic concepts. They learn to:

- Formulate big essential questions (both analytical and integrative) that drive personal inquiry and engagement and expand understanding, integrate concepts, and deepen meaning.
- Use graphic organizing tools like concept maps to discern, clarify, visualize, and integrate conceptual relationships and patterns and to identify misconceptions that impede understanding.
- Design prototypes and plan and conduct experiments; generate, collect, and evaluate data; make conjectures and hypotheses; and evaluate claims of validity based on multiple forms of evidence.

Creative disciplinary and interdisciplinary problem solving

These strategies enable children to discern patterns of wholeness and connection between and within concepts and domains. They learn to:

- Know why, how, and where information should be gathered and used to solve a problem or respond to a question.
- Evaluate the context, evidence, soundness, and veracity of multiple forms and sources of information for complex problem solving from differing and often paradoxical perspectives.
- Recognize integrating concepts between, among, and beyond disciplines to enhance disciplinary, interdisciplinary, and transdisciplinary learning and inquiry.

- Learn the modes of knowledge representation and inquiry unique to specific domains in order to integrate multiple ways of knowing and strategies for problem solving.

"How did you learn in school today?"

"Every way of knowing becomes a way of living . . . ," says Parker Palmer. "Every epistemology becomes an ethic . . . every mode of education, no matter what its name, is a mode of soul-making."[4] How we come to know has profound implications for the learning self we define and the mind we create. The conditions for how we learn create the context for how we choose to live. Our processes for learning become our acquired mode of thinking. Perhaps we should ask our children a new question when they come home from school. Along with, "*What* did you learn in school today?" we should ask them, "*How* did you learn in school today?" It is the answer to this question that holds the greatest potency for mind shaping. I keep coming back to what is for me a radical relationship: mind shaping is world shaping. When we change our minds, we change our choices. When we change our choices, we change our behavior. When we change our behavior, we can change the world.

"Scientists *Do* Come *from* Greenfield!"

I'd like to tell you a story about Matthew Knisley, a student from my institution, and *how* he was invited to learn "in school." Matthew came to the Illinois Mathematics and Science Academy when he was fifteen, a very bright child from Greenfield, a small rural town in Illinois. Against the counsel of many who doubted Matthew could become a scientist—because, in his words, "No scientist has ever come from Greenfield"—Matthew applied to IMSA and was accepted.

Like all other sophomore students, Matthew was plunged into our core science program, Scientific Inquiries. Students and teachers do exactly as the name implies: they inquire about science. Scientific Inquiries is an integrated program connecting the deep organizing principles and concepts of physics, chemistry, biology, and earth and space science, around significant interdisciplinary questions—questions that are designed to engage students meaningfully and actively. One such question is, "How do I come to understand the natural world and my place in it?"

One of the requirements of Scientific Inquiries is a personal plan of inquiry. Students pose a question they have been intrigued by or wondered about, and they pursue it as far as it leads them. For many of our students who have excelled at schooling but not necessarily at learning, this is often a rude awakening. They don't know how to frame a question. They don't even know the questions they have because they have been hidden for so long. Their schooling was never about questions; it was only about answers.

Matthew's conversation with his teacher went something like this:

"Matthew, what questions do you have?"

"I don't know."

"What have you always wondered or been curious about?"

"I don't know."

"Has there been anything you read recently in a journal, or a text-book, or a newspaper that grabbed your attention and you were puzzled or intrigued by it?"

And suddenly Matthew replied, "Yes!" He had read an article in a local newspaper that described some bones that had been uncovered in a makeshift grave not far from his home. Through forensic testing and DNA sampling, scientists were able to determine that the bones belonged to a female and that she had likely been killed with an axe.

Matthew was intrigued by how scientists knew this. He finally had his question. Living near his uncle's farm, he had access to all sorts of bones—from cows, sheep, goats, deer, chickens, and turkeys—and he and his father had spent many weekends hitting them with various instruments just to see what happened to the bones. They were observing the distinct physical evidence of the different "weapons" on the bones. As Matthew pursued answers to his question, he became fascinated by what he was beginning to understand. His inquiry deepened. He learned about sophisticated DNA testing and became highly knowledgeable about biochemistry and genetics. He developed interests in paleontology, forensics, and anthropology. Because of the nature of his expanding inquiry, his teacher scheduled an appointment for him at the Field Museum of Natural History in Chicago with a noted paleontologist.

Matthew described the day he went to meet with the paleontologist in this way. "I took the train to Chicago and then hopped a bus to the Field Museum of Natural History. I started climbing the steps and I looked up and saw the words Field Museum of Natural History in huge letters. I stopped dead in my tracks on the steps and said out loud, 'I *am* a scientist. Scientists *do* come from Greenfield!'"

Our children's gifts and talents will astonish us when how they learn in school is naturally right—when they learn just as life does.

GENERATIVE LEARNING PROCESSES CREATE SYSTEM COHERENCE

Processes that are resonant and congruent with the system's identity enable the community to "live its mission" and embody it in its actions.

Processes are both the creative (novelty-generating) and self-regulatory (order-creating) ways our systems explore possibilities, measure and monitor achievement, generate and transmit information, and get their work done. They are the known and observable behaviors, operations, and rules by which a system achieves and advances its learning purpose and objectives. Collaborative and creative processes help to establish the essential relationships necessary for goal achievement.

Systems are really constellations of processes that manifest themselves in structures. It is our system's processes, not its structures, that manifest and yield system order and coherence. How we do our work (that is, our processes) emerges from who and why we are as a system. While identity is the source of system meaning, processes (cognition, generation of novelty, and self-organization) are its sources of order and coherence. A system cannot manifest its identity—cannot realize its mission and goals—unless its processes are congruent with and advance its purpose. How we learn, work, and achieve together shapes who we become.

The mission-driven and creative work of generative and life-affirming systems is accomplished through diverse, inventive, nimble, and collaborative relationships, not command and control. Their freedom to explore and creatively engage stimulates the emergence of new capacities, possibilities, and relationships.

In control-based and centralized hierarchical systems that characterize the current story of learning and schooling, the work (often externally mandated) largely gets done through rigidly prescribed, inflexible, and often nonnegotiable processes. These "my way or the highway" processes ignore the attraction and synergy of shared purpose, fluid information exchange and generation, and diverse communication networks essential to engage the system and advance its creative work. More detrimental is that process rigidity almost ensures that the system's desire, energy, and astonishing capacity for learning, growth, and change will be extinguished. The more control based the system's learning and creative processes are, the less creative, adaptive, and resilient it will be, and the less it will genuinely learn.

We have likely all experienced the deflation and sense of loss of knowing that we could truly have advanced our system's unique purpose and goals—if only we had been asked to use our imagination and creativity to do what really works. But without explicit invitations and expectations to create, risk, and experiment, we stop exploring and trying. We also stop seeking novelty, inventing, dreaming, and learning. In order to preserve our selves, our deepest and most inventive self goes into hiding, and with it, the organization's vitality and generativity erode. Our capacity to discover and create comes when we are free to explore and surprise. Learner autonomy is essential for system creativity.

Generative and self-organizing processes are the essence of our new system's vitality and its transformative change process. They bring and hold the system together and enable it to achieve its purpose and continually learn. If a community ceases to learn and ceases to increase its capacity for self-creation, ultimately it is not sustainable.

Unlike reductive systems that seem to stifle or prevent organizational creativity and innovation, generative and life-affirming learning environments flourish and continue to create, learn, and change through purposeful dialogue and inquiry, exploration, and invention. They seek novelty and intentionally create conditions to enable internal and external information to challenge the system. They confront issues, intentionally raise uncomfortable questions, seek external counsel and insights, explore conflicting viewpoints, and reevaluate assumptions. Generative systems plan, but they do so from two contexts: the strategic and the emergent. They create goals, define objectives, generate metrics, and design strategies. But they also continuously scan the environment for new possibilities. They build on what works in the system. They harness the energy that emerges from success and continuously learn their way into the future.

They also play; encourage trial balloons; reward experimentation, mistakes, and "failure"; create catalytic prototypes of new ideas and initiatives; and welcome the messiness of following one's passion. They recognize that like the rest of life, the system and all its members require freedom to discover and invent in order to find out what really works in achieving the system's learning purposes. They trust that the creative processes generated through the freedom to explore will result in new possibilities and new forms of order and stability far more complex, innovative, and adaptive than who they currently are. They know that absent an expectation to continually create, the system cannot thrive, and deep learning is less likely.

In generative schooling systems, there is a dynamic congruence between the system's identity and its processes for getting its work done. *Who* the organization is (its identity) is inextricably connected to *how* it is (its processes of learning and change). There must be coherence and resonance between how the system learns, the way it works, and the work itself. This is extremely important because designing and implementing processes incongruent with organizational purpose and beliefs create cynicism and erode trust. Life-affirming systems do not create processes that are antithetical to their mission. Processes must enable the organization to become its purpose. They must embody our natural curiosity and desire for connections, and stimulate our natural capacity to learn and create.

Leadership Inquiries *About* Learning *and* Schooling Processes

Creating generative learning and schooling systems means engaging our communities in deeper questions about learning and schooling processes. I offer the following questions to get you started:

- *How does the mission-driven work of our system actually get done?* What are our processes for: whole system planning; program evaluation; stimulating and rewarding innovation; creating new "products" and services; designing innovative and personalized curriculum; allocating financial resources; establishing program priorities; engaging the community in decision making; challenging the status quo; adopting new programs and discarding old ones; recognizing and celebrating contributions and achievements; seeking and communicating critical and potentially disruptive information; assessing individual, team, and institutional performance; revisiting our vision and beliefs; honoring our history and stories?

• *What simple and generative processes (actions, operations, behavioral routines) might we create to increase our potentials for thinking creatively together, discovering what is important to us, and integrating our collective work?* What do we currently do and what might we do to simulate, encourage, recognize, and sustain individual and collective learning, creativity, discovery, risk, experimentation, and novelty? Is our system an inquiring system? How do we create spaces that welcome the exploration of big questions?

• *How do we really want our children, our selves, and our system to learn to know, do, be, and live together?* What thinking and reflecting processes will better prepare us for collaboratively engaging in messy, ill-structured problems? How do we collectively resolve system conflicts?

• *What conditions might we create to enable our children to believe in and celebrate their own possibilities, work for the common good, engage in passionate inquiry, and "lose" themselves in learning about something they love?* How do we help them understand the natural world and their place in it? How might we immerse them in wonder, awe, and a sense of belonging to something much bigger and more transcendent than themselves?

Sustainability

Weaving and Mapping Networked Learning Patterns

System learning patterns are dynamic and self-generating networks.

SEVERAL YEARS AGO, I PRESENTED A WEEK-LONG seminar on the new story of learning and schooling to a distinguished group of Jordanian and Saudi Arabian educational leaders. The first three days went quite well, but on the fourth day, several participants told me that the new story of learning I proposed was not needed in their countries. Their children, they said, simply did not have the same problems with learning and schooling that American children did. Taking a chance, I asked if they would be willing to invite some of their students to our seminar so we could ask them questions and listen to their experiences as learners. They agreed.

For two hours we listened as these high school students poignantly described their hopes and dreams for the future—and their deep desire to uniquely contribute to their communities and the world while they are young. They spoke of their yearning for connection, meaningful dialogue, and authentic relationships with adults, their wish to live and work in peace, and their commitment to engage with us in solving the complex problems within the human community.

In story after story, these young people emotionally described how so many of the current expectations, processes, and structures of schooling were silencing their spirit and inhibiting them from authentically engaging in meaningful and relevant learning. They talked about being embarrassed by their obsession with getting good grades and top scores on tests because they knew this took precedence over real learning. They said they felt guilty that they did not spend time helping others because the competition to achieve was so fierce. They were quite aware that their focus on test scores reinforced rapid memorization, not deep understanding, but said they had little choice: this was what "the system" required.

They spoke from the heart and gave voice to the losses they so deeply felt. The room was very quiet.

The students' deep desire for meaning, purpose, belonging, and authentic connections with adults was quite clear. I did not have to say, "I told you so." These young men and women had spoken for themselves. Sadly, this lesson was one I had learned in many countries around the world: regardless of geography and culture, the learning and teaching patterns of our current story of schooling are quite similar, and they do not support deep and connected learning because they are antithetical to how we naturally learn.

In the current story of learning and schooling, learning information is viewed as proprietary. It is determined by the system and can be accessed only through an expert—a teacher, a textbook, or some other external source. The pattern of learning and teaching is linear and hierarchical. To get to the idea or subject, the student must go through an intermediary. If we were to map this pattern, we'd see a straight vertical line with arrows going from students through teachers to subjects. This deeply embedded and habitual pattern of teaching as transmission, and learning as acquisition, is now perceived as truth. This pattern must be broken. To transform our current system, we must transform its patterns of teaching and learning relationships. We must transform the patterns by which students can engage in exploring the "grace of great things."

The patterns within the new story are profoundly different. Learning information is not owned and dispensed by the teacher; it is abundant, accessible, open-sourced, and continuously constructed by students and teachers learning together in community. The pattern of learning and teaching is a dynamic, self-generating network. Each learner can access the subject and construct his or her own meaning by engaging with others. If we map this pattern, we would see a dynamic web, with arrows going in all directions. Rather than the teacher being both the expert disseminator and arbiter of access, she is the expert designer, learning partner, and constructor of meaning.

Coherent and dynamic patterns of learning within diverse learning networks enable the generation and flow of individual and collective (system) intelligence and creativity throughout the system. The more diverse, collaborative, and intricate the system's learning networks and patterns of learning relationships, the healthier and more sustainable it will be. Generative systems are interconnected learning networks rooted in the abundance and connections of community.

Pattern Recognition Helps Us Make Sense *of* Our World

Our brains are naturally pattern seeking and sense making, and we learn and construct meaning from discerning patterns embedded in a holistic context. We experience a sense of wholeness and connection when we recognize and understand deep patterns. Discerning patterns in seemingly disparate information or processes enables us to experience

---

Beliefs That Ground Generative Learning and Schooling Patterns

- *Deep understanding gained through pattern recognition and concept integration promotes wholeness and the flow of knowledge within and between domains.* Disciplinary knowledge and understanding can best be encouraged if we teach disciplinary, interdisciplinary, and transdisciplinary organizing principles, patterns, and concepts in a coherent and integrative context.

the resonance of deep and sustaining order. The ability to recognize and formulate patterns is essential to deep understanding because patterns are essential to meaning construction.

We are born within a patterned whole—the web of life—and learning is innately pattern seeking and creating. Seeking and generating patterns are how we make sense of our experience. Hence, disciplinary learning is best facilitated when coherent patterns (representations) of knowledge, major concepts, and organizing principles are presented within a holistic and connected context. Patterns create the sense-making contexts for future learning. They create the models and maps for disciplinary, interdisciplinary, and transdisciplinary navigation.

Patterns also serve as the foundation for developing expertise within a domain. Expertise develops not only from extensive knowledge but also from a honed capacity to discern the hidden order—patterns—within domain-specific knowledge and to organize large quantities of information in a way that facilitates rapid access. The distinctions between expert and novice learners are rooted in their capacity to create vibrant and intricate knowledge networks and then fluidly access them. Experts create multiple, coherent representations and organizing frameworks of knowledge. This capacity to perceive and sort familiar patterns of knowledge and understand their strategic implications is a defining attribute of expertise.

Within disciplinary domains, patterns represent the organizing conceptual configurations (schema) of principles, constructs, concepts, and modes of inquiry. The extensive knowledge networks essential to developing expertise enable experts to structure, represent, interpret, and apply knowledge in ways not yet available to novice learners. One of the most common capacities of expert learners is their ability to "chunk (categorize and classify) information into familiar patterns."[1] Without a well-defined and deep understanding of the organizing conceptual structure of the domain, this would not be possible.

Recognizing the organizing patterns (knowledge networks) within and among disciplines is one of the most important goals of learning. It is essential to our children's ability to meaningfully link new knowledge to their prior and current knowledge and experience. It enables deep conceptual understanding, facilitates retention, and allows knowledge to be creatively transferred to problems or situations not previously encountered. Pattern recognition is a prerequisite for complex and integral thinking. The brain learns best when information is presented in patterns of relevant and meaningful connections.

Impoverished Mind Making

Unfortunately, the current conditions of schooling mitigate against meaningful, coherent, and ordered representations of knowledge (patterns). By requiring our children to focus on acquiring excessive amounts of fragmented and inert information without the context to understand and make sense of it, we have compartmentalized their learning to such an extent that the discipline's essential coherence, integrative patterns, and meaning are lost. Over time, retention is far less likely because there is no holistic context (schema) within which to place new information. Hence, new information is placed into "old" schema, and tenacious misconceptions result.

I have called this disconnected process *impoverished mind making.* Because the most significant work of our time will be integrative, the growing minds of our children must be immersed in learning landscapes that enable them to see the world through an integral lens. This will require an understanding of the deep patterns inherent within and between domains of knowledge. While experimentation, objective analysis, and deep disciplinary understanding are essential for synthesis, integration, and transdisciplinary thinking, they do not naturally lead there.

As a result, we need to create conditions that make these interdisciplinary and transdisciplinary relationships (patterns) explicit. Paradoxically, discerning interdisciplinary connections actually deepens disciplinary understanding, for not all the secrets of a discipline are uncovered through linear analysis. Many are illuminated when viewed through the lens of interconnections. Integral minds can more likely be grown in learning environments that immerse children in wholeness and invite them to "think the world together."[2] Without the context of the whole from which meaning emerges, our children are lost in a stream of endless parts. It is no wonder they are confused, and misconceptions emerge. The unfortunate reality is that we have confused them by design. One of the goals of deep learning is to ensure that the integrity, coherence, beauty, elegance, and wonder of each discipline are revealed and understood.

We have designed learning experiences that do not enable our children to make the rich connections required for genuine understanding. Our ability to see ourselves as either connected to or alienated from the world and one another is largely shaped by the context of our worldview, and our worldview is largely shaped by the way we have come to know the world through the "languages" (disciplinary concepts, constructs, principles, ways of representing knowledge and modes of inquiry) we are able to "speak" or not. How disciplinary context is presented, how its unique modes of inquiry, its enduring questions, and its grand conceptual organizers are offered to students all profoundly influence who they become and how they perceive and make sense of the experiences around them. Our current conception of learning is defined not by deep disciplinary understanding but by shallow content acquisition. Students can memorize a lot of facts, but devoid of deep disciplinary context—patterns of knowledge and meaning construction—their learning has no meaning, relevance, or power.

Integral Thinking Is Patterned Thinking

We need to teach our children disciplinary concepts, content, and skills; but equally important, we need to imbue them with a sense of disciplinary patterns of reasoning, imagination, and intuition. Children simply cannot connect what they do not know.

Integral thinking can come only from deep disciplinary understanding within a connected learning environment. We must teach students the patterns, structures, and language of the disciplines, and create concept-centered curricula focused on their unifying constructs and organizing principles. Unless they are immersed in learning conditions that enable them to become truly "multilingual" in the world's disciplinary languages, our children are robbed of their capacity to know fully and belong wisely.

For all these reasons, our children need continuous practice in connecting disciplinary and interdisciplinary concepts and symbol systems in real-world problem solving. For example, asking students to create a concept map of the scientific, ethical, financial, and legal issues involved in stem cell research enables them to visualize these complex issues in a coherent and integrated way. The process of mapping multiple interdisciplinary concepts illuminates their hidden patterns and makes their relationships visible. Making patterns visible is the heart of teaching.

Retention, meaning, and integration are fostered when patterns are noticed, understood, and connected into a disciplinary "story." Our students' potentials will astonish us if we create the conditions and tools for them to learn deeply. If we want our children to demonstrate high levels of complex understanding, engage in rigorous and imaginative inquiry, and study problems of significance to them, collaborative and exploratory learning environments that honor all of who they are and how they learn must be created, by design. Patterns provide the conceptual maps for deep understanding and sense making within and between disciplines.

GENERATIVE SYSTEM PATTERNS ARE *the* PATTERNS *of* SELF-GENERATING NETWORKS

The pattern of a living system is not a control-based hierarchy; it is a self-generating network. Like all other living systems, our learning communities must be organized as learning webs and learning networks. Organizing our systems as multiple learning networks is the key to system generativity. It is this pattern that is the source of system integrity, wholeness, and connections. The more diverse and intricate the system's networked patterns are, the more intelligent, innovative, and resilient the system will be. The hidden geography of deeply rooted network patterns grounds and reconnects us to our system's history and nourishes our need for meaning and belonging. Networks enable the continuous flow of communication within our systems. Organizing our learning system as a network enables us to create learning environments that embody our commitments and purpose and resonate with the vibrancy of life.

The culture of any school and system emerges from the diversity of its relationships and the intricacy of its self-generating networked patterns. It is the pattern of relationships manifested in structures that allows the system to be recognized. Patterns create and sustain our system's stories. The network pattern of natural living systems must be the pattern of generative learning systems. This is the most significant dimension of system transformation. These relational webs are created as the system's members repeatedly engage with one another in advancing the system's work. Cross-functional networks are a primary example. To solve an institutional problem, for example, people can access and use the resources from anywhere in the system. They are not confined to what is available in their department. They now have all the institution's resources at their disposal. Generative patterns emerge from generative processes that enable the system to be true to its self. Processes that stimulate rapid innovation, experimentation, and imaginative modeling enable the system to explore new ideas quickly and see what works. Such systems not only reflect the networked patterns of life and learning, but generate more life and more learning—more novelty and more wholeness.

System patterns are often illusive because they are difficult to observe and quantify. We see their effects, but not the patterns themselves. That is why they are seldom recognized. They come into being as a result of repeated sequences of very small acts or events. It is only when we step back to explicitly connect and actually map these events that we can discern their patterns and assess their impact on our systems. The systemic properties of generative schooling are largely the properties of their networked relationships and processes. In an interconnected world, we need to understand the dynamics of webs and how they work so we can create conditions that invite their emergence, by design.

How we cocreate our system's identity and collectively engage in its work; the nature and frequency of the learning information we seek, generate, use, and share; how our community creatively learns together; and how we teach and learn: all these comprise the organized and repeated configurations of relationships that constitute the system's patterns. These patterns become embodied in structures. When we talk about the systemic properties of our school systems and schools, we are really talking about the properties of their patterns of organization, communication, and learning and teaching relationships.

Because our schools are embedded in our culture and reflective of its worldview, it should not surprise us that their formal patterns of relationships are largely control- and power-based hierarchies. The patterns inherent in this worldview remain a dominant and potent source of our language and mental models of schooling and learning. Change the patterns—the configurations of learning, teaching, communicating, and problem-solving relationships—within a system, and you change the system: its culture and its structures.

ENCOURAGING SELF-GENERATING NETWORKS

Within most school systems, we find at least two different patterns of relationships: formally established hierarchies and the informally emergent networks. Formal patterns of relationships are typically embodied in positional structures and rooted in expertise and experience. Who engages and works with whom is generally visible in the "boxes and lines" of authority depicted in the system's organization's chart.

Most of us recognize, however, that although some of these formal organizational relationships ensure the stability of the system's infrastructure (finance, security, maintenance, legal), they do not stimulate or generate the system's innovation, creativity, and continuous learning. Breakthrough thinking and authentic learning arise when everyone can openly engage in advancing the system's shared learning purpose. Our system's boundless creative capacity to generate new knowledge emerges only when people are connected and when abundant and freely flowing information can move naturally and quickly through it.

System novelty and creativity are far more likely to emerge through relationships fostered in self-generating networks than in positional hierarchies. Despite the need for some formal authority relationships to maintain system security, we will naturally create informal networks because we simply want to be connected. However, unless the system explicitly encourages and invites multiple networks to develop around its real work, these informal networks will generally not be focused on advancing the system's learning purpose; in fact, they could undermine it.

Discerning leaders and generative schooling systems recognize that space and time must be explicitly created for self-generating learning networks to be cultivated and thrive. The formal system must intentionally create conditions for the emergence by design of learning networks and communities of practice that invite the creativity, imagination, and innovativeness of the system around shared purpose. It is only through the existence of these dynamic networks that the creative patterns of life can thrive. While this may be challenging to us, it is natural for our children.

Our children live in a world of self-generating networks: networked video games, e-mail, instant messaging, blogging, chatrooms, and open source operating systems. Having grown up on the Internet—itself a self-generating networking—the network pattern is the most natural for them. They exist and navigate in a self-generating and networked world where everything—outside of school—is connected. The fragmented and disengaged context of schooling makes the pattern recognition essential to sense making very difficult.

Reconnecting to the deepest patterns of life reinforces the simple truth that in an interdependent world, it is relationships, not things, that create more life. This is true of all institutions, but especially our schools, whose purpose is learning. When generative learning networks are able to thrive, a school will come to life. The radical new system of learning and schooling is a self-generating learning network that cannot be bounded or boxed.

Leadership Inquiries *About* Learning *and* Schooling Patterns

Creating generative learning and schooling systems means engaging our communities in deeper questions about learning and schooling patterns. I offer the following questions to get you started:

• *What is the hidden geography—the landscape and culture—of our system?* What are our patterns (networks) of communicating, sharing, and generating information and ideas? What are the patterns of learning and teaching between teachers and students, students and students, and teachers and teachers? What are the beliefs and assumptions that ground our patterns of learning, connecting, and belonging? How have we integrated both linear (hierarchical) and networked patterns in our system's organization?

• *If we drew a map of the configuration of our working relationships, learning networks, and decision-making and communication pathways, what would our map look like?* Is our system's diversity and intricacy sufficient to advance and sustain our shared purpose (identity)? What might we do to increase its complexity and variety? Who intentionally collaborates with whom in the course of the system communicating, connecting, and doing its work? What relational patterns are embodied in our learning and teaching structures—especially curriculum, instruction, assessment, and professional development? How shall we change our patterns of teaching and learning? What new patterns do we now seek?

• *What is the nature and quality of the multiple networks of our system?* How are learning and communication networks encouraged and sustained? How do they serve our learning purpose? What are our networks for creating knowledge or experimenting with ideas or prototypes? What is the role of technology in facilitating real and virtual learning networks and local and global communities of practice?

• *To what degree do our learning and working networks promote innovation, collaboration, and interdependence?* What are our simple "rules" (patterns of relationships) for generating new ideas, innovations, and experimentation and fluidly distributing intelligence throughout the system?

Stability

Creating Flexible, Temporary, and Adaptive Learning Structures

System learning structures are flexible, adaptive, temporary,
and responsive to new learning.

I RECENTLY LEARNED ABOUT A CLASS OF FIFTH- TO
eighth-grade special education students who were asked by their
local community to tackle a civic problem: the need to change a road
pattern in the community so the local airport could add a runway.
These ten to fourteen year olds threw themselves into the project with
great energy: they carefully crafted the problem statement and decided
what they knew and needed to know. Then they explored multiple
issues related to wetlands in the area, took surveys of businesses and
home owners along the existing and proposed route, did extensive traf-
fic counts, studied the number of accidents at a dangerous Y intersec-
tion, pored over maps from their state's department of transportation,
and invited state transportation officials to their class to share information and answer questions.

At the end of their project, the students presented their recommendation to the state department of transportation, proposing that

the existing road configuration be changed from a Y to a T. Because this would require cutting down many trees, they also recommended that two trees be planted for each one cut down. The officials listened attentively, thanked the students for their thoughtful proposal, and told them that they were not required to replace trees that they cut down.

Two years later, the students read a news story on the front page of the local newspaper: the state department of transportation had finally decided what to do about the road: they were going to change the configuration from a Y to a T, and replace two trees for every one they cut down![1]

Learning is a process of exploration and discovery. It thrives within contexts and conditions (structures) that stimulate and encourage our pursuit and construction of meaning. How and what we perceive, think, and hold as truth is shaped by the multiple contexts and structures within which we continuously learn. Cultural norms, peers, the Internet, and the media often immerse us in shallow contexts for learning. However, to sustain a vibrant democracy, the context of formal learning must ensure that deep thinking is nurtured in a culture of inquiry and imagination.

Despite all the other competing contexts in which we learn, our homes, our communities, and our schools are the dominant environments and places where our learning self is initially defined and often solidified. If we do well in school and are praised and rewarded for being "smart," we carry this affirmed and confident learning self into everything we do. And if we do not do well in school and are ignored or marginalized for not being "smart," we carry this demeaned and shamed learning self with us as well, a silent and invisible albatross that diminishes our future learning capacity. We become afraid, tentative, and risk averse. Learning becomes unnatural.

It is within this context of defining the learning self that the structures of schooling have their greatest potency for mind shaping. Within living systems, structures are the physical embodiments of the system's identity and patterns of relationships and the visible and temporary forms created to sustain it. While patterns are qualitative and invisible, structures are quantitative and tangible. In healthy living systems, structures are continuously adapting and changing. When meaningful information challenges its current forms, it must adapt to sustain its deeper purpose. Old structures are no longer able to hold the new self being formed. This emergence of new or modified structures keeps the system alive.

Learning Changes *the* Structure *of the* Brain

Structural adaptability (plasticity) is also true of the human brain as we learn. Our brain is a complex adaptive system. Although we do not know the extent to which the brain changes as a result of experience (learning), or the role of cultural contexts in brain shaping, we do know that the interplay between genes and experience influences the unique shape (the networks of connections) of our brains.[2] Each person's combination of intelligences is therefore uniquely configured.

If learning influences the structure and organization of our brains, then the nature and quality of the environments in which learning

---

Beliefs That Ground Generative Learning and Schooling Structures

- *Learning is demonstrated, assessed, and credentialed by multiple forms of evidence* and by exhibitions and performances of deep understanding, anytime and anywhere. Learning time is variable. Learning is assessed whenever the learner is ready and credentialed when the learner demonstrates learning. Learners actively participate in the assessment of their own and their peers' learning.

- *Rigorous, meaningful, reliable, and legitimate assessment of deep learning is dynamic, flexible, and systemic.* It includes both quantitative and qualitative evidence of understanding. It is self-correcting and ongoing and is demonstrated in authentic contexts and settings that enable complex responses.

- *Meaningful curriculum must be connected to the learner's lived experience,* the community's needs, and the world's problems. Life must be the curriculum for schooling.

occurs are crucial. Our brain's search for meaning is innate. Because meaning is constructed through patterning and because deep under-standing is more likely encouraged in challenging inquiry-based envi-ronments and thwarted in fearful or threatening ones,[3] we must design learning conditions and structures that are congruent with how we learn and that stimulate our natural desire for learning. Such environments are messy, ill structured, highly interactive, imaginative, "seriously" playful, and brain and learning compatible.

Deep learning is profoundly relational. It is all about engagement and meaning. Deep learning occurs when children create a relation-ship between themselves and what they want to learn, between them-selves and their peers, between themselves and their teachers, and between themselves and their communities. Learning structures must actively encourage these learning relationships. They must be muta-ble, adaptive, and responsive to new information. Currently they are not. We lack relational contexts for knowing, relational strategies for teaching, relational curricula for meaning making, relational assess-ments for understanding, and relational learning environments for belonging.

Schooling systems and their learning and teaching structures are connected webs of relationships. Their components of curriculum—instruction, assessment, and professional development—have no meaning devoid of the whole and the context within which they are embedded.

GENERATIVE STRUCTURES *of* SCHOOLING ARE FLEXIBLE *and* ADAPTIVE

So too with the structures of schooling. They must flow from the prin-ciples and processes of what we now know about living systems and learning. This means they must be flexible and adaptive to the chang-ing needs of learners and learning environments. The current struc-tures of schooling, largely manifested through historically mandated, nonadaptive, and rigid frameworks of curriculum, instruction, assess-ment, and professional development, were designed using erroneous principles of human learning and profound misconceptions of the conditions essential for deep understanding. As a consequence, these structures are irreconcilable with our natural ways of learning and the creative and exploratory processes of life itself. The results? A prescriptive, uniform, and often incoherent curriculum that is unchallenging, overly saturated with facts, fragmented, and lacking in disciplinary and interdisciplinary depth, relevance, connections, and meaning. Nonadaptive and formulaic instructional approaches rooted in efficient and detached transmission. And a depersonalized, competitive, punitive, and high-stakes testing system that is nondiagnostic and disengaged from the learners' need for continuous and immediate feedback on their own learning.

These fragmented and immutable structures mark the current environment of learning. Now, however, we have the knowledge to create learning and teaching structures that nurture creative inquiry, experimentation, innovation, and deep learning. These environments:

- Do not abandon standards. They establish relevant, coherent, and meaningful expectations for significant student learning designed to develop integral habits of mind.[4]

- Do not abandon formal curriculum. They redesign it so children engage with the concepts and inquiry strategies of multiple disciplines by using their modes of inquiry to solve real-world problems within the community.

- Do not abandon instruction. They transform it to enable teachers, students, mentors, and practitioners to actively engage in cocreating knowledge and inquiring together.

- Do not abandon evaluation, measurement, and assessment. They create multiple indicators and strategies for securing continuous feedback and evidence (both formative and summative) on the quality of their children's learning.

- Continuously share this learning information with the children so they develop their own internal learning authority.

These environments do not abandon the structures of learning and schooling that are essential for disciplined meaning making; they redesign them in concert with the generative identity, information, relationships, processes, and patterns of life. No longer is an externally created, one-size curriculum, instructional strategy, or assessment system mandated for all. These structures are informed by external contexts, but they are created by the system and are continuously evaluated, adapted, and changed as new learning and information emerge. Buoyed by these adaptive and more personalized structures, children feel connected. They know what they need to learn and why, and they are able to imaginatively explore and continuously learn anytime, anywhere, and in any place. Generative structures for learning are congruent with the process of life. Our brains are structurally flexible and spontaneously adaptive. The processes of learning must be as well. The identity we choose and the processes we design create the system dynamics that shape our organizational structures.

The SYSTEM'S IDENTITY MUST GROUND ITS STRUCTURES

In generative learning and schooling systems, structures are explicitly designed to enable the system's fundamental learning identity, learning information, learning relationships, and learning processes and networks to become manifest. Structures embody the system's learning expectations and commitments. If we begin a systemic change process by first trying to change structures, the structures not only drive system identity; they become the system's identity. We water the structural leaves of schooling, but that nourishment never reaches the deepest roots of learning.

This understanding is fundamental to designing a radical new system of schooling: *the system's identity must ground the design of its structures, not the other way around.* The first step is to cocreate a clear, coherent, and compelling identity around deep learning; only then can we design generative structures that embody our purpose. Deep learning is more likely stimulated and nurtured in natural learning systems—a network designed according to the ways life organizes itself for sustainability. How a system is organized has enormous influence on its capacity to become and live its purpose. In healthy and vibrant learning systems, structures are adaptive and can re-form as the system discerns new possibilities, new interpretations, and new expressions of self.

We commonly make two fundamental errors when it comes to trying to impose systemic change: we forget we are engaging with life, and we fail to remember that we are part of a dynamic, interdependent, self-generating system. That's why we so often fall into the engineering and efficiency trap and think we have to start with structural change. Either we begin our organizational change efforts by thinking we need to fix the structure, or we conclude our change efforts with structural changes as the final dimension of our work. Perhaps it's because structures are the most visible part of schooling and their visibility suggests immediate attention, but based on what we understand about how transformation occurs in living systems, it is both the wrong place to begin and false security to believe change will ever be finished.

The POWER of GENERATIVE LEARNING STRUCTURES

Within a schooling system, there are numerous structures that manifest the system's purpose and embody its patterns and processes for doing its work. The crisis of meaning emerging from our current system of schooling comes from its identity and design as a deficiency-based and remedial model of learning that has become calcified in rigid, permanent, and disconnected structures out of sync with the creativity and adaptability of learning. The new system is profoundly different. To illuminate its distinctions, we'll focus briefly on three schooling structures: curriculum, instruction, and assessment.

Many important books have been written in recent years about each of these structures. My purpose is not to reiterate what has already been advanced. Rather, it is to name the principles of generative and life-affirming design essential to manifesting the new story and system of learning and schooling within each of these three structures. These patterns and design principles create the language and map from which the new learning and schooling terrain will emerge.

Before we explore each of these components, I'd like to share a personal story that exemplifies the power of intentionally designed generative learning structures to invite and evoke deep learning. Several years ago, I attended a conference designed to challenge perceived learning and capacity boundaries, stretch awareness of our unexplored and unknowable potentials, and invite a new learning identity and sense of self. In opening the conference, the leader raised four questions and asked the group to respond by raising our hands. These questions were:

- How many of you can't sing?
- How many of you can't write?
- How many of you can't paint or draw?
- How many of you can't dance?

There were two hundred adults in the room, and everyone raised their hands at least once. She followed this question with two more: "Where were you and how old were you when you first learned what you could not do, when you first learned that you could not sing, or write, or paint, or draw, or dance, or?"

I recalled the woman who told me she hadn't sung since the third grade, not even in the shower. Now, with sadness, I realized that in third grade, I had learned that I could not draw or paint, and I had not done so since that time.

Everyone had his or her own story, but the pattern was unmistakable: each of us had learned in school (mostly by fifth grade) what we could not do. I particularly remember the young woman who "couldn't write," married a writer, and then even stopped writing Christmas cards. But then something unfolded that felt magical. For the next four days, we practiced doing what we believed we couldn't do. We sang passionately with a skilled singing coach. We wrote creatively with a renowned writer. We painted freely with a gifted water-color artist. And we danced almost effortlessly. Some of us thought our "products" needed much more work, and others were astounded at how good they really were. But it didn't matter. We had been invited into a place we had never been except when we were very young, and it provoked a fundamental shift in who we were now and who we saw ourselves to be as learners. We clearly could do what we had believed for years we could not.

The conference leader had brilliantly designed generative and life-affirming conditions and structures that enabled each participant to reconnect to what had been severed and lost. Through trusting coaching relationships with experts; immersion and practice in writing, singing, dancing, and painting; slow time; and emotional reconnection with who we were becoming, we were transformed as learners. The young woman who "knew she couldn't write" has since written several children's books.

How smart are we really? How capable are we really? The truth is, we have no idea. The power of learning invitations and conditions to shape learning identity and performance is profound.

We turn now to three defining process structures: curriculum, instruction and assessment, and the design principles that enable us to create their generative learning terrain. We begin with curriculum.

A CURRICULUM *for* LIFE IS ALL *About* LOVING *the* QUESTIONS

I first encountered the construct of curriculum for life in the writings of Howard Gardner and Veronica Boix-Mansilla.[5] Using this context, they named several universally human questions they believed children must actively engage in in order to deeply understand their world and their connections to it. I offer their questions as a context for the new curriculum:

- *Identity and history:* Who am I? Where do I come from?

- *Who is my family?* What is the group to which I belong? What is the story of that group?

- *Other people, groups:* Who are the other people around me, and what other parts of the world do they live in? How are they similar to and different from me? How do they look? What do they do? What is their story?

- *Relations to others:* How should you treat other people? How should they treat you? What is fair? What is moral? How do you cooperate? How do you handle conflicts? Who is the boss, and why?

- *My place in the world:* Where do I live? How did I get there? How do I fit into the universe? What will happen to me when I die?

- *The psychological world:* What is my mind? Do others have minds? Are they like mine? What are thoughts, dreams, and feelings? Where do my emotions come from? How can I handle them? How do I remember things? How do I communicate?

- *The biological world:* What about other creatures? What does it mean to be alive, dead? Do animals think? What about plants? How are animals related to one another, to the world of plants, to humans? Is there a substance of life? How is it created?

- *The physical world:* What is the world made up of? Why do things move? What do we know about the sun, the earth, the stars, the water, the rocks—their origins, their fate?

- *Forms, patterns, sizes:* Why do things look and feel the way they do? What regularities are there in the world? How do they come about? What is big, biggest, and how can you tell?

After I read these questions, I became curious about some of the questions my own faculty was asking our students. Table 10.1 lists some "big questions" IMSA faculty embed within our curriculum.

For some, these questions may appear far too soft and lacking in disciplinary coherence and complexity to constitute a formal and rigorous curriculum. But deeply exploring really good questions can take us into the depths of disciplinary, interdisciplinary, and transdisciplinary thinking and problem solving. Knowledge generation is provoked by inquiry—by truly great questions whose exploration profoundly illuminates and deepens our understanding. It is the truly great question that captures our sense of wonder and imagination and invites us to discover the essence of who we are, why we are here, how we come to know, and how we belong. Great questions are portals to a future of unknown possibilities. Several years ago, I was asked by an interviewer, "If you could, what's the one piece of advice you would give to all students?" My answer was simple: "Ask questions that matter. Ask questions that make a difference. Ask questions that you love so that as you live your life seeking the answers, you will find joy."

For schooling to be generative and life affirming, the curriculum must tell a coherent, connected, and powerful story of wholeness, meaning, connections, and belonging. It must tell the story of our oneness with the universe, with the web of life, with the web of human experiences, and with each other. It must help children discover and tell their own story. In a relational universe, all of life is connected.

TABLE 10.1. *"Big" Questions for Deep Learning*

The Four Pillars of Learning	*"Big" Questions for Deep Learning*
Learning to know	What does it mean "to know"?
	How do I come to know the natural world and my place in it? What is the system of which we and life are a part?
	What are the dimensions of reality, and how do we come to know reality? What constitutes the "real world"?
	How can we know our own mind or the world outside our mind?
	What do we mean by "truth"? What is a "fact"? Are there "fixed truths" or values, or are human actions and endeavors culturally relative?
	What is the relation of us-as-observer to that which is observed? How do we characterize the interface, and what about some possible results of such a connection?
	How can we tie the present to an unknown, rapidly changing future?
	What do we currently believe that is probably wrong?
	We are our history, so who are we?
	How do things work in the physical world? What are the implications and responsibilities that come with this knowledge?
	How do we know what we know? What is the relationship between public knowledge (that which society recognizes as "true") and private conscience (that to which one has a personal commitment)?
Learning to do	*How* have I learned what I know?
	What am I eager to explore, invent, and discover?
	How do I most enjoy solving problems and resolving conflicts?
	What kinds of questions and challenges do I want to devote my life to?

TABLE 10.1. *"Big" Questions for Deep Learning, Cont'd.*

The Four Pillars of Learning	*"Big" Questions for Deep Learning*
Learning to be	Who am I? What are my assumptions? How do my assumptions affect what I know, what I believe, and what I do or don't do?
	What is my work, and how is it living out? How do I make sense of my environment? How does what I know and do come together to define my worth?
	What do I believe in, and why do I believe it?
	What is consciousness? What is the mind? What is specifically human about our minds?
	What is sacred?
	What is important in life?
	What am I willing to die for (or live for)?
	Are there absolutes in my life, or in life? If so, how can they be discovered?
	What is life all about? Why are we here? What do I believe in? What must I fight for, and what must I fight against?
	What is my place on this earth—for now, for the next few years, forever? What is my story?
Learning to live together	How do I sustain the belief that I can leave the world a better place?
	How can I learn to live and work with others? How do I relate to others?
	What is my relationship to the natural world, the universe, and its inhabitants, and so what?

Our children do not know this timeless story and therefore do not know they are an essential part of its wondrous evolution. A curriculum for life ensures that the deeply human story embedded in the richness, complexity, beauty, and unity of knowledge is experienced by our children.

FIVE DESIGN PRINCIPLES *for*
a CURRICULUM *for* LIFE

What principles might we use to design a curriculum for life that engages children in the human questions necessary for deeply understanding the world and their place in it? We must ensure:

1. *The curriculum is centered on real-world problems framed by the learner's prior knowledge and lived experiences and the community's and real-world's needs.* Grappling with complex and compelling questions and relevant and meaningful ill-structured problems engages the learner's passion, curiosity, and imagination in trying to make sense of the environment, figure things out, and develop a sense of his or her own efficacy and power as a learner. The curriculum for life makes this encounter with life possible and connects children to their growing identity as self-directed learners.

2. *The curriculum is based on inquiry and structured around essential questions embedded in the human experience.* Learning experiences grounded in the organizing principles, core concepts, and modes of inquiry and truth verification that uniquely define each disciplinary domain promote mindful investigation, knowledge generation, and critical thinking. Understanding the principles and concepts within a domain illuminates its patterns and brings coherence and meaning to its knowledge and theoretical claims.

3. *The curriculum is integrative—explicitly and continually linking principles and concepts within, across, between, and beyond disciplinary domains.* Discerning connections enables children to see the fundamental unity, patterns, and relationships of knowledge. Curriculum experiences that engage students in individual and collective reflection allow them to create meaning, discern wholeness, and internalize a sense of belonging and connection. It is important to note, however, that deep interdisciplinary and transdisciplinary understanding and application are not fully possible without deep disciplinary understanding. Our children simply cannot connect what they do not know.

4. *The curriculum is competency driven—focused on developing the habits of mind and being (higher-order thinking and perceiving)*

internalized by thoughtful practitioners. This is made possible when children are immersed in continuous practice within and across disciplines. For example, we frequently hear educational slogans that promote science (it could be any discipline) *for* all students. The curriculum for life carries a decidedly different message: it says science and scientific thinking *by* all students. If children are not actively engaged in the doing of a discipline, the solving of a problem, the writing and acting of a play, or the creation of a product, they remain observers of life and cannot participate in its cocreation. Multiple and rich opportunities for immersion in doing the work of a domain are essential for mindful inquiry.

5. *The curriculum activates and honors the unique potentials of each child.* When generative and life-affirming conditions are created for our children's learning, their goodness and genius will astonish us.

Complex problem resolution is more likely when children have been immersed in complex learning experiences that call them to engage their multiple potentials to discern and connect the dots. This is enhanced when we teach children about systems of all kinds and engage them in systemic thinking. This systemic mental model offers them a dynamic and connected map for discerning often hidden patterns and interconnections. Understanding our kinship with life and living systems is an imperative not only for the planet but also for human health and well-being. Our children must understand that they are a part of the web of life and their behavior either enhances or diminishes the web's vitality and sustainability.

Teaching *for* Understanding

The story at the beginning of this chapter illustrates the excitement that can be generated when we teach for understanding. The fifth graders whose research influenced the actions of their community recognized that to resolve the problem they were confronted with, they had to understand its complexities. This high school-age student reflects on the value of the deep understandings made available through problem-based learning:

Imagine you are in a course for the first time, expecting a traditional classroom setting. Instead of your instructor attempting to spoon-feed you information, she says you are part of a risk assessment panel and your duty is to determine the best location to build a super theme park in Southern Illinois. Or perhaps there is a hurricane threatening the coast of Florida, and it is your responsibility to issue warning and evacuation plans to keep the population safe. Wouldn't this experience be far more exciting than a typical class and motivate you to take responsibility for your own learning? Problem-based learning requires a student to experience intellectual frustration, witness firsthand the power of collaboration, and deal with ambiguity. These skills will continue to gain importance in our increasingly complex global society.[6]

Teaching is one of those endeavors that intrigues and often confounds us. "What exactly do great teachers *do*?" is often a question we ask. Is teaching an art or a science, or is it an integration of both? What is the role of a teacher in an environment designed to foster personalized learning, inquiry, and deep understanding?

An IMSA math teacher who teaches a course entitled Mathematical Investigations (MI) offers the following response. I quote it in its entirety because it so beautifully captures the answer to these questions:

To an MI observer, teaching an MI classroom looks like a teacher's dream job . . . very little at-the-board "lecture" on some days, and instead, the teacher is milling about the room, looking over students' shoulders, and intermittently asking or answering questions. Even first-time MI students sometimes wonder, "When is the teacher going to "teach"?

But looks can certainly be deceiving! Teaching MI is far more exhausting than preparing lessons and lecturing could ever be. In the traditional format, the teacher is almost always in control of what happens next; everything is predictable, planned, and polished. There is often a sense of "I taught it, so they now know it" that follows. Unfortunately, there is little way to actually validate that sense until a formal assessment is given, and by then, it's way too late for some kids.

The word "teaching" takes on a whole new meaning in the MI classroom. It goes well beyond standing at the board and dispensing content, methodologies, and algorithms organized in a manner that makes perfect sense to the well-educated (and well-meaning) teacher. It now means letting go, *listening, assessing,* responding, questioning, probing, *listening,* clarifying, watching, *listening,* guiding (but not just telling), and *assessing* EVERY student, EVERY day. There is a delicate balance of timing that must be maintained of when to let the students grapple with a new or difficult idea, and when to intervene, help them make necessary connections and "see the big picture." There is a constant need to "think on your feet" as students ask questions that even the seasoned teacher does not anticipate. There is a need for enough self-confidence and mathematical understanding to let the students watch YOU grapple with a challenging problem so that they can see you as a model problem solver, even if that means you make a mistake in front of them (something that the traditional teacher wouldn't dream of!). There is a need to be able to answer students' questions with questions that lead them to the answers they thought they couldn't get. There is a need to hear the misconceptions that truly underlie their initial response—"I don't know how to do this one."

And once you think you've mastered all of that, you get a new class of students, and you have the grand opportunity to start all over again. You find the balance again, perhaps in a different place; because all students are different, and teaching MI actually lets you see that and react to it. The MI teacher has the gift of hearing students talk about the mathematics in their language, using their constructs. You learn to read how each student in your class thinks about mathematics, and you have the privilege of adjusting your instruction to suit all of those needs; that is simply impossible in a traditional classroom. Results on formal assessments are rarely surprises; such tests are merely opportunities for the students to demonstrate their knowledge in a more formal manner.

What does the MI teacher do? Oh. Not much![7]

Her response tells me that Parker Palmer had it just right: teaching is a profound and constantly unfolding and evolving integration of what he calls the "tangles of teaching." These tangles, he says, have three sources: the need to deeply understand the content of what we teach; the need to deeply understand and wisely respond to the individual, social, and emotional complexities of our children; and the need to understand who we are as teachers. "We teach who we are," Palmer says. "Good teaching requires self-knowledge. . . . The human heart is the source of good teaching."[8]

Teaching who we are is illustrated by another IMSA teacher:

> If we are to develop ways to make active student discovery happen, take hold, and endure, we must define who we are in the classroom. A teacher who facilitates discovery, who creates the environment that makes discovery possible must realize it is not an environment only for students, but that the interrogative mood includes the teacher as well.
>
> It is not enough to ask questions that evoke responses. One could do that all day and cover nothing but fact. The teacher must raise questions that genuinely puzzle the teacher.
>
> Facilitating discovery is the ultimate intellectual exposure because the way to encourage thinking is to be thinking yourself.[9]

Many years ago, as a brand-new sixth-grade teacher, I faced my ultimate intellectual exposure during an encounter with students I never anticipated. We were studying the fascinating culture of the Bushmen of the Kalahari desert as part of our world history unit. I had designed the class to be highly interactive. Students were working in teams—very uncommon thirty-five years ago—and the curriculum was largely *National Geographic* magazines and encyclopedias, not textbooks. The children appeared quite captivated and fascinated by this remarkable culture, and I felt everything was going according to plan.

Then one day, when one of the teams was presenting their research, a student blurted out, "I know you won't like this, but I don't believe the Bushmen really exist!" Half the class laughed. The other half stared in silence. I was stunned. I wondered how he could possibly have gotten this idea. Hadn't he remembered reading *National Geographic*? Hadn't he remembered seeing all the pictures of Bushmen? How could he believe they didn't exist? I didn't know then what made me do what I did next, but in looking back, I can see that it was the beginning of living into the new story for me. I looked around the room, where all the pictures of the U.S. presidents were hanging. I grabbed the picture of Abraham Lincoln, tore it off the wall, ripped it up, and said, "Jamie, I am *so* glad you said this, because I never believed Abraham Lincoln existed either!"

The class went berserk—accusing me of everything from ignorance to insanity, including lack of patriotism. When they finally settled down, I asked everyone to pick up a chair, move it into a circle, sit quietly for a moment, and think about what had just happened. I then invited them to comment if they wished to—one at a time, so we could all really listen to one another. Amid all of their eleven- and twelve-year-old emotions of disbelief and outrage toward me and the student who had started this, emerged something I wasn't expecting: a deep and passionate desire to really know. My actions had thrown them off, completely destabilizing their world. They thought they knew how to decide if something was true and who to believe. But now they weren't sure. I had taken away an illusory safety net.

The next day we began a very different conversation. We talked about truth and how we know something is true when we cannot see it or are not there. We asked countless questions:

- What exactly is truth?
- Can something be true at one time and not another? Who decides?
- What experts should we believe? What are reliable sources that we can trust?
- How can we verify what experts say?
- How do historians arrive at saying something is true?
- How is it different from scientists?
- How shall we decide if the Bushmen really do exist?

From that moment, I had different children in my classroom. The questions had engaged their curiosity and their passion, and they became skeptical and thoughtful inquirers—an essential disposition for lifelong learning. They read the newspaper differently, listened to their parents and me differently, and, most important, asked each other different questions: How do you know? What evidence have you gathered and from whom? How have you verified it? Their laser-like intensity astounded me. They had begun a learning journey they would continue for the rest of their lives.

Five Design Principles *for* Teaching *for* Understanding

What principles might we use to design instruction so that our children experience teaching as a relational, cocreative, and live encounter with great questions and great ideas and so that their hearts and spirits are welcomed in learning? We must ensure that teaching is:

1. *A relational, personal, communal, and transformative process of cocreation between teachers and learners.* Teachers and learners are deeply and often playfully engaged in mindful and challenging investigation—in safely wondering together, cocreating meaning, and experiencing the unfolding mysteries and revelations of the natural world and the human experience. They improvise together, experiment together, seek novelty together, play together, risk together, and create new truth together. The climate is challenging and engaging but not threatening.

2. *Focused on ensuring that each student acquires knowledge, develops an understanding of disciplinary and interdisciplinary concepts and knowledge structures, and learns a broad repertoire* of critical and analytical thinking, reasoning, and inquiry strategies that enable her to process and make sense of what she has learned.

3. *Personalized and grounded in fostering each learner's construction of meaning* through exploring prior knowledge, uncovering preconceptions and assumptions, and actively engaging each learner's unique constellation of intelligences.

4. *Centered on the personal and communal exploration of great questions* and the creative framing and resolution of complex and ill-structured problems and issues relevant and meaningful to the learner. Teaching must create a safe practice field for dynamic inquiry, innovation, and playful exploration. Great teaching is teacher designed and student directed.

5. *Developing each child's confidence and internal authority for lifelong learning.* Great teaching must ensure children have the metacognitive skills and strategies necessary to assume control over their own

learning. This includes discerning and correcting their misconceptions, understanding their strengths and how they learn best, monitoring their own learning goals, and assessing their own understanding.

Great teaching for great learning is clearly not only about what we are asking our children to learn; more important, it is about *how* we are asking our children to learn. Again, Parker Palmer's insights are profoundly important: "Every way of knowing becomes a way of living. . . . Every epistemology becomes an ethic. . . . Every mode of education, no matter what its name, is a mode of soul-making."[10] To this I would add, every epistemology gives rise to a pedagogy: how we teach is based on how we believe we come to know.

Ensuring this quality of teaching is learned and sustained requires vibrant communities of practice—professional learning communities that are also competency driven, inquiry based, problem centered, and integrative.[11] These dynamic and collaborative partnerships and networks enable teachers to explore teaching practice, exchange and challenge instructional strategies, collectively analyze and use student learning data, and engage and support one another in innovative systemic change. For far too long, teaching has been an isolated act. Closing the classroom door has often meant closing the door to meaningful dialogue, peer observation, reflection, and deep learning. We must create conditions that encourage and sustain communities of practice.

Within IMSA, for example, there are two process structures for enhancing instruction and professional practice. One is a "call for dialogue" (optional), and the other is annual faculty presentations. A "call for dialogue" can be issued by a faculty member at any time and is open to anyone in the community. While these calls vary, they provide an opportunity for professionals to engage one another in non-evaluative conversations about teaching and learning. Typically, calls for dialogue center around faculty candidly describing a lesson that didn't seem to work and asking for feedback on what they might do differently. Calls for dialogue are not mandatory workshops on best practice. They are collegial and voluntary inquiries about professional practice and its impact on student learning.

Faculty presentations offer similar opportunities for learning and exchange. Faculty prepare brief written abstracts of what they will present in a thirty-minute time frame. Abstracts are compiled and distributed ahead of time so faculty can choose the sessions they wish to attend. Here are several examples of abstracts to give you a sense of what is shared.

Assessment of Mathematical Investigations-2 Exams

After an exam on matrices in Mathematical Investigation-2, I video-taped three students presenting their solutions to two problems. The aim of this work was to gain a better understanding of how well students are able to demonstrate their understanding of mathematical concepts on timed written exams. I will show portions of the video-tapes and discuss what I have learned.[12]

An Experience with Projects: Balancing Structure and Flexibility

My Mathematica class offers a challenge to create assignments that are challenging, possible for all, and grade-able. I have made some progress in my ability to create and define these projects, but there's still plenty of room for improvement. I will share some of my goals, my attempts, and the results. (Note: It is not necessary to know anything about Mathematica or even much of anything about mathematics to follow most of my presentation).[13]

Changing My Spots

I've always known that I am intimidating to students—they bluntly tell me so on each student survey. But I couldn't figure out exactly why they see me this way. Last year when doing an unrelated study with my students, they unexpectedly helped me discover several of my behaviors which they see as intimidating. This year I have been making a concerted effort to change these behaviors. I'm still not seen as Mr. Snuggly, but this year's student surveys sure read differently.[14]

Using Student-Generated Rubrics to Improve Student Performance and Encourage Metacognition

Students usually want to do their best; therefore, I am always looking for ways to clarify expectations without being overly prescriptive.

Adapting an idea from my colleague, I asked French III students to develop an assessment rubric for a culminating oral presentation of a unit on Francophone poetry. I will show the process in which students engaged, provide copies of the final rubric, and show one or more video clips of the oral assessment. Performance has consistently improved for all students.[15]

I have attended many of these presentations, and they have been powerful. When peers decide to become vulnerable to one another and authentically and nondefensively share their practice and their questions, profound insights can emerge and thinking, and behavior can change.

Schooling systems that intentionally design time and space for the creation and sustainability of communities of practice and reflective inquiry invite a vital and self-correcting practice field for continuous and meaning-filled professional learning.

ASSESSMENT GENERATES CONTINUOUS FEEDBACK *About* STUDENT UNDERSTANDING

In living systems, feedback (assessment) is neither a monster nor a process and structure to be feared. Quite the contrary: living systems are sustained through the flow of continuous and abundant information about their learning purpose.

Learners, schools, and the systems of which they are a part also require continuous, abundant, and transparent information about their learning. However, our current obsession with only one kind of feedback—annual performance and ranking on national and state high-stakes achievement tests, often unconnected to the curriculum—completely distorts the natural and essential purpose of feedback, which is to deepen student understanding by illuminating knowledge and conceptual insights, and gaps and misconceptions. By mechanizing its procedures, granting indefensible high stakes to its conclusions, inaccurately interpreting the meaning of its results, and not questioning the consequences of its totally quantitative and comparative test scores, we allow these standardized and once-a-year multiple-choice tests to "distribute" student achievement along a bell-shaped curve and "define" the learning, potential, and success of our students and the competence of our teachers.

If it were not so tragic, it could be viewed as an astounding act of hubris—believing we could actually create a one-size-fits-all assessment system to definitively and conclusively determine the achievement and promise of each one of our children, without asking them to actually demonstrate their knowledge and understanding in multiple ways over extended periods of time. But its unintended and insidious effects linger long past the years of formal schooling, and they cast an ominous shadow over the minds and hearts of our children. Years of hearing labels like "failure," "underachiever," or "slow learner" become internalized so deeply that a new "deficient" learning self emerges—one who no longer sees possibilities or promise, but sees only peril and the need to protect its fragile self.

Our children crave meaning-filled, honest, continuous information about their learning, given within the context of an affirming and respectful environment designed to help them succeed through the ways they learn best. In such an environment, there is no one right way to learn or demonstrate learning proficiency and no one-size assessment to fit all students. Every child is unique. Our instructional work is to create personalized learning conditions that develop the potentials of each child. Our assessment work is to create multiple assessments—including tests—that enable each child to demonstrate his or her learning proficiency and mastery. In such a system, there is no normatively prescribed achievement distribution. Everybody can get an A.

FIVE DESIGN PRINCIPLES *for* ASSESSING DEEP LEARNING

What principles might we use to design generative assessments and assessment systems that are congruent with our children's need for continuous and meaningful feedback (information) on their learning that will provide evidence of deep understanding and integral habits of mind and will sustain their learning over time?

We must ensure that assessment for deep learning is:

1. *Generative (ongoing and cyclical) and focused on continuously deepening learning and understanding by teaching children how to monitor and regulate their own learning and that of their peers.* Assessment is a natural and essential process of learning, but the structures we have designed—largely summative, norm-referenced, high-stakes tests—do not serve this self-monitoring purpose. In high-stakes testing, students are detached recipients, not engaged collaborators. Students must actively participate in monitoring, regulating, reflecting on, and assessing their own learning. All students must have the opportunity to deeply learn a core of essential knowledge and organizing principles within and across domains. However, how that knowledge is assessed must be driven by their unique potentials and ways of knowing. Students have input in designing assessment rubrics and are encouraged to demonstrate their understanding in ways that are compatible with how they learn best.

2. *Coherently and explicitly integrated within curriculum and instruction.* Generative assessments cannot be separate evaluation structures disconnected from the curriculum in which our children are engaged. We must assess the curriculum we ask our children to learn.

3. *Structured so all learners can demonstrate their learning when they are ready through multiple forms of evidence that encourage them to integrate knowledge across disciplines.* These include public defenses, performances and exhibitions, concept maps, mathematical and scientific models, musical and artistic products, software programs, diagrams, problem logs, Web pages, learning journals, or integrative learning portfolios.

4. *Meaningful, reliable, valid, fair, and transparent.* Assessment must not only be useful to the system in adapting and adjusting curriculum and instruction, but it must provide learning information meaningful to the learners, their parents, and the community.

5. *Diagnostic, ongoing, flexible, and systemic.* Assessment for deep learning must include objective and quantitative assessment, as well as personal and qualitative evidence of understanding. It must also be self-correcting and be demonstrated in authentic contexts and settings that enable complex responses. Superficial, one-time, ranking, and sorting-based evaluation is not a sound measure of deep learning or understanding. It does not provide evidence of the depth and quality of a student's understanding and does not allow him or her to demon-

strate interdisciplinary and transdisciplinary connections. Generative assessments are not one-time snapshots; they must enable patterns of learning proficiency to emerge. Multiple assessments must provide a picture of each learner's development and performance over time, and reliable and valid evidence of the system's desired learning outcomes. Advances in computer-adaptive assessment may lead to a far more meaningful and personalized system of assessment and instruction. By adjusting the difficulty and complexity of test questions each child receives according to his or her proficiency level in responding, adaptive assessment illuminates patterns of understanding that can serve as a map for further learning and teaching.

REDESIGNING OTHER CRITICAL STRUCTURES

Other critical learning and teaching structures must also be flexibly redesigned if the new story is to become manifest. These include structures of:

- Learning space and location (within the school and within the larger community)
- Learning time, not seat time (schedules, learning year)
- Grading, monitoring, documenting, and reporting student and system learning to students, parents, and the community
- Student advancement and credentialing
- Mentoring, advising, coaching, and personalized learning
- Student clustering for collaborative, intergenerational learning
- Stimulating innovation and experimentation
- Parental and community engagement in learning
- Recognitions and celebrations of learning

Designing these structures to create the new learning and schooling landscape will require fundamental reconceptions. Rigid schooling structures cannot drive generative learning purpose. Adaptive, personalized, flexible, and responsive structures enable learning to thrive. Rigid schooling structures are the "boxes" we are often told to "think outside of." But this admonition carries an assumption that the boxes are basically sound. Maybe they are not. If all of us are consistently encouraged and challenged to think out of the box, perhaps there is something fundamentally wrong with the box.

Table 10.2 depicts in condensed form the profound differences between the landscape of the current prescriptive and uniform story of learning and schooling and the generative and life-affirming new story. (For a more complete story, see "The Two Stories of Learning and Schooling Contrasted" at the end of the book.)

LEADERSHIP INQUIRIES *About* LEARNING *and* SCHOOLING STRUCTURES

Creating generative learning and schooling systems means engaging our communities in deeper questions about learning and schooling structures. I offer the following questions to get you started:

• *How have I experienced great learning? What learning conditions—curriculum, instruction, assessment, time—encouraged and invited it? As a system, what must we invest in to build our capacity to create these conditions for our children?* What would our children say if we asked them when and how they experienced great learning? What does our system feel like to our students, teachers, parents, and community?

• *What are the nature and quality of the learning experiences and structures that are more likely to nurture integral and wise minds?* What experiences can we create and embed in our structures that connect children to themselves, others, and the natural world so they feel a sense of connection and belonging? How do our current structures support personalized, engaged, and active mind shaping?

• *What flexible and adaptive structures might we create to become a living learning laboratory for integral teaching, integral schooling, and integral leadership?* What might we do to dislodge the structural constraints on our system's learning and creativity? What learning, teaching, and governing structures must we now reimagine in order to create another way? How might we create more time for deep learning for reflection, innovation, discovery, and creation?

• *What current structures are stifling our system's capacity and our capacity to learn deeply and develop internal learning authority, create and experiment, and actively engage in developing the fullness of our children's and our own potentials?* What must we do to ensure our learn-

TABLE 10.2. *The Current Reductive Story and the New Integral Story: A Synthesis*

	The Current Reductive Story: Prescriptive and Uniform Transaction	The New Integral Story: Generative and Personalized Engagement
Mental model of learning and schooling	Deficiency and memory: analyzing, "fixing," and remediating identified learning limitations; accepting external authority for learning	Abundance and meaning: activating, developing, and connecting unknowable learning potentials; developing internal authority for learning
Learning identity	Passive acquisition and pragmatic compliance; short term	Purposeful and transformative engagement; lifelong
Learner identity	Disengaged and conforming recipient: receive inert information	Active and inquiring cocreator: construct meaning
Teaching identity	Transmitter: convey preselected information; dispenser	Mentor: weave deep understandings; cocreator
Learning information	Static and limited: externally prescribed, controlled, and perceived as irrelevant	Dynamic and abundant: externally responsive, self-generated, accessible, and imbued with meaning
Learning relationships	Contractual: individualistic, competitive, and fear based	Collaborative: inclusive, interdependent, and trust centered
Learning processes	Mechanistic: acquisition based and risk averse	Creative: inquiry based and exploratory
Learning patterns	Prescribed and hierarchical: fragmented—focused on parts	Self-generated and networked: holistic—focused on the whole
Learning structures	Immutable and standardized: permanent and nonresponsive to new learning	Flexible and adaptive: temporary and responsive to new learning
Quality of minds	Reductive: shallow, fragmented, and rigid	Integral: holistic, connected, and resilient

ing and teaching structures are and remain adaptive, flexible, and mutable? What are the silos that exist in our system, and what can we do to offer them another way? What are we measuring in our system? What does this cause us *not* to measure or notice? How might our current infrastructure systems—human resources, finance, legal, facilities, security, and so on—become more adaptive and flexible so they better manifest our purpose and connect our work?

II

A Generative Community for Integral Learning

Aspen Grove Revisited

*We have to see the world differently if we are
to live in it more harmoniously.*

—Margaret Wheatley, *Leadership and the New Science* (1999)

W E BEGAN OUR JOURNEY INTO THE LANDSCAPE
of the new story by visiting an imaginary yet possible new learning community: the Aspen Grove Center for Inquiry and Imagination.
We explored its songline—its learning context and conditions—and
became aware of how the "naturally right" design principles of living
and learning systems might guide our design of a generative new *system* of learning and schooling.

We return now to Aspen Grove to reflect on each aspect of its generative design.

GENERATIVE LEARNING IDENTITY

The heart of Aspen Grove's commitment to holistic learning and the
nurturance of integral and wise minds is purposeful and transformative

engagement, creative and collaborative inquiry, and meaning construction. The community believes that each child possesses abundant and unique potentials, that knowledge and meaning are constructed by the learner, and that learning is an exploratory, relational, and recreative process. Its vision is to invite and deepen the potentials of each child by engaging his or her intellectual, emotional, physical, and spiritual ways of knowing in great ideas, relevant problems, and challenging real-world questions. Aspen Grove is designed to embody a holistic, integrative, and generative theory of learning, achievement, and child development:

- Knowledge of how we naturally learn creates the system's integral learning identity and drives the design of generative processes and structures.

- A clear learning purpose to activate and develop the abundant potentials of each child has been formalized by the community.

- Children develop internal authority for learning by actively engaging with parents, teachers, mentors, and peers in co-creating their own personalized learning plan.

Aspen Grove says to its children, "Wherever you are on your learning journey, we will meet you there."

Generative Learning Information

Aspen Grove believes that deep learning requires unimpeded and continuous access to multiple forms and sources of information. This includes information *for* learning and information *about* learning. As a result, the community holds itself accountable for developing and assessing mutually agreed-on learning outcomes. Authentic and frequent evidence of student and system learning drives instructional and programmatic decision making:

- Using advanced technologies, students access and generate knowledge from numerous sources. Textbooks are only one resource.

- Problem-based learning teams share and analyze research results and discuss them electronically with teams from across the nation and around the world. Community panels review student team recommendations in open public forums.

- National and international practitioners from multiple disciplines are engaged in dialogue with students.

- The community participates in learning conversations through the local cable networks.

- Every student has a personal learning portfolio—a continuous digital record of her learning as it unfolds.

GENERATIVE LEARNING RELATIONSHIPS

Aspen Grove understands that learning is a relational and social process and is significantly shaped by personal and community engagement. The environment stimulates collaborative learning relationships and views teachers as mentors and coconstructors of knowledge with students. Families are actively engaged in their children's learning. Vibrant communication pathways keep the community and the system connected to how well its children are learning, encourage the sharing of information, and stimulate innovation. Aspen Grove has created an ecology of relatedness and community around learning:

- Intricate stakeholder networks connect the system to its learning purpose.

- Clusters of children of multiple ages, teachers, mentors, graduate students, and community members work and learn together. Older children mentor younger children, and every child has an advocate. Intergenerational learning is prevalent. Alliances and partnerships are created to extend learning opportunities.

- Curricular frameworks grounded in essential concepts are developed by faculty and staff in collaboration with the learning board and the community's learning network.

- Faculty and external experts collaborate on disciplinary, interdisciplinary, and transdisciplinary curriculum design.

- Staff and volunteers from many of the community's learning institutions and health agencies are connected to the life of Aspen Grove.

- Aspen Grove is integrated into the vibrant learning web of the community and its families and is inextricably connected to other learning communities. This creates a generative learning network and an extended community of learning and practice. Learning takes place in the context of community.

GENERATIVE LEARNING PROCESSES

Aspen Grove understands that learning is a natural, purposeful, and creative process of acquiring and generating knowledge and constructing meaning within a social context. As a result, the system and all its learners are immersed in exploration—experimenting with new ways of working, organizing, improvising, and innovating as they learn:

- Students engage in the essential questions of the human experience and in the curriculum for life. They are immersed in deep disciplinary, interdisciplinary, and transdisciplinary inquiry. The development of integral and wise minds is explicitly nurtured.

- Students learn how to learn, how to frame and pose questions, and how to engage in systemic and imaginative problem framing and resolution.

- Students develop deep knowledge and a fluid repertoire of skills and strategies essential for more complex understanding.

- Students are imaginative and not fearful. They are encouraged to seek, explore, and generate new ideas, products, and solutions. They know that failure is part of exploration. They experiment, tinker, and wander into innovation.

- Learning and organizational processes activate the creativity and learning potentials of each child and enable the system to achieve its purpose in adaptive and novel ways.

- Learning experiences engage students in paradox, uncertainty, and ambiguity. Learning is playful and spirit filled.

GENERATIVE LEARNING PATTERNS

Aspen Grove has created dynamic and self-generating community learning networks for continuous learning:

- Multiple learning and teaching networks deepen and expand the community's learning goals. These include networks between students and students, students and teachers, students and community members, students and expert practitioners, teachers and expert mentors, and teachers and community members.

- Communities of practice, both real and virtual, deepen understanding of promising practices and help to resolve complex community-based problems.

- The curriculum is coherent, concept centered, and designed around the deep organizing patterns and principles of the disciplines.

GENERATIVE LEARNING STRUCTURES

Learning and teaching structures are flexible and adaptive to individual learning needs. They are personalized, responsive to new learning information, and often temporary:

- Aspen Grove's physical structure and space are alive. It feels like an experimental laboratory, a hands-on interactive museum, an entrepreneurial think tank, and a reflective retreat center. Nature is embedded in its surroundings.

- Schedules, time structures, learning spaces, and locations are flexible and adaptive and are driven by children's inquiry and learning needs. Teachers collectively establish time parameters for learning and change them as needed. Learning occurs anytime and anywhere. The community is the classroom.

- Learners are not grouped by traditional age or grade cohorts. Rather, the unique learning goals, interests, and needs of each learner drive the creation of multiage learning clusters.

- The curriculum is driven by learning competencies that are inquiry based, integrative, and centered on significant community and global issues and problems.

ASPEN GROVE IS ONE NODE *in a* DIVERSE *and* VIBRANT LEARNING SYSTEM

What must not be lost in reflecting on Aspen Grove is that its dynamism, generativity, and stability are sustained by its systemic connections to other integral learning communities. It is not isolated. Aspen Grove is only one node in a vibrant and intricately connected learning system—a network of diverse and vibrant learning communities. Unlike our current P–16 "nonsystem" (preschool through college), Aspen Grove and other new schools are all one system and the children have access to the resources of the entire system. Each school is part of a dynamic learning ecosystem designed for learning innovation and coherence. Creating conditions for developing the abundant learning potentials of each child drives system processes and structures. The system is held together by shared learning purpose, abundant information, and intricate communication and feedback networks.

We can cite many examples, nationally and internationally, of individual schools designed according to the principles of life and learning.[1] Fortunately, there will always be individual genius. The critical issue, however, is that with few exceptions, these schools are not networked and are not a part of a generative learning system. What they learn cannot be shared within a whole system because there is no whole, and there is no system. Despite their individual genius, they can be viewed as idiosyncratic and often become marginalized. Because their intelligence, wisdom, and learning remain unconnected, they are not available to provoke the entire system and ignite the emergence of large-scale transformation.

We must learn from these schools, and they must learn from one another, but to do so they must be connected in a generative learning network that moves them out of the shadow and into the light of public conversation. This conversation must now be centered on the inextricable linkages between our children's abundant learning potentials, the conditions we create to activate them or not, the nature and quality of the minds we are nurturing into existence, and the power of these minds to imagine and shape a more hopeful future for all. The essential public conversation must be about generative and life-affirming mind shaping and sustainable world shaping.

Schools are not corporate learning businesses; they are natural learning systems. Students are not markets; they are dynamic cocreators and generators of knowledge and meaning. Schooling is not a private contract to fix innate learning deficiencies; it is a public covenant to develop innate and abundant potentials. Learning is not an isolated or anonymous transaction; it is a communal and personal process of transformative engagement.

We have allowed the conversation on public education to become hijacked by economic principles and metrics. To be sure, economics is a legitimate dimension of any public discussion on matters of public policy, but when it comes to educating the minds of those who will shape our future, it cannot be the driver. The driver must be our commitment to wisely educate knowledgeable, imaginative, ethical, and compassionate minds.

Until our system of schooling is designed to reconnect the natural and abundant creativity and power of our minds, hearts, and spirits in learning, our children will not develop the fullness of their unknowable potentials, and their capacity for imaginative and wise world shaping will be diminished. Until our system of schooling becomes "naturally right" by design, we will not realize our evolutionary potential. It is not enough for our children to compassionately bear witness to suffering. They must have the intellectual, emotional, creative, and spiritual capacity to diminish it.

WHAT WILL IT TAKE?

I began this book with a question: "What will it take to create a generative and life-affirming system of learning and schooling that liberates the goodness and genius of all children and invites and nurtures the power and creativity of the human spirit for the world?" You now have my answer: it will take a radical new story of learning and schooling:

- Rooted in the songline of unity, wholeness, creativity, connections, belonging, and freedom flowing within the universe

- Grounded in a new understanding of life and living systems, and how we come to know and construct meaning
- Designed according to the organizing principles of living systems and the generative principles of human learning

This will take:

- Common language and an articulation of the "design principles" of life and learning that must ground the new story of learning and schooling
- New mental models and maps for thinking about our world and reconceiving learning systems and organizations
- Naming and embracing a deeper, more holistic integrative and moral purpose for formal learning and schooling
- Continuous generation, distribution, and use of knowledge about learning and the conditions most likely to foster the growth of integral and wise minds
- Collaborative transdisciplinary inquiry and research, integrating the domains of traditional knowledge with indigenous knowledge
- Catalytic and transformative prototypes—new forms of learning and schooling that mirror the autonomy, creativity, and interdependence of life
- Purposeful integration of the principles of living systems and learning into the design of curriculum, instruction, assessment, professional development, and other processes and structures of schooling.

And this will require:

- Vibrant and connected learning places, where it is safe to experiment and to fail, where new ideas are explored and tried, and new structures and processes for deep learning are designed
- A new cultural narrative and commitment for creating a just and sustainable world that works for all, with lifelong learning at its center

- Elder leadership and a commitment to engage our communities in a new and deeper conversation

From these new conversations, new dreams can be born, new stories can be told, new maps can be created, and new learning landscapes can be brought to life.

WE ARE *in the* MIDST *of a* TRANSFORMATION *of* CONSCIOUSNESS

I believe we are in the midst of a silent yet discernable transformation of consciousness. Our cultural mind is slowly shifting from fragmentation and reductionism, expressed in excessive competition, unbridled acquisition, winning, short-term thinking, and isolated self-interest, to integration and interdependence—collaboration, shared purpose, and global sustainability.

Unparalleled advances in technology and research have led to new knowledge of how we learn and how human systems grow, evolve, learn, and re-create themselves. We must use this new knowledge to radically reframe our discourse on learning and our redesign of schooling. In place of linear machine-based metaphors, we have fluid biological metaphors that place the current context and conditions of schooling in dynamic opposition to our new knowledge of learning. There is a profound disconnect between the world we want to create, the integral and wise minds needed to imagine and create it, and the fragmented, competitive, and individualistic minds currently being developed and rewarded in so many of our schools. Integral thinking can emerge only from a holistic and integral system of learning and schooling, designed with the principles of life and learning.

Figure 11.1 depicts the map of the new story, grounded in developing integral habits of mind and embedded in the songlines of life in learning. This map represents the landscape of generative learning and schooling designed to nurture integral habits of mind. The presence of intention adds intricacy and complexity to the system's dynamics and organization. In addition, the specific purpose of integral learning further increases the system's dynamism and complexity. Walking these songlines and following this map, our shared intention and collective action will evoke a new reality. Together we

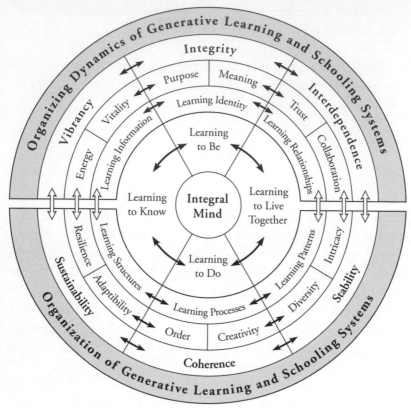

Figure 11.1. The Map of Generative Learning and Schooling
Note: The curved arrows indicate the dynamic movement and synergy between system organizational dynamics (identity, information, relationships) and system organization (processes, patterns, structures). The vertical arrows indicate the fluid interaction and interdependence of these properties in order to achieve the system's purpose of integral learning.

can create a generative new landscape of learning and schooling—by design.

I have come to view our new map as a kaleidoscopic web of intricately connected and dynamic relationships in continuous motion. Webs, or networks, are the fundamental and sustaining pattern of life. They illuminate the intricate patterns of symmetry, interdependence, and wholeness present in the natural world and all living systems. They encourage us to see a mosaic of infinite connections; to observe wholeness, harmony, integration, and coherence; and to experience the resonance and restorative power of deep patterns and order. They enable us to reflect on the profound truth that at the deepest levels of the cosmos, life, learning, and our own experience, there are inherent unity, order, connection, and meaning—the songline of an "implicate order" that is embedded within all of life.[2] Webs remind us that the perceived fragmentation and lack of connection in our lives is a temporary illusion; that parts have meaning only in relationship to the whole; that relationships, not objects or things, create meaning and patterns; that connected diversity creates infinite variety; and that the self is always illuminated in relation to other. Devoid of the self, relationships cannot be sustained. Devoid of relationships, the self struggles for context and meaning. Together, the embedded song of unity, integration, and order emerges.

Life and learning are journeys filled with astonishment, wonder, awe, boundless creativity, limitless possibilities, and the inherent freedom to be and become. As a dynamic symbol of the continuous unfolding, spontaneous creativity, and integrative wholeness of life and learning, webs embody the ever emerging song of deep order out of apparent randomness, unity out of separateness, harmony out of dissonance, and wholeness out of fragmentation.

The vibrant and intricate web of humanity is woven with human threads spun from the roots of life's deepest song—that inextinguishable and inherent drive to freely and spontaneously create one's self and connect with and belong to other life. It is this purposeful desire to be and to belong that is life's sustaining grace.

It is this songline of life in learning—the songline of wholeness, meaning, connection, belonging, and continuous self-creation—that must now serve as the root of a new cultural narrative and a radical new story and system of learning and schooling. We must create generative and life-affirming learning communities that invite our children into the wondrous and boundlessly creative dance of life in learning. To do so requires uncommon leadership. This is our next exploration.

A Call for Leaders

I2

The Right Moment

Answering the Call

You must give birth to your images.
They are the future waiting to be born.
Fear not the strangeness you feel.
The future must enter you long before it happens.
Just wait for the birth, for the hour of new clarity.

—Rainer Maria Rilke, *Letters to a Young Poet* (1929)

SOMETIMES THERE ARE MOMENTS IN HUMAN history that seem to beckon awakenings. They perturb us to reevaluate our beliefs, assumptions, and reigning cultural stories. They challenge us to synthesize and integrate seemingly disparate forms of knowledge into new relationships, new patterns, and new theories. They invite us to invent new language, new rules, and new structures. They call us to create and live into new stories of possibility. These moments grace us with enlightened insights and more soulful understanding. They fill us with wonder and amazement. They open us to life and to the invitation to reclaim the fire and light that reside within us all to change the world.

The ancient Greeks called this time *kairos,* the "right moment."[1] It is a time of awakening. It is a time of radical changes in perceptions, imagery, and stories. It is a time when reality embraces possibility. I believe we are in such a moment. It is now our time to author a radical new story of learning and schooling that will create decidedly different minds for the future now waiting to be born.[2]

At this time of *kairos,* we are morally charged to ask ourselves: What does it mean to be fully human? Which qualities of the human mind, heart, and spirit must be nurtured if we are to create a global civilization worthy of the light that resides within us? What might we learn and dream together? How shall we live? Do we wish to be conquerors, consumers, or stewards? How shall we reconnect to the web of life to which we belong?

We live with escalating social, economic, and educational injustices and with sobering and unsustainable paradoxes. Increasing knowledge and economic growth for some can coexist with increasing ignorance and devastating poverty for many. And although we have the structural, technological, and scientific knowledge and tools and the financial and political resources to restore balance to our wounded world, we seem paralyzed, afraid, or simply unwilling to do so. Ill-conceived, nonsystemic, and partial solutions become predictably mired in political and economic bureaucracies, institutional inertia, arrogant considerations of self-interest, and unbridled, ethically imperiled, and publicly licensed greed and consumption.

We can no longer pretend that knowledge acquisition, economic growth, and material progress disconnected from the web of life and the values of the commonweal inevitably result in prosperity for all, advance the human condition, or protect and preserve the natural world. There is a holistic, integrative, and morally wise context for our thinking and our behavior, and it resides within the songline of life in learning.

I believe that the interlocking complexities of our escalating global problems currently seem to elude or defy resolution not because they are too complex but because our thinking lacks an integral and wise context. We are not used to thinking in the holistic, systemic, imaginative, and connected ways essential for shared discernment and problem resolution. Although we are born with an innate capacity to think, act, and create in integral ways, there is a profound disconnect between the minds needed to imagine and create a sustainable and just world and the reductive, competitive, and isolated minds currently being developed and rewarded in our society and our schools.

The stakes have never been higher and the possibilities never greater. It is my belief that the quality of our children's growing minds is not commensurate with the enlightened leadership required in the twenty-first century. A world dominated by excessively competitive and acquiring minds who cannot think holistically, systemically, long term, and wisely is dangerous. It is our responsibility to nurture the growth of integral minds and ground our leadership, learning, and schooling in the principles of life and learning. The power of our minds must transcend the power of our might. These disquieting words of Vaclav Havel remain a stirring wake-up call: "Without a global revolution in the sphere of human consciousness, nothing will change for the better in the sphere of our Being as humans."[3]

We now need leaders who reconnect us and our systems to life— who evoke spirit, invite soul, and liberate the fullness of our community's intellectual, emotional, and spiritual potentials. We can no longer pretend that our interior lives are separate from the "real world" and our rigorous pursuit of deep learning. Our system of schooling has lost its connection to deep learning, and this estrangement has severed its ability to evoke the wholeness, meaning, connectedness, and creativity our children so desperately seek. This enormous hunger for a transcendent story of meaning, purpose, and belonging is not being fed in the old places. To unleash the genius, goodness, creativity, and wisdom of our children and our systems and increase their individual and collective knowledge, vibrancy, inventiveness, and shared sense of purpose, we must be engaged in new work. Our system's capacity for reflection, exploration, imagination, and connectedness depends on the conditions we create by design, that enable life and deep learning to flourish.

It is time to let go of our false ideas about school system change and move from believing we can control change to delighting in the idea that we cannot. Our work as leaders is not to prescribe, but to evoke and liberate—to create generative conditions for deep learning by design that embody the creative processes of life and learning and invite our children to astonish us.

THINK WISELY *and* ACT BOLDLY

Our exhausted and malnourished world cries out for enlightened leaders who know we must reconnect schooling to the deeper, more holistic, connected, and creative songline of life in learning. To do so requires that we create natural learning environments by design.

Can there be any doubt that the fullness of our humanity and the sustainability of our planet rest with the transformation of human consciousness and the emergence of decidedly different minds that can think anew?

This book is a call to your leadership. It is a call to stir and engage the fullness of your attention and desire to think and act differently, capture the depth and breadth of your imagination and courage, reclaim and amplify your voice, and put your name on cocreating a holistic, interconnected, and wise story of learning and schooling in harmony with life and the human spirit. It is this radical new story that can liberate the goodness and genius of our children for the world. It is this integral and wise story that can reweave humanity's fragmentation and bring our children's learning back to life.

Calls are not initially about strategy. They are about possibility. They are not about how to do something; they are about what to say yes to. They are not about rationality; they are about resonance. A call is about embracing our soul's voice and work and coming home to rejoin and belong once again, to our own life.

Our children are born to learn—to question, risk, wonder, generate new knowledge, seek and forge connections, creatively explore the mysteries of life, and imaginatively participate in world making. They are born scientists, mathematicians, musicians, writers, scientists, artists, poets, dancers, philosophers, inventors, pioneers, and explorers. They are also social and spiritual beings. Deep learning—learning that nourishes the deepest roots of all of who we are and invites, energizes, and integrates all our natural potentials and ways of knowing—is the kind of learning essential for our children to fully belong to and creatively and wisely engage in the world.

Our Children Need Wise Mind
Makers *and* Soul Guides

G. K. Chesterton once observed, "Education is simply the soul of a society as it passes from one generation to another."[4] Most people believe that it is education that will save us. But this bland, sweeping, and unexamined assertion reduces us into continuing to uncritically support and tinker with the current story of schooling. It is education that will save us, but not *any* kind of education—only education of a certain kind: only education that is generative and life affirming; that invites, engages, and integrates the fullness of our children's capacities and ways of knowing; and that nurtures the creation of integral minds committed to the creation of a truly just and wise global civilization. Only education that develops our capacity to become more fully human is truly worthy of the human spirit. Only education that invites deep learning and reconnects us to life will light and sustain the fire within.

Our children are yearning for healthy, meaning-filled engagement with adults. They seek genuine mentors—real mind makers and soul guides who can authentically challenge and engage them in discovering and developing their voices and gifts and can create genuine practice fields for their work in the world. They do not want to be marginalized, patronized, or thought not yet ready. They want to be seen and heard as serious learners, participating freely in and belonging fully to their communities because they share in its important and complex work. It is their engagement with us that will create meaning and enable our children to participate with discipline, imagination, and passion in advancing the human condition and sustaining the global home in which we live.

Our children want to learn and engage in lives of meaning, purpose, connection, and contribution while they are still young. They do not want to be held in a state of suspended animation until we think they are ready to become visible and active in the world. Moreover, the world is not served by keeping them physically sequestered and cognitively, emotionally, and spiritually disengaged for so long. Our children don't want to be passive observers in their own learning. They want to be in the center with us, bringing their own talents and stories to life—and the world needs their energy, passion, and creative commitment now more than ever before.

We Can Create Learning Habitats That Are Naturally Right

We can design natural and nourishing learning habitats for our children. We can design environments that invite and integrate their deepest thinking, curiosity, imagination, creativity, and passionate pursuit of possibilities. And we must. We cannot lose another generation to the old story.

Too many children emerge from schooling very clear about what they cannot do, but few emerge with an evolving clarity about their own efficacy as learners and their capacities for unique contributions to the world. Our children are eager to engage with us in reimaging our collective future. We must enable them to develop the integral and wise habits of mind to do so. As elders, we must teach our children to hear and sing the deeper song.

13

Elder-Leadership
Changing the Current Story

*For centuries we met by the fire—not as managers, executives, or
consultants—but as storytellers, teachers, and enchanters. Our voices
served as the light in the darkness. Our work is now . . . to align
ourselves with this flow of creative energy . . . it is important
that our voices be clear.*

Michael Jones, "From Performance to Presence" (2003)

L EADERSHIP IS AN ILLUSIVE CONSTRUCT. UNDER-
girding our search for clarity seems to be a need to analyze and
define its critical attributes and then package them for replication. Our
desire to understand both the pragmatism and mystery of leadership is
framed by a powerful yet faulty mental model: that leadership is all
about individual talent. That it is about what leaders do to direct and
manage people, resources, and systems. That if we master the strategies and tactics of successful leaders, our schools (and systems) will
respond as we intend—with increased achievement, productivity, and
robustness. Experience tells us that this is a profound illusion.

As we have discovered, schools are living systems. They adapt and
change just as life does: when they choose to, when new information

meaningful to their identity is noticed and disturbs the system into creating new patterns, structures, and processes to do their work. Leaders can perturb, challenge, and inspire living systems, but try as we might, we cannot mandate what really matters. Command-and-control algorithms of leadership do not govern their dynamics. Like life, leadership is first about identity: we lead *who* we are. As "storytellers, teachers, and enchanters," we lead from our deepest center of purpose and meaning. Radical leaders take responsibility for their internal life, knowing that the shadow or light they project can change the heartbeat of their organization and alter its future.

As we create conditions for the design of a generative and life-affirming system of learning and schooling, our first question is, "Who is the self that leads?" Generative and life-affirming learning environments can be created only if as leaders, we first become that which we are trying to create. Our leadership must be rooted in meaning, wholeness, connections, and belonging and in the processes, patterns, and structures nature uses to learn, heal, and organize itself for sustainability. We must engage our communities in inquiry and dialogue about the conditions of learning and schooling that can reconnect the minds, hearts, and souls of our children in learning. We must talk about deep learning and the nurturance of integral habits of mind as the fundamental purpose of schooling. From this new conversation will emerge a vibrant new system of new schools: generative learning communities that liberate our children's potentials for imaginative and wise world shaping.

This chapter shines a light on a radical conception of leadership. For the work that is needed in the world now, for the work that is needed to develop deep learning and integral and wise minds, and for the work that is needed to create generative and life-affirming systems of learning and schooling by design, radical leaders are needed more than ever before. And as Michael Jones says in the epigraph to this chapter, "It is important that our voices be clear."

Elder-Leaders Hold *the* Context, Consciousness, *and* Soul *of* Their Culture

The words *leader* and *leadership* are often misunderstood, so I have chosen the word *elder* to frame the context of radical leadership now required to create and sustain the new story of learning and schooling. Elders are called to teach and cocreate a covenant of meaning and belonging with the young; nurture and prepare them through life-affirming stories and initiations; infuse their present with the wisdom of the past; and affirm their future possibilities.

Elders hold the context (story), consciousness (meaning), and soul (wisdom) of a culture. They reconnect us to our deepest self, the song-line of life in learning, our collective humanity, and our capacities to cocreate a worthy future. They teach us to notice and mindfully attend to the patterns and stories of our present moments, and they offer a vision of the deep connections and interdependence of all living things. Elders offer the gift of stewardship to the next generation. They are the wise storytellers and cultural weavers, weaving the tales and threads of connection, coherence, creativity, community, and continuity into a story of meaning and belonging. They are the ones who say to our youth, "Now is the time for you to become yourself."[1]

To indigenous people, the concept of elder is a natural one. But to Western minds, it is a foreign and often disquieting idea. We typically hold up as our elders those who are the oldest, not the most wise; those who are the most successful and wealthy, not the most visionary and introspective; those who artfully negotiate contracts, not who generously create covenants; those who live among the famous, not who engage with the young; those who seek attention and notoriety, not who cherish silence and reflection; those who live only in the now, not who wisely learn from and honor the lessons of the past in order to evoke a sustainable future.

Western leaders aggressively drive toward speed, individualism, acquisition, and competition. Elders slowly call us to the promise of what it means to be fully human. They reconnect us to the human spirit, help us to clarify and claim our life's work, and offer us timeless stories of reciprocity, cooperation, interdependence, justice, and love.

Western leaders entice us to seek and acquire more of the culture's possessions. Elders ask us to embrace "enough" and to connect to humanity's deepest roots; seek truth, beauty, and goodness; use our deepening knowledge and understanding of learning and life to create right and whole relationships with one another and the earth; and create global institutions that serve our most enduring human purposes.

Western leaders seem to focus on the objective, the easily and quickly quantifiable, and the often prescribed solutions contained in the rule of law. Elders honor and evoke the ways of knowing that also come from the heart, the soul, and the spirit. They call us to be morally just, and they embrace the rule of life. Elders connect us to the essence of who we are and what it means to be fully human. They illuminate our path and give us a place to stand.

Our culture must reconceive leadership. Elder-leaders must be invited to speak deep and transcendent truths to the world again. It is these leaders who can help us and our children reconnect to the indigenous parts of our being. It is this reintegration of all of who we are that grounds the new story of learning and schooling. The time is now for the elder-leaders of our time to give voice to this new story of learning and schooling, call us to reconnect learning to the songline of life, and create conditions that enable this new story to be manifested.

In the Prologue, I shared my profound experiences with Australian Aborigines. They awakened me to the realization that flowing through the structures, processes, and patterns of every culture, system, and institution is a songline—a powerful narrative of beliefs and stories that shapes our identity, behavior, cultural maps, and landscapes within which we create our world. As we travel these landscapes, we nourish and sustain them. Our songlines and their emergent stories, maps, and landscapes continue to shape our consciousness and what we perceive, create, and become.

The fragmented cultural story that sustains the current map and landscape of learning and schooling is slowly eroding the intellectual, emotional, and spiritual health of our children and the health of our global society. Our children have become disconnected and schooling disabled in a relational and learning-abundant universe. They have become estranged from the fullness of their astonishing potentials and from the web of life. Despite our best intentions, the fragmented landscape of schooling inhibits the creative and courageous engagement with life that our children are yearning for.

Changing *the* Story *of* Learning *and* Schooling

It has become clear to me that the landscape changes when the map changes. The map changes when the story changes. To change the current landscape of schooling, we must first and fundamentally change its story and ground it in the unifying and whole songline of life in learning. Our children have been "storied" to "think the world apart," in Parker Palmer's words. We must give them a new story and language within which to "think it back together." It is this songline of abundant potentials and generative learning that will allow them to embrace their interdependence with all living things and reclaim their relationship to one another. It is this new learning landscape that will invite our children to embrace their multiple ways of knowing and restore the profound imbalance created by honoring only one way of knowing that pervades schools and our classrooms. Exploration, creativity, imagination, passion, wonder, and awe lie at the heart of life and learning. They must also be at the heart of schooling.

Recall my account of how the Aborigine elder changed the story of the Rainbow Serpents. The old story of lust, envy, mistrust, conquest, revenge, and death—The Firestorm—was transformed into a new story of wholeness, trust, generosity, harmony, relationships, and love—The Gift. This was an act of love filled with hope and a deep belief in our collective yearning and commitment to bring forth the emergent new world struggling to be born. I understand now that it was the creative field evoked by the joined presence of Western and Aboriginal leaders that enabled the new story to emerge: our engagement cocreated the new story.

It is our responsibility as elder-leaders to bring this new story and its new map and landscape to life in the learning of our children by engaging our communities in new conversations that will evoke its creation. It is this new story that will enable the creation of a generative and life-affirming system of learning and schooling. It is this new system that in integrating intelligence and love in action can educate integral and wise minds into being. We turn now to our new conversation.

Creating the Radical New Story of Learning and Schooling

I would like to beg you, dear Sir, as well as I can, to have patience with everything unresolved in your heart and to try to love the questions *as if they were locked rooms or books written in a very foreign language. Don't search for the answers, which could not be given to you now, because you would not be able to live them. And the point is, to live everything.* Live *the questions now. Perhaps then, someday far in the future, you will gradually, without even noticing it, live your way into the answer.*

—Rainer Maria Rilke, *Letters to a Young Poet* (1929)

S AYING YES TO AN IDEA IS USUALLY FIRST A matter of the heart. It often begins with a whisper but gradually generates a resonance that cannot be silenced. There is no greater force for transformation than a community that has discovered who it is and what it cherishes. Together with their children, every community must now engage in conversations around radical questions of life, learning, and schooling and the nature and quality of minds needed for a sustainable future. These conversations will enable us to reclaim the creative energy of life and learning that so naturally flows within all living systems and create generative systems of learning and schooling that liberate and ignite the goodness and genius of all of our children for the world.

It is our role as elder-leaders to name both the context and the container for this new conversation to begin. It is this conversation that creates the context for system discernment—understanding who we are—and system coherence—understanding why and how we belong together. It is this conversation that can lead to a new way of being in and for the world. It is this conversation that calls forth the great work of our time.

The essence of elder-leadership is not only to awaken and develop our remarkable individual capacities; it is to awaken and develop our community's remarkable capacities to:

- Proclaim its highest possibility.
- Name and manifest its beliefs.
- Create and articulate its fundamental learning purpose.
- Discover and live into its deepest self.
- Wisely choose the provocations and information it notices, seeks, creates, shares, and uses to deepen learning.
- Create vibrant networks for continuous learning, communication, and belonging.

The commitment of leaders to create conditions that integrate the system's generative identity, information, and relationships around deep and connected learning is at the center of our new landscape for educational transformation. It is this integration that serves as the crucible for the emergence—by design—of life-affirming processes, patterns, and structures that bring the new story to life.

Why do we feel so impotent to challenge and change the pathologies of our current landscape of learning and schooling? We made them up in the first place as a response to the perceived learning needs of the times. And times have changed. We now need courageous leaders everywhere who know it is the right time to call their communities into new conversations from which new stories and new possibilities can emerge.

The New Work *of* Elder-Leadership

The new work of elder-leaders is to create conditions for the design of generative learning and schooling. It is to deepen and expand the abundant intelligences, creativity, imagination, and wisdom of the whole system so that everyone learns and the system's learning purposes and commitments are achieved. By embracing the principles of life and learning that naturally connect the system to its deepest self—to the meaning and purpose of its work in the world—elder-leaders invite continuous learning and the cocreation of new possibilities and new worlds. A community cannot be alive and thrive unless it continues to learn—unless it continues to deepen its observations, interpretations, and understandings of its self.

Elder-leaders create conditions for the dynamic integration of the system's identity, information, and relationships and for the emergence of the system's processes, patterns, and structures.

We've previously explored the properties of generative systems of learning and schooling. We briefly revisit them to frame the new work of leadership.

Generative Learning Identity

Our educational system is in great turbulence as its invisible yet timeless songline of wholeness, interdependence, meaning, abundant potentials, creativity, and deep learning desperately struggles to emerge. The only way through this turbulence is to return to the center—to the integrity of its fundamental and transformative learning purpose—so we can find firm ground on which to stand. Clarity at the core is both the ground and fire that will sustain the new learning story and light its path.

Our schools will have the capacity for self—reference and self-organization only when there is a clear, compelling, and generative self around which to organize, when our system's generative beliefs about learning, vision for learning, purpose of schooling, and core learnings are known and shared, and when elder-leaders intentionally create the following conditions:

• Engage the entire system in dialogue about its identity (self) as a whole, interdependent, and dynamic system—not a series of independent and isolated parts; continuously connect the system to the meaning and power of its essential learning identity, and create clarity at the core.

• Honor the story and voice of each person, and stimulate individual awareness of belonging to a deeper system purpose that is congruent with his or her own.

• Invite and tell founding and sustaining stories and enroll the community in connecting to its legends and traditions; honor elders, heroes, warriors, and healers; share challenges, achievements, disappointments, joys, sorrows, and acts of courage; name life-affirming and life-diminishing patterns of learning relationships; encourage awareness of what to embrace and what to let go.

• Enroll the community in naming and publicly declaring its beliefs, values, vision, and learning purpose.

• Invite the community into understanding that there is no self without other, that individual freedom and autonomy can emerge only within the context of shared identity and relationships, and that paradoxically we are freer when we are more connected.

• Awaken and invite possibility thinking.

GENERATIVE LEARNING INFORMATION

Meaningful information that continuously deepens the system's capacity to achieve its essential learning purpose is the sustaining energy in generative systems of learning and schooling. Abundant, freely flowing, and shared information about student and system learning enables it to sustain its vibrancy and capacity for continuous learning.

In order to ensure the system remains alive, awake, aware, and adaptive, elder-leaders create the following conditions:

• Engage the whole system in determining, generating, and accessing the information it requires to achieve its learning purpose (identity); ensure the creation of systems (processes, patterns, and structures) for continuous feedback and for seeking, generating, sharing, using, and evaluating information essential to achieving the system's learning purpose.

• Ensure the system is infused with abundant information about the totality of the children's learning by explicitly bringing complex and often conflicting or paradoxical information into the system and moving it everywhere.

• Promote courageous conversations, individual and collective inquiry, and the generation of new knowledge.

• Keep rules for noticing, processing, responding, and integrating information simple, realizing that the greater the system's ability is to process information meaningful to its identity, the greater is its collective intelligence, creativity, adaptability, and sustainability.

• Promote and stimulate openness to new knowledge and new ideas; ensure that engaging in paradox, uncertainty, and ambiguity are safe encounters.

• Invite everyone to continuously scan the environment for new information and new possibilities and to bring them into the system.

GENERATIVE LEARNING RELATIONSHIPS

Despite education's preoccupation with reforming structures, it is the system's kaleidoscopic webs of learning relationships that sustain the collaboration necessary for transformation. By linking all members of the community into conversations and networks of meaning, intricate communication networks and feedback loops establish the system's capacity for engagement and interconnection around shared identity and purpose. They promote system dynamism, interdependence, and resiliency.

The new capacities generated by new relationships are the system's invisible source of energy and power. Within this context, elder-leaders create the following conditions:

• Encourage the creation of dialogue and communication networks that continuously circulate information about learning throughout the system and connect the system to more of its self.

• Promote diversity of all kinds and purposefully connect it; without meaningful connections around the system's work, diversity can cause fragmentation.

• Create space, time, and capacity for collective inquiry about and collaborative accountability for their mission; seek and live truth telling.

• Cultivate organizational coherence while building capacity to adapt to discontinuous change.

• Continuously seek new alliances and new partners in order to expand their networks and increase connections around the system's work.

• Trust that people will contribute wisely and well and that they will promote the best interests of their system if they are engaged in meaningfully connecting their personal purpose to the system's identity and purpose.

• Embody love as the most potent source of relational capacity.

The essence of elder-leadership is to invite continual individual and collective learning that deepens each person's and the system's learning potentials. It is to create meaning-filled conditions that enable the system to continuously renew and recreate its self.

By connecting every dimension of the system to its self (self-reference), encouraging and explicitly infusing it with abundant information, and establishing and sustaining intricate and dense webs of relationships based on shared and mutually created meaning, elder-leaders promote continuous learning and system coherence. Dynamic and fluid processes, generative patterns and networks, and flexible and adaptive structures can emerge spontaneously or by design when the system's life-affirming identity, information, and relationships are generatively integrated.

GENERATIVE LEARNING PROCESSES

Processes—actions, procedures, operations—are the underlying self-regulating and creative ways the system innovatively achieves its purpose, generates and transmits information, gets its work done, and explores its possibilities.

In order to ensure the design of generative and self-regulatory processes, elder-leaders engage in creating the following conditions:

• Create an agile, exploratory, risk-taking, and innovative culture, and cultivate a spirit of inquiry, play, and wonder.

• Encourage frequent and rapid experimentation and the generation of catalytic prototypes just to see what works.

• Recognize and celebrate inventiveness, innovation, novelty, creativity, and failure.

• Challenge the system to design generative processes that ensure collaboration, dismantle barriers to connectedness, are congruent with the system's identity and values, and recognize and celebrate learning.

GENERATIVE LEARNING PATTERNS

Patterns give our systems their form and shape—their essential properties, characteristics, and uniqueness. The nature, quality, culture, and "feel" of any school or school system and whether it is adaptive, resilient, and alive emerge from its patterns of learning and engagement. Change the pattern, the rules for connecting, and you change the system. It is the pattern of networked relationships that allows the system to be recognized.

In order to maintain the generativity of the system's learning patterns, elder-leaders engage in creating the following conditions:

• Take time to discern the deep, emerging patterns (stories) within and external to the system and make them explicit to the whole system; invite the system to learn from emerging realities and shape its future; name and encourage others to name the institution's emerging stories.

• Foster the creation of diverse, vibrant, and intricate learning and communication networks throughout the system.

• Encourage the creation of networks that manifest the system's desired patterns of learning relationships and keep the system connected to its self.

GENERATIVE LEARNING STRUCTURES

Structures are the visible dimensions of our systems—the departments, divisions, and functional teams that organize the system's work. They embody our system's patterns of relationships and manifest its processes. In order to enable the emergence of more dynamic, adaptive, and imaginative structures, elder-leaders create the following conditions:

• Challenge the system to design generative structures that support and deepen system identity, information, and relationships.

• Encourage structural experimentation congruent with the system's beliefs, mission, and goals.

• Ensure the fundamental structures of curriculum, teaching, assessment, professional development, leadership, community engagement, governance, and learning time remain flexible, adaptive, and responsive; and explicitly advance deep learning and the system's transformative learning purpose.

If we are to create a generative and life-affirming system of learning and schooling, our communities must be engaged in a new conversation.

The NEW SLOWER *and* DEEPER CONVERSATION

Our new conversation is a slower and deeper one, imbued with mindful intent. Unlike the rapid, percussive, and volleyed conversations of most organizations—where speed, volume, verbal agility, and positional power dominate—these conversations are about deep learning, deep questions, deep knowledge generation, and deep wisdom creation. Several times each year, the IMSA community is invited to convene in what we call a slower conversation. These voluntary conversations continuously invite us to:

• Explore, clarify, and reconnect to our community's deepest sense of meaning and purpose.

• Look within, across, and through divisions and roles, and notice the inherent interconnections and interdependence within our system.

• Name those beliefs, assumptions, and mental models that dishonor our relationships, diminish our trust, stifle our creativity, thwart our innovation, or inhibit our responsiveness to new information critical to our integrity and sustainability.

• Commit to new principles of collaboration and belonging together in the work.

• Nourish our spirit and the spirit of our community.

• Continuously cocreate a future worthy of who we are.

This new conversation requires us to pay attention, listen deeply, give voice to our own truths, suspend judgment, and honor the self, truth, and wisdom of the other. Slower and deeper conversations are fundamentally about reestablishing ties and grounding system transformation in relationships imbued with meaning and purpose. When we surrender to the center that deep conversation makes available to us, we discover that everything is connected, relationships are all there is, and if we create time to ground our work in the deep connections and commitments that unite us, we would be astonished by the energy, passion, and love we are eager to give to our organizations, our communities, and our world.

Of all the well-intentioned strategies and interventions leaders may conceive and implement, slower and deeper conversations are simple and powerful means to shift the system's ground and move it closer toward its deepest purpose. These conversations and the questions of identity and meaning they provoke are the crucible for the emergence of the new story of learning and schooling.

Within dynamic living systems, questions about meaning and purpose serve as a magnet for ensuring the system remains true to its self. Questions emerge from both current system context and the system's visions of its future possibility. Responding to "who are we now" and "who we wish to become" are fundamental to developing deep system meaning. Especially during times of turbulence or uncertainty, meaningful questions hold enormous power because human systems are drawn in the direction of powerful questions. Perhaps now is the time for you to name the questions you are holding that can engage your community in creating the generative new story of learning and schooling for your children.

The system's commitment to continuously engage in a dialogic process of inquiry and self-creation is the source of its capacity to design a generative and life-affirming story and system of teaching and learning. Lived patterns create the narrative contours—the stories of our institutions. If we were more adept at discerning and understanding our system's patterns before they unfolded and became manifest in our stories and behavior, we could intervene in their unfolding and choose the stories we wish to live into. We must be conscious of the patterns we are in and the ones that are emerging undetected. Firestorm or Gift? The choice will shape our world.

I hope it is now clear that we become the stories we tell ourselves about ourselves. It is our work as elder-leaders to name the patterns and the stories so our communities have a choice in creating their own narratives, maps, and landscapes for the future.

I have worked with many remarkable educators, parents, children, and business leaders striving to create generative and life-affirming communities. Their lives and commitments have given me many insights. Here are some of the most important to me:

GENERATIVE IDENTITY

- What matters most cannot be mandated. Individuals will construct their own meaning. A shared and collective vision can be created by bringing the whole system into its own re-creation.

- Living systems need boundaries. Absent boundaries, there can be no self. But in generative systems, boundaries do not come from structures; they come from the system's shared identity and purpose.

- The transformation of our learning and schooling systems begins with the transformation of self. There is no other way.

GENERATIVE INFORMATION

- Knowledge is power, and although most organizations either horde it or dole it out, the more it is shared, the more intelligent, engaged, and resilient the system can become, and the greater is its capacity for transformation. Information freely shared is the organization's energy source. Possibility thinking is contagious.

GENERATIVE RELATIONSHIPS

- We all want to be a part of something meaningful and more transcendent than ourselves, and we have no choice but to learn. Our system must constantly stimulate deep and continuous learning.

- Trusting relationships generously nurtured are our system's heart-line. Relationships built on control destroy the vitality and creativity of living systems.

- Paradoxes are unsettling, and most people schooled in the old paradigm find ambiguity and turbulence frightening. A community must embrace and care for one another in paradox.

GENERATIVE PROCESSES
- The journey toward system sustainability is grounded in continuous learning and the creation of conditions that ensure system vitality and coherence.
- Natural living systems creatively do what works. Human systems must choose life as our mentor.

GENERATIVE PATTERNS
- Meaning is cocreated through an awareness of context. When the context changes, everything changes. Context is what grounds the system's design principles.
- Educational transformation must be grounded in the principles and patterns of life and learning. The new story of learning and schooling is not about restructuring and reengineering; it is about reclaiming and reconnecting.
- Complex behavior-like learning does not need to have complex rules. Simple rules will yield profoundly complex results.

GENERATIVE STRUCTURES
- Models are informative, but models cannot be transferred from one system to another. They must be cocreated, not replicated, by the people working in their own environment and community.

What will it take to create a generative and life-affirming system of learning and schooling that can liberate the goodness and genius of our children? Where do we go from here? We cannot create that which we have not become. It is now our time to put our names on the new story of learning and schooling.

IT IS NOW OUR TIME

Several years ago, a graduate of IMSA was matter-of-factly recounting some of her remarkable achievements as part of an advanced leadership training experience in Kenya for students ages fourteen to eighteen. In the two weeks she was in Kenya, she wrote a formal business plan to build and fund several clinics and she created a 501(c)3 foundation to raise the funds required to launch the first one. She also secured an agreement from a medical school in the United States to supply both medicine and the medical students. She asked me if I would serve on her board.

I was astounded at her achievements at so young an age, and I asked her why she thought our society did not seem to recognize or value the enormous talents of our youth and their potential to contribute to the world while they are still young. "Why do you think we make you wait so long?" I asked.

Her reply was sobering. "That's one of the things about my experience in Kenya that surprised me the most," she said. "It didn't surprise me that students my age could do amazing things—it surprised me that no one expects us to."[1]

What are we waiting for? Expecting children to do amazing things is the essence of the new story of learning and schooling, and creating learning conditions by design that invite them to do so is its foundation. When we create learning environments that welcome and develop their unknowable potentials, our children's gifts and talents will astonish us.

The deep desires of our children to name and own their own lives is reflected in a thinking log entry that a young IMSA student wrote several years ago. Its honesty and poignancy capture the essence of the new story of learning and why it is so essential. At the end of her reflections, she poses a question we must respond to:

> I wish I could still draw. When I was in grammar school I used to draw pretty decently. I love to draw in pencil and chalk. Art of all kinds intrigues me, but I also love music and painting, and carpentry and metal working, and dancing, and sewing and embroidery, and cooking.
>
> I want to dance in my old ballet class, play my clarinet, draw thousands of pictures, really good ones, create beautiful poems and pieces of woodwork, cook and sew for my children, decorate my home, have a good marriage, be an active volunteer, go to church, be an astrophysicist, go to Mars, and understand all my questions about life.
>
> That's not too much to ask, is it?

What is so powerful and unsettling about this young woman's question is that as young as she is, she has already discerned what she loves and what is integral to her life, and she wants to pursue it passionately and embrace it without apology. She wants to live a connected and whole life but isn't sure she can, and she asks us (and herself) if this dream is really too much to ask. In the new story of learning, dreams are the places learning often begins.

I began these final chapters with my belief that we are living in a time of *kairos*. I close by calling you into this moment when reality embraces possibility.

It is now our time to give voice, form, legitimacy, and momentum to a radical new story of learning and schooling—a story that waters the deep roots of learning and creates the context for nurturing integral minds that can begin to shift the current cultural narrative. This radical story will promote the design of learning landscapes that can liberate our children's goodness and genius for the world and reconnect them to the abundance, wonder, and mystery of the web of life. It is this deep story of meaning, wholeness, connection, and belonging that we and our children so desperately need now.

It is precisely during times of heightened vulnerability, fragmentation, ambiguity, uncertainty, and often despair that people yearn for new stories that reconnect them to what they believe they have lost. They seek meaning-filled and hopeful stories that give voice and form to their deepest longings and dreams. It is during these moments of *kairos*—of awakening and transformation—that new dreams unfold, new stories are written, and new storytellers and dreammakers emerge. I am reminded of the wise words of Ben Okri: "Stories are the secret reservoir of values; change the stories individuals or nations live by and tell themselves, and you change the individuals and nations."[2]

I return to the question that frames this book: "What would it take to create a generative and life-affirming system of learning and schooling that liberates the goodness and genius of all children and invites and nurtures the power and creativity of the human spirit for the world?"

I believe our path is clear. It will take the synergy of our individual and collective intention, leadership, and action explicitly connected around shared purpose. It will take a radical new story rooted in the generative songline of life in learning. It will take a new covenant with our children.

And so we have come full circle. This book is a call and an invitation born out of conviction that we and our communities know what is needed to nurture the minds of our children and honor the deep mystery that lives within them. It is a call to declare a new path, awaken to the songline that imperceptibly weaves through humanity and the natural world, and use its clarity and deep resonance to tell a new story and a create transformative landscape of generative learning and schooling.

Minds, hearts, and spirits nourished in this generative and life-affirming landscape can, with discipline, passion, and wisdom, access their remarkable potentials to imagine and create a compassionate and sustainable world that works for all—a wise global society that is worthy of our lives. When we immerse children in this generative learning landscape, we water the roots of an enlightened global consciousness that can restore life's sacred balance.

As elder-leaders we are responsible for speaking deep and transcendent truths into the world and for naming and sustaining the generative and life-affirming songline embedded in the universe and the natural world through continuous learning. As elders, we can offer a radical new story that can change everything. We must "think what nobody yet has thought" about learning and schooling and its inextricable connection to life and then, holding this new story, live into it with passion and courage. It is this story that will bring our children back to the songline of life in learning, that will always tell them where they are, that will always bring them home. "The visions we present to our children shape the future," Carl Sagan reminds us. "It matters what those visions are. Often they become self-fulfilling prophecies. Dreams are maps."[3]

Please do not wait for others. Courage is the capacity to claim what we imagine. If you are carrying this new story in your heart, now is the time to step forward. There is a place in the world for your unique voice, and it carries a message that must be heard. Start anywhere, but begin the conversation, and tell the new story that brings learning and schooling to life.

Afterword:
A Letter to My Grandchildren

Throughout this book, you have been invited to reflect on your own learning and leadership odyssey and reconnect your leadership with the songline of life. "The Swan," a poignant poem by Rilke, captures this journey and the soul of the new story and new learning landscape.[1] In it, Rilke describes the swan's two states of being as she navigates two profoundly different environments and contexts of belonging. The first is the swan's response to land; the second is the swan's response to water. Although swans can indeed maneuver on land, their awkwardness in navigating belies their natural majesty and grace. It is not until the swan leaves the land and enters the water that her land-based clumsiness dissipates into regal and effortless gliding. *It is only when the swan finds her natural place of belonging that she becomes herself.*

So too with our children. When our children are able to immerse themselves in their naturally right place of learning and belonging—in generative and life-affirming learning communities that allow them to once again become who they really are—their awkwardness and limitations seem to dissipate, and their gifts can take our breath away. We could very likely train the swan to navigate the land more gracefully, but at what cost? Water is the swan's natural habitat. It is where she most belongs.

My hopefulness at this time comes from a deep belief that as we realize that mind shaping is world shaping and that integral education holds the human future, we will choose to author a generative story of learning and schooling—a new cultural narrative that enables us to create thoughtful, vibrant, and soulful learning communities that invite and nurture the depth, color, texture, and unknowable potentials of each child.

I close this book with a letter to my grandchildren in celebration of the song that resides within each of them, hoping that with our help, they and their generation will dream of a just and sustainable world and create the maps to guide their journey.

• • •

Dear Austin, Ryan, Sarah, Jacob, and Alana,

I have been wanting to write to you for quite some time. Now seems like the right moment. I do so just in case you begin to give up on yourself. Just in case you doubt your remarkable and unique potentials and gifts. Just in case you wonder why you're here and what your life means. Just in case you begin to question your dreams and your deep capacity and right to pursue them. Just in case you feel disconnected, overwhelmed, and pressured to give in to all the voices that try to constrain and narrowly define who you are, what you are good or not good at, and what you should do with your life. Just in case you're not sure how you fit or belong. And just in case you dismiss as impossible or as nonsense your genuine capacity to change the world.

I share my notes with you just in case you will need help in figuring things out in the often strange neighborhoods you will encounter throughout your life. Just in case the lessons embedded in these notes give you meaning and hope. Just in case they invite you to reconnect to the web of life and learning that joins us all.

Despite all the cultural messages to the contrary, you are born into a world of abundance, wholeness, and love. It is a world of unity, order, connections, relationships, and continuous learning, and it will support and sustain you if you accept its open invitation to imagine, dream, discover, and continue to learn and become all that you can be. You must explore the magic and mystery that live inside you and "sing the song" that is uniquely yours to sing. I have heard it many times. It is beautiful and it belongs only to you. If you do not live your song and continue to nourish it, you will not be visible to the world. Your song is your gift to the world.

So here are my notes, and I send them with love.

1. *Slow down and learn something very well. Let go of right answers and illusions of objectivity, control, and predictability, and listen to your intuition and your heart.* Live from the inside out. Do not participate in your own diminishment, and always walk in the direction of your own learning and healing.

2. *Do everything with the seventh generation in mind.* The future is being born now in everything you do or do not do. Live a life of wholeness and connection. You are the seeds of a sustainable world. You are the mapmakers of our future.

3. *Honor and celebrate life in all its forms, be gentle with the earth, and absorb and embrace the wonder and beauty that surround you.* Beauty changes people. If you stop listening to nature, you will not be able to hear one another.

4. *Be a steward of your gifts, your passion, and your dreams.* The world desperately needs your imagination, your courage, your passion, and your commitment. Small stories have never stirred the soul. Dream big dreams, and create new realities worthy of your life. Be faithful to your own image of possibility, and remember that the price of passion and commitment is the shattering of personal illusions of safety. Be visible in the world so it can find you. You are grander than you can imagine.

5. *Say yes to belonging.* There is a songline woven into the universe, the earth, and life itself, and it is one of wholeness, coherence, connection, and relationships. There is no such thing as alone or lost in the web of life.

6. *Find your own voice, speak your own truth, and choose faith and hope over cynicism.* All are choices, and cynicism will never invite the potential for goodness and genius that lives within you.

7. *Pay attention, and listen for the sacred that lies hidden in the ordinary.* Your spirit and soul breathe best when you are still. So slow down, cherish silence, and listen for what wants to emerge. Percussive conversations do not welcome your inner voice. It is the depth of your attention that allows you to access the depth of your own identity.

8. *Decide what you want your name on.* Your name is everything. It is your identity and your integrity. Remember your name, and

reclaim your life for the world. Put your signature on impossible causes; they are the ones most worthy of who you are.

9. *Invite yourself into a life of learning, and choose the questions you want to be holding for your life.* Your boundless capacity to learn and grow your mind is the path to transformation—yours and the world's. New minds can shape new possibilities, and new possibilities can create new realities. You can indeed shape the future. Be mindful of what you learn and how you learn it. Seek connections and wisdom. Understand the meaning of "enough." Embrace wonder, welcome surprise, and always, always keep learning.

10. *Remember that contrary to the voices, images, sounds, and messages that surround and bombard you, your life is about:*

Your integrity, not your position

Your voice, not your power

Your name, not your title

Your calling, not your career

Your legacy, not your success

So think and learn more slowly. Listen to your heartsong. Honor the voice of possibility that calls you. Notice what diminishes you and what makes you come alive. Embrace your questions, treasures, and gifts with gratitude. Passionately commit to impossible causes. Love generously, and pay attention to the deeper song that connects all of life, including your own. Believe in your own goodness and genius, and always, always keep learning. You can be the ones to imagine and create a just, compassionate, and sustainable world for us all.

I know that you won't learn these "lessons" just by my telling them to you. My hope is that if you keep them in a safe and quiet place and take them out from time to time as you grow, they may begin to enter your heart and guide your journey. They may cause you to notice different things and to see with new eyes. Then perhaps one day, you will take them out and add your notes and pass them on to your children.

Love,

Grandma Steph

American Psychological Association Principles for Learner-Centered Education

1. *Nature of the learning process.* The learning of complex subject matter is most effective when it is an intentional process of constructing meaning from information and experience.

2. *Goals of the learning process.* The successful learner, over time and with support and instructional guidance, can create meaningful, coherent representations of knowledge.

3. *Construction of knowledge.* The successful learner can link new information with existing knowledge in meaningful ways.

4. *Strategic thinking.* The successful learner can create and use a repertoire of thinking and reasoning strategies to achieve complex learning goals.

5. *Thinking about thinking.* Higher order strategies for selecting and monitoring mental operations facilitate creative and critical thinking.

6. *Context of learning.* Learning is influenced by environmental factors, including culture, technology, and instructional practices.

7. *Motivational and emotional influences on learning.* What and how much is learned is influenced by the learner's motivation. Motivation to learn, in turn, is influenced by the individual's emotional states, beliefs, interests and goals, and habits of thinking.

Source: Lambert, N. M., and McCombs, B. L. (eds.) *How Students Learn: Reforming Schools Through Learner-Centered Education.* Washington, D.C.: American Psychological Association, 1998 (pp. 16–22).

8. *Intrinsic motivation to learn.* The learner's creativity, higher order thinking, and natural curiosity all contribute to motivation to learn. Intrinsic motivation is stimulated by tasks the learner perceives to be of optimal novelty and difficulty, relevant to personal interests, and providing for personal choice and control.

9. *Effects of motivation on effort.* Acquisition of complex knowledge and skills requires extended learner effort and guided practice. Without learners' motivation to learn, the willingness to exert this effort is unlikely without coercion.

10. *Developmental influences on learning.* As individuals develop, there are different opportunities and constraints for learning. Learning is most effective when differential development within and across physical, intellectual, emotional, and social domains is taken into account.

11. *Social influences on learning.* Learning is influenced by social interactions, interpersonal relations, and communication with others.

12. *Individual differences in learning.* Learners have different strategies, approaches, and capabilities for learning that are a function of prior experience and heredity.

13. *Learning and diversity.* Learning is most effective when differences in learners' linguistic, cultural, and social backgrounds are taken into account.

14. *Standards and assessment.* Setting appropriately high and challenging standards and assessing the learner as well as learning progress—including diagnostic, process, and outcome assessment—are integral parts of the learning process.

Howard Gardner's "Multiple Intelligences"

Linguistic: The "sensitivity to spoken and written language, the ability to learn languages, and the capacity to use language to accomplish certain goals."

Logical-Mathematical: "The capacity to analyze problems logically, carry out mathematical operations, and investigate issues scientifically."

Musical: "Skill in the performance, composition, and appreciation of musical patterns."

Bodily-Kinesthetic: "The potential of using one's whole body or parts of the body . . . to solve problems or fashion products."

Spatial: "The potential to recognize and manipulate the patterns of wide space . . . as well as the patterns of more confined areas."

Interpersonal: "The capacity to understand the intentions, motivations, and desires of other people and, consequently, to work effectively with others."

Intrapersonal: "The capacity to understand oneself, to have an effective working model of oneself—including one's own desires, fears, and capacities—and to use such information effectively in regulating one's own life."

Naturalist: "The capacity to distinguish among members of a species; to recognize the existence of other neighboring species; and to chart out the relations, formally or informally, among several species."

Existential [not yet determined by Gardner to be an intelligence but still under serious consideration]: "The capacity to locate oneself with respect to the furthest reaches of the cosmos—the infinite and the infinitesimal—and the related capacity to locate oneself with respect to such existential features of the human condition as the significance of life, the meaning of death, the ultimate fate of the physical and psychological worlds, and such profound experiences as love of another person or total immersion in a work of art."

Gardner, H. *Intelligence Reframed: Multiple Intelligences for the Twenty-First Century.* New York: Basic Books, 1999, pp. 41–43, 49, 60.

The Two Stories of Learning and Schooling Contrasted

	The Current (Reductive) Story: Prescriptive and Uniform Transaction	*The New (Integral) Story: Generative and Personalized Engagement*
Mental model of learning and schooling	*Deficiency and memory:* Analyzing, "fixing," and re-mediating identified learning limitations; accepting external authority for learning.	*Abundance and meaning:* Activating, developing, and connecting unknowable learning potentials; developing internal authority for learning.
Learning identity *What is the nature of the mind-brain?*	*Passive acquisition and prag-matic compliance—short term* Mind is a linear, precision-based reasoning "machine."	*Purposeful and transformative engagement—lifelong* Mind is a messy, creative process.
	Brain is a structurally static mechanism—a blank slate, a hard drive, or a hard-wired computer.	Brain is a complex, adaptive, structurally malleable system—a dynamic "plastic" network.
	Intelligence is singular, stable, fixed, and solely determined by heredity.	Intelligences are dynamic multidimensional potentials influenced by heredity and en-vironmental activation.
	Emotions and feelings distort reason and scholarship.	Emotions and feelings are es-sential to deepen reasoning and scholarship.

What is the nature and focus of the learning self?	*Disengaged and conforming recipient:* Receive inert information	*Active and inquiring cocreator:* Construct meaning
	Externally directed learner (driven by external mandates).	Self-directed learner (driven by personal purpose).
	Passive, disconnected, and competitive; learning is focused on acquisition: learning to know and learning to do; separated from natural world.	Engaged, meaning seeking, and collaborative; learning is focused on inquiry and on developing competence and expertise: learning to know, learning to do, learning to be, and learning to live together; connected to natural world.
What is the nature of the teaching self?	*Transmitter:* Convey preselected information; dispenser	*Mentor:* Weave deep and emergent understanding; cocreator
	Convey and monitor externally prescribed standards, content, and skills for achievement mastery; diminished autonomy and creativity; manager.	Cocreate contexts and conditions for engaged learning: deep conceptual understanding, disciplinary and interdisciplinary knowledge and skills, knowledge generation and use; significant autonomy and creativity; cocreator, coach, and role model.
Learning Information *What is the nature of information collected, shared, and used to increase learning and ensure system congruency?*	*Static and limited :* Externally prescribed and controlled; perceived as irrelevant	*Dynamic and abundant:* Externally responsive, self-generated, and accessible; imbued with meaning
	Delayed and sporadic feedback to teachers; erodes authentic instructional decision making.	Immediate and continuous feedback to teachers and the entire system; enables authentic instructional decision making.
	Quantitative summative measurement of achievement; precise measurement is the preeminent and irrefutable arbiter of worth; largely single-source norm-referenced tests.	Quantitative and qualitative formative and summative assessments of multiple measures and evidence of understanding; meaning is preeminent.
Learning Relationships *What is the nature of learning and teaching relationships?*	*Contractual:* Individualistic, competitive, and fear based	*Collaborative:* Inclusive, interdependent, and trust centered
	Relationships are simplistic and linear, and prescribed	Relationships are complex and webbed, and generative feed-

feedback lines are not explicitly connected around learning; an authentic learning community—a community that continuously learns—does not exist; learner tries to "fit."

Teaching and learning relationships are formally differentiated, prescribed, and hierarchical; students are subordinate to teachers' positional authority and presumed expertise; dominance and division drive external rewards.

There is no relationship between the knower and the known; teachers transmit and interpret information and serve as the gateway to information.

Learners learn independently and in isolation from and in competition with their peers; inquiry is individual.

Teachers are isolated from one another; competition, not collaboration, is preeminent; classroom management is focus; disciplinary teams are disconnected; promising practices are not shared.

back loops are seamlessly connected around learning and meaning; an authentic intergenerational learning community exists; learner knows he or she belongs.

Teaching and learning roles are collaborative; learning is a cocreative process where students and teachers learn together, exchange insights, and mutually deepen understanding; meaning and intrinsic motivation drive learning.

There is a relationship between the knower and the known; students and teachers coconstruct meaning; teachers are mind makers—mentors who help students "make up their own minds."

Learners learn interdependently and collaboratively; they are connected to and not in competition with their learning peers; inquiry is communal.

Teachers engage with one another in formal and informal dialogue about learning and teaching; their own plans of inquiry are shared; disciplinary and interdisciplinary teams collaborate; a community of shared practice is present.

Learning Processes	*Mechanistic:* Acquisition based and risk averse	*Creative:* Inquiry based and exploratory
What is the nature and purpose of learning?	Learning is a linear, sequenced, inert process of incrementally acquiring decontextualized information and skills; outcomes are predetermined, learning sequences are prescribed, and mastery or expertise is a concrete state to be individually achieved.	Learning is a natural, playful, purposeful, and imaginative process of exploration, constructing meaning and developing deep understanding within a social context; focus is on inquiry and creative, constructive, and adaptive engagement with change.

What is the nature of knowing? (epistemology)	Achievement variance decreased; predictability sought.	Learning complexity increased; novelty and newness encouraged.
	Detached: objectively verifiable, analytically experimental; empirical and observational knowing are the most rigorous and culturally respected.	Relational: personal, integrative, communal, and transformative; honors all the ways we come to know.
What is the nature of teaching?	Uniform to meet needs of curriculum; focused on answers and telling.	Personalized to meet needs of learner; focused on inquiry and dialogue.
	Transmit essential content and skills; focused on ensuring adequate achievement on tests.	Develop whole minds; ensure deep understanding and creative use of knowledge.
	Paradoxes and creative conflicts are ignored or trivialized.	Paradoxes and creative conflicts are embraced and illuminated.
Learning Patterns *What is the nature of learning and teaching patterns?*	*Prescribed and hierarchical; fragmented—focus on parts*	*Self-generated and networked; holistic—focused on the whole*
	System control is established through positional and power-based hierarchical relationships.	System order is continuously created through self-generating learning networks and relationships focused on the community's explicitly shared learning purposes and goals.
	Content is presented in discrete unconnected units and often decontextualized from the domain's integrating concepts from which understanding and meaning are derived.	Learners are actively engaged in developing disciplinary and interdisciplinary concepts and skills and modes of inquiry that enhance meaning and understanding.
	Conceptual relationships within, between, and beyond the disciplines are generally secondary to content and coverage.	Conceptual relationships within, between, and beyond the disciplines are explicitly discussed; connections (patterns) form the context of learning and teaching.
Learning Structures *What is the nature of learning, teaching, and schooling structures?*	*Immutable and standardized:* Permanent and nonresponsive to new learning	*Flexible and adaptive:* Temporary and responsive to new learning
	"One size rigidly and permanently fits all": Curriculum,	Continuous feedback and diagnostic assessments of learn-

	learning sequence, instructional strategies, assessments, time for learning, space for learning, efficiency and coverage, and not the learner's unique potentials, prior interests, knowledge, and experience, are the foundations for designing learning and teaching structures; diverting from this model to meet individual learner needs is the exception; school is a place for receiving information.	ing help to determine learner's personalized pathways; developing understanding and "whole minds" by identifying the learner's unique potentials, prior knowledge, experience, and interests are the foundations for designing all learning and teaching structures; every student is an "exception"; school is a practice field for mind making.
Curriculum	Driven by externally prescribed content.	Driven by learners' questions and ideas.
	Descriptive and topical; detached from experience; artificial and neatly packaged.	Coherent and connected to prior knowledge and experience; real-world, messy, and ill-structured experience.
	Closed, shallow, and uniformly sequenced.	Open, complex, and flexibly sequenced.
	Large amount quickly acquired.	Smaller amount slowly and deeply understood.
	Emphasis on quantity and breadth of coverage; excessive amount of prescribed grade-specific, discrete content "bits"; content delivery narrowly organized by "efficiency structures" (grades, courses) and not the logical organizing principles and conceptual structures of the disciplines; emphasis on "what's tested."	Emphasis on quality and rigor of thinking and depth of understanding; core disciplinary, interdisciplinary, and transdisciplinary organizing principles, concepts, knowledge, and inquiry processes are foundational and create the broad and deep context for connected understanding; content organized according to the patterns and structure of each discipline; "curriculum for life" is the foundation.
	Disembodied; not linked to learner's prior knowledge and experience.	Embedded in context; linked to learner's prior knowledge and experience.
	Focused on content segmentation and information acquisition.	Focused on core concept integration and knowledge acquisition and generation.
Instruction	Instruction rooted in detached epistemology; focused on "tested" achievement.	Instruction rooted in relational epistemology; focused on deep learning and understanding.

	Mostly didactic instruction delivered to large groups of chronologically aged peers (telling); mode of teaching directed to linguistic and mathematical-logical intelligences.	Multiple adaptive strategies used to ensure meaning and understanding for each learner (mentoring); inquiry-based, problem-centered, and integrative strategies used to enhance engagement; teaching modes serve multiple intelligences.
Assessment	Little or no feedback to learner; learner is guarded from knowledge of his or her own learning.	Ongoing feedback to learner; learner is coparticipant in continuously generating and using knowledge of his or her own learning.
	Provides single summative high-stakes standardized tests to demonstrate learning.	Provides multiple formative and summative assessments to demonstrate deep learning.
	Isolates students from monitoring and regulating their own learning.	Enrolls students in monitoring and regulating their own learning (assessment for learning).
	Contrived, prescheduled at benchmarks determined by instructional time, not learning; objective, external, quantitative, standardized, and high stakes; punitive consequences for poor performance; failure is punished; focused on extrinsic rewards.	Authentic, continuous, and ongoing feedback according to learning needs: objective, external, quantitative *and* subjective, anecdotal, qualitative; multiple forms of evidence of understanding; failure is viewed as essential to good learning; focused on intrinsic rewards (assessment of learning).
Time	Predetermined lockstep seat time—blocks, schedules, grades; time is the independent variable; "one time" fits all; speed of information acquisition is valued; turbocharged environment.	Adaptive to learner needs, and readiness to demonstrate understanding; time is variable; time allocated for "slow" learning and knowledge creation; reflective and engaged environment aligned with how students naturally learn.
Space	Formal learning happens best and most efficiently in formal classrooms; school is a building—geographically and architecturally defined.	Learning is not defined by formal classroom space or by geographical location, but by context and conditions; learning occurs in community, in classrooms, with peers, in an online community engaged in

		a problem, in museums, and with mentors; "school" is the nerve center of a dynamic, intergenerational, living-learning network.
Quality of Minds *What is the nature and quality of minds?*	*Reductive:* Shallow, fragmented, and rigid	*Integral:* Holistic, connected, and resilient
	Intellectually unaware of what he or she really understands and ill prepared, insecure, and fearful when confronted with new problems he or she has not been taught.	Aware of who he or she is as a learner; possesses strong sense of learning self; confident and energized by ability to navigate the "wilderness."
	Lacking sense of personal efficacy.	Possesses sense of personal efficacy and meaning.
	Unable to see patterns of relationships.	Able to integrate disparate information and find patterns and connections.
	Lacking in deep understanding; can't transfer information learned to real-world issues; lacking in curiosity; conforming.	Possesses deep understanding; able to transfer learning to real-world problem resolution; insatiably inquisitive; pioneering.
	Sense of fragmentation, isolation, and alienation.	Sense of wholeness, connection, and belonging.
	Alienated or disconnected from global issues and issues of transcendence.	Connected to global issues of sustainability and issues beyond oneself.
	Disenfranchised from nature and the web of life.	Deeply connected to the natural world; sees self as a cocreator in the web of life.

Notes

Preface

1. Enabling legislation, Illinois Mathematics and Science Academy (Springfield, Illinois, 1985). For more information about the Illinois Mathematics and Science Academy, go to http://www.imsa.edu.

2. F. Capra, The *Hidden Connections: Integrating the Biological, Cognitive and Social Dimensions of Life into a Science of Sustainability* (New York: Doubleday, 2002), 37.

3. I began my inquiry into the world of new science in 1987 with James Gleick's book, *Chaos: Making a New Science* (New York: Viking, 1987). Other pioneers included: J. Briggs and F. D. Peat, *Turbulent Mirror: An Illustrated Guide to Chaos Theory and the Science of Wholeness* (New York: HarperCollins, 1989); K. Kelly, *Out of Control: The Rise of Neo-Biological Civilization* (Reading, Mass.: Addison-Wesley, 1994); M. M. Waldrop, *Complexity: The Emerging Science at the Edge of Order and Chaos* (New York: Simon & Schuster, 1992); F. Capra, *The Web of Life: A New Scientific Understanding of Living Systems* (New York: Anchor, 1996); S. Kaufman, *At Home in the Universe: The Search for Laws of Self-Organization and Complexity* (New York: Oxford University Press, 1995); D. Zohar, *The Quantum Self: Human Nature and Consciousness Defined by the New Physics* (New York: Morrow, 1990); S. Goerner, *After the Clockwork Universe: The Emerging Science and Culture of Integral Society* (Edinburgh: Flores Books, 1999).

4. T. N. Hanh, *The Miracle of Mindfulness,* trans. M. Ho (Boston: Beacon Press, 1976), 103.

Gratitudes

1. C. Sagan, "Dreams Are Maps: Exploration and Human Purpose," *The Planetary Report,* Sept.–Oct. 1992, 4.

Prologue

1. D. Abram, *The Spell of the Sensuous* (New York: Vintage Books, 1977), 164, 165, 166.

2. Abram, *The Spell of the Sensuous,* 166.

3. C. Sagan, "Dreams Are Maps: Exploration and Human Purpose," *The Planetary Report,* Sept.–Oct. 1992, 1.

Chapter One

1. B. Okri, *Birds of Heaven* (London: Phoenix, 1996), 34.

2. M. Schneps and the Science Media Group of the Harvard-Smithsonian Center for Astrophysics, *A Private Universe: Misconceptions That Block Learning* (Cambridge, Mass., and Washington, D.C.: Harvard University and the Smithsonian Institutions, 1988).

3. P. Palmer, *The Courage to Teach: Exploring the Inner Landscape of a Teacher's Life* (San Francisco: Jossey-Bass, 1998), 49.

4. J. Delors (ed.), *Learning: The Treasure Within: Report to UNESCO of the International Commission on Education for the Twenty-First Century* (Paris: United Nations Educational Scientific and Cultural Organization, 1996) explicated these "four pillars" of learning. They are explored further in Chapter Three of this book.

5. F. Capra, *The Web of Life: A New Scientific Understanding of Living Systems* (New York: Doubleday, 1996), 290.

Chapter Two

1. D. Suzuki and A. McConnell, *The Sacred Balance: A Visual Celebration of Our Place in Nature* (Richmond, Va.: Greystone Books, 2002).

2. F. Capra, *The Hidden Connections: Integrating the Biological, Cognitive, and Social Dimensions of Life into a Science of Sustainability* (New York: Doubleday, 2002), xix.

3. R. N. Caine and G. Caine, *Making Connections: Teaching and the Human Brain* (Alexandria, Va.: Association for Supervision and Curriculum Development, 1991), 27.

4. For a review of the mind/brain/body system, the following authors and works provide significant insight: A. Damasio, *Descartes' Error: Emotion, Reason and the Human Brain* (New York: Avon, 1994). A. Damasio, *The Feeling of What Happens: Body and Emotion in the Making of Consciousness* (San Diego, Calif.: Harcourt, 1999). A. Damasio, *Looking for Spinoza: Joy, Sorrow and the Feeling Brain* (San Diego, Calif.: Harcourt, 2003). J. D. Bransford, A. L. Brown, and R. R. Cocking, *How People Learn: Brain, Mind, Experience, and School* (Washington, D.C.: National Academy Press, 2000). G. Caine, R. N. Caine, C. McClintic, and K. Klimek, *12 Brain/Mind Learning Principles in Action: The Fieldbook for Making Connections, Teaching, and the Human Brain* (Thousand Oaks, Calif.: Corwin Press, 2005). M. Diamond and J. Hobson, *Magic Trees of the Mind* (New York: Penguin Putnam, 1998). R. Sylvester. *A Biological Brain in a Cultural Class-*

room, 2nd ed. (Thousand Oaks, Calif.: Corwin Press, 2002). R. Restak, *The Secret Life of the Brain* (Washington, D.C.: Joseph Henry Press, 2001).

5. Capra, *The Hidden Connections,* 14.

6. F. Capra, *The Web of Life: A New Scientific Understanding of Living Systems* (New York: Doubleday, 1996), 161.

7. Capra, *The Web of Life,* 269.

8. Capra, *The Web of Life,* 227.

9. Capra, *The Web of Life,* 158.

10. My study and understanding of the significance and applicability of the living systems perspective and the systemic view of life to the reconceptualization and transformation of human systems (organizations) was illuminated and deepened in seminars and multiple conversations with Margaret J. Wheatley, Myron Kellner-Rogers, and Fritjof Capra. These conversations began in a dialogue series on self-organizing systems that Wheatley and Kellner-Rogers established in 1992 at Sundance, Utah, through the Berkana Institute. Wheatley is Berkana's founding president. Capra joined these conversations during 1996–1997. Later we became part of an extended inquiry group called Inquiring Friends. Our inquiries were far-reaching, but our focus was always on the transformation of human systems. It was during the Berkana dialogues that the domains (identity, information, and relationships) and the phenomena (processes, patterns, structures) of self-organizing systems within the context of organizations were studied. Wheatley's, Capra's, and Kellner-Roger's writings were also seminal to my thinking and understanding; see, for example, M. Wheatley, *Leadership and the New Science: Learning About Organization from an Orderly Universe,* 2nd ed. (San Francisco: Berrett-Koehler, 1999) and *Turning to One Another: Simple Conversations to Restore Hope to the Future* (San Francisco: Berrett-Koehler, 2002); Capra, *The Hidden Connections* and *The Web of Life;* and M. Wheatley and M. Kellner-Rogers, *A Simpler Way* (San Francisco: Berrett-Koehler, 1996).

11. Capra, *The Web of Life,* 171.

12. A. Lubow, "Inspiration: Where Does It Come From?" *New York Times Magazine,* Nov. 30, 2003, 69–70.

Chapter Three

1. N. M. Lambert and B. L. McCombs (eds.), *How Students Learn: Reforming Schools Through Learner-Centered Education* (Washington, D.C.: American Psychological Association, 1998), 505.

2. K. Plinske, "Creating Conditions for Developing and Nurturing Talent: The Work of School Leaders," in S. P. Marshall, M. Ramirez, K. Plinske, and C. Veal (eds.), *National Association of Secondary School Principals Bulletin, Education for the Gifted and Talented,* 1998, *82*(595), 75–84.

3. Although the term *integral mind* is not mine, as far as I know, the context, meaning, and definition I bring to it are my own. Sally Goerner has an imaginative and compelling chapter on the integral society in her book *After the Clockwork*

Universe: The Emerging Science and Culture of Integral Society (Edinburgh: Floris, 2001). K. Wilbur, *A Theory of Everything: An Integral Vision for Business, Politics, Science, and Spirituality* (Boston: Shambhala, 2001), remains the most scholarly and provocative in his explication of an integral vision.

4. J. Delors (ed.), *Learning: The Treasure Within: Report to UNESCO of the International Commission on Education for the Twenty-First Century* (Paris: United Nations Educational Scientific and Cultural Organization, 1996).

5. P. J. Palmer, "The Violence of Our Knowledge: Toward a Spirituality of Higher Education" (The Michael Keenan Memorial Lecture, Berea College, Berea, Ky., Nov. 1993), 2.

6. J. Watson in P. J. Palmer, *The Courage to Teach: Exploring the Inner Landscape of a Teacher's Life* (San Francisco: Jossey-Bass, 1998), 108.

7. B. McClintock in Palmer, *The Courage to Teach,* 55–56.

8. P. H. Ray and S. R. Anderson, *The Cultural Creatives: How 50 Million People Are Changing the World* (New York: Harmony Books, 2000), 242.

9. H. Gardner, *Intelligence Reframed: Multiple Intelligences for the Twenty-First Century* (New York: Basic Books, 1999), 33–34.

10. Gardner, *Intelligence Reframed,* 34.

11. H. Gardner and V. Boix-Mansilla, "Of Kinds of Disciplines and Kinds of Understanding," *Phi Delta Kappan,* 1997, *78*(5), 382.

12. Palmer, *The Courage to Teach,* 107.

13. Illinois Mathematics and Science Academy, Scientific Inquiries Program, 2004. For more information, go to www.imsa.edu.

14. B. Nicolescu, "Charter of Transdisciplinarity" (adopted at the First World Congress of Transdisciplinarity, Convento da Arrabida, Portugal, Nov. 2–6, 1994). http://nicol.club.fr/ciret/english/indexen.htm.

15. J. Garrison, "Wisdom University: Building a Global Learning Community" (Oakland, Calif.: Wisdom University, Dec. 2004), 1–13.

16. Thanks to Kathleen Plinske for permission to use her comment.

Chapter Four

1. C. Sagan, "Dreams Are Maps: Exploration and Human Purpose," *The Planetary Report,* Sept.–Oct. 1992, 4.

2. P. P. Cousineau, *Once and Future Myths: The Power of Ancient Stories in Modern Times* (Berkeley, Calif.: Conari Press, 2001), 118.

3. P. Cousineau, *Once and Future Myths,* 125–126.

4. I have drawn part of its description from the design and work of the Illinois Mathematics and Science Academy's dedicated research space, the Grainger Center for Imagination and Inquiry.

5. IMSA's core competency is "the ability to conceive, design, develop and demonstrate exemplary competency-driven teaching and learning experiences and materials in mathematics and science that are inquiry-based, problem-centered and

integrative." Illinois Mathematics and Science Academy, "Defining IMSA's Core Competency: A Report to the IMSA Community," Apr. 2001.

6. For more information about IMSA's problem-based learning program, personalized learning program, four-semester core mathematics sequence (entitled Mathematical Investigations), introductory science program (entitled Scientific Inquiries), and annual presentation day for students to present their research, inquiry, and mentorship projects, all of which are discussed in this chapter, go to http://www.IMSA.edu.

Chapter Five

1. Illinois Mathematics and Science Academy. The author of these "Rules for Belonging Together" was Brian Quinby, former resident counselor at the Illinois Mathematics and Science Academy.

2. K. Plinske, "Creating Conditions for Developing and Nurturing Talent: The Work of School Leaders," in S. P. Marshall, M. Ramirez, K. Plinske, and C. Veal (eds.), *National Association of Secondary School Principals Bulletin, Education for the Gifted and Talented,* 1998, *82*(595), 79.

3. H. Gardner, *Intelligence Reframed: Multiple Intelligences for the Twenty-First Century* (New York: Basic Books, 1999), 34.

4. R. Sylvester, *A Biological Brain in a Cultural Classroom,* 2nd ed. (Thousand Oaks, Calif.: Corwin Press, 2002).

5. G. Caine and R. N. Caine, *Making Connections: Teaching and the Human Brain* (Alexandria, Va.: Association for Supervision and Curriculum Development, 1991).

Chapter Six

1. K. Plinske, "Creating Conditions for Developing and Nurturing Talent: The Work of School Leaders," in S. P. Marshall, M. Ramirez, K. Plinske, and C. Veal (eds.), *National Association of Secondary School Principals Bulletin, Education for the Gifted and Talented,* 1998, *82*(595), 80.

Chapter Seven

1. This phrase was inspired by the work of Phil Cousineau, who described an odyssey as a "courageous journey that changes everything" and a mentor as "a mindmaker"—someone who helps the young make up their own mind. In P. Cousineau, *Once and Future Myths: The Power of Ancient Stories in Modern Times* (Berkeley, Calif.: Conari Press, 2001), 118–119.

2. K. Plinske, "Creating Conditions for Developing and Nurturing Talent: The Work of School Leaders," in S. P. Marshall, M. Ramirez, K. Plinske, and C. Veal (eds.), *National Association of Secondary School Principals Bulletin, Education for the Gifted and Talented,* 1998, *82*(595), 80–81.

Chapter Eight

1. M. Scherer, "Do Students Care About Learning: A Conversation with Mihaly Csikszentmihalyi." *ASCD Educational Leadership,* 2002, *60*(1), 14.

2. S. L. Brown, "Evolution and Play," in P. Cousineau, *Once and Future Myths: The Power of Ancient Stories in Modern Times* (Berkeley, Calif.: Conari Press, 2001), 162.

3. S. Brown, in the PBS series, *The Promise of Play,* 2000. To learn more about this series, go to http://www.instituteforplay.com/2promise_of_play.htm.

4. P. J. Palmer, "The Violence of Our Knowledge: Toward a Spirituality of Higher Education" (The Michael Keenan Memorial Lecture, Berea College, Berea, Ky., Nov. 1993), 2.

Chapter Nine

1. J. D. Bransford, A. L. Brown, and R. R. Cocking (eds.), *How People Learn: Brain, Mind, Experience, and School* (Washington, D.C.: National Academy Press, 1999), 20.

2. P. Palmer, *The Courage to Teach: Exploring the Inner Landscape of a Teacher's Life* (San Francisco: Jossey-Bass, 1998), 62.

Chapter Ten

1. Thanks to Rebecca Jaramillo, a teacher at Norwood Elementary School, Peoria, Illinois, for relating this story to IMSA problem-based learning director Debra Gerdes.

2. S. Blakeslee, "How Does the Brain Work?" *New York Times,* Nov. 11, 2003, D4.

3. R. N. Caine and G. Caine, *Making Connections: Teaching and the Human Brain* (Alexandria, Va.: Association for Supervision and Curriculum Development, 1991), 63–64.

4. Illinois Mathematics and Science Academy has developed Standards of Significant Learning. For more information, go to http://www.imsa.edu.

5. H. Gardner and V. Boix-Mansilla, "Teaching for Understanding in the Disciplines and Beyond," *Teachers College Record,* Winter 1994, 198–218. Permission received from Howard Gardner.

6. K. Plinske, "Creating Conditions for Developing and Nurturing Talent: The Work of School Leaders," in S. P. Marshall, M. Ramirez, K. Plinske, and C. Veal (eds.), *National Association of Secondary School Principals Bulletin, Education for the Gifted and Talented,* 1998, *82*(595), 78–79.

7. Thanks to Janice Krouse, IMSA mathematics curriculum assessment leader, for her comments.

8. P. Palmer, *The Courage to Teach: Exploring the Inner Landscape of a Teacher's Life* (Jossey-Bass: San Francisco, 1998), 2, 3.

9. Thanks to Michael Casey, IMSA English faculty, for his comments.

10. P. J. Palmer, "The Violence of Our Knowledge: Toward a Spirituality of Higher Education" (The Michael Keenan Memorial Lecture, Berea College, Berea, Ky., Nov. 1993), 2.

11. Illinois Mathematics and Science Academy's Core Competencies. For more information, see http://www.imsa.edu.

12. Thanks to Steve Condie, IMSA mathematics faculty, for permission to use his abstract.

13. Thanks to Ruth Dover, IMSA mathematics faculty, for permission to use her abstract.

14. Thanks to Micah Fogel, IMSA mathematics faculty, for permission to use his abstract.

15. Thanks to Willa Shultz, IMSA world language faculty, for permission to use her abstract.

Chapter Eleven

1. There are numerous national and international models and movements—individual schools, systems, coalitions, and consortia—illustrative of the emerging new story of learning and schooling and embodying many of its generative beliefs and design principles. Some of these programs are described in P. Senge and others, *Schools That Learn: A Fifth Discipline Fieldbook for Educators, Parents, and Everyone Who Cares About Education* (New York: Doubleday, 2000), and on the Edutopia Web site (www.edutopia.org). Other examples include: Central Park East Secondary School, New York City; Charter High School for Architectural Design, Philadelphia; Coalition of Essential Schools, created by Ted Sizer; Eco-Literacy programs promoted by the Center for Eco-Literacy, Berkeley, California (Fritjof Capra); Francis W. Parker Charter School, Devens, Massachusetts; Gateway High School, San Francisco; Key Learning Community (K–11 School), Indianapolis, Indiana; and Metropolitan Regional Career and Technical Center (The Met), founded by Dennis Littky and Elliot Washor. Other programs are the Reggio Emilia Primary Schools in Italy; Waldorf Schools, around the United States and internationally; and Shikshantar: The People's Institute for Re-Thinking Education and Development, Udaipur, Rajasthan, India.

2. D. Bohm, *Wholeness and the Implicate Order* (London: Ark Paperbacks, 1980).

Chapter Twelve

1. W. Van Dusen Wishard, "Between Two Ages: Get Used to It!" (address delivered to the Coudert Institute, Palm Beach, Fla., Dec. 1, 2001).

2. Illinois Mathematics and Science Academy (IMSA). IMSA's Standards of Significant Learning (SSLs) are designed to educate what we have called "decidedly different minds." For more information on IMSA's SSLs go to http://www.imsa.edu.

3. V. Havel, address to a Joint Session of the U.S. Congress, Feb. 21, 1990.

4. G. K. Chesterton, *Illustrated London News,* July 5, 1924.

Chapter Thirteen

1. P. Cousineau, *Once and Future Myths: The Power of Ancient Stories in Modern Times* (Berkeley, Calif.: Conari Press, 2001), 162.

Chapter Fourteen

1. Thanks to Anitra Sumbry for permission to use this story.
2. B. Okri, *Birds of Heaven* (London: Phoenix Press, 1996), 21.
3. C. Sagan, "Dreams Are Maps: Exploration and Human Purpose," *Planetary Report,* Sept.–Oct. 1992, 4.

Afterword: A Letter to My Grandchildren

1. R. M. Rilke, "The Swan," in *The Selected Poetry of Rainer Maria Rilke,* ed. and trans. S. Mitchell (New York: Vintage Books, 1989), 29.

Index